SEAMUS HEANEY
POET
OF CONTRARY
PROGRESSIONS

RICHARD FALLIS, *Series Editor*

© Jennie Summerall

SEAMUS HEANEY
POET
OF CONTRARY
PROGRESSIONS

Henry Hart

SYRACUSE UNIVERSITY PRESS

First Paperback Edition 1993

97 98 99   6 5 4 3 2

The paper used in this publication meets the minimum requirements
of American National Standard for Information Sciences—Permanence
of Paper for Printed Library Materials, ANSI Z39.48-1984.♾™

Library of Congress Cataloging-in-Publicaton Data

Hart, Henry, 1954–
    Seamus Heaney, poet of contrary progressions / Henry Hart.—1st
ed.
        p. cm.
    Includes bibliographical references and index.
    ISBN 0-8156-2536-7 (alk. paper) 0-8156-2612-6 (pb.)
    1. Heaney, Seamus—Criticism and interpretation. I. Title.
PR6058.E2Z69   1991
821′.914—dc20   91-12017

For Susannah

HENRY HART has taught in the English departments of The Citadel and The College of William and Mary. He is an editor of *Verse*, an international poetry journal, and has published widely on modern poetry, in such journals as *The Southern Review*, *Twentieth Century Literature*, *Contemporary Literature*, *Michigan Quarterly Review*, and the *Journal of Modern Literature*. His essay, "Seamus Heaney's Poetry of Meditation," was co-winner of the annual prize for literary criticism given by *Twentieth Century Literature* in 1987. He is the author of *The Poetry of Geoffrey Hill* and a collection of poems, *The Ghost Ship*.

CONTENTS

PREFACE

LIKE MOST BOOKS, this one began in a state of uncertainty and delight. I had been fascinated by Seamus Heaney's poetry from my college days, and hoped someday to investigate it more thoroughly. While in Oxford completing a book on Geoffrey Hill, I decided to fly to Belfast just before Orange Day in order to witness at first hand the sort of sectarian turbulence that informs Heaney's poetry from beginning to end. I also planned to visit the libraries at Queen's University and St. Joseph's College of Education, where Heaney had studied and taught. Some of the uncollected poetry and prose I found in student journals in these libraries made it into the book, and I would like to thank the librarians for their help in locating it. Most of my research and much of the actual writing, however, was done in the Bodleian Library at Oxford, and to the librarians there I am also indebted. Summer grants from The Citadel and from The College of William and Mary made the trips to England possible, and I thank both institutions for their generosity. A grant from the Virginia Foundation for the Humanities allowed me to spend a term in Charlottesville that was as enjoyable as it was productive. It was there that I finished most of the writing and revising of the book.

Many of the chapters originally appeared as essays, and I am grateful to the editors of those journals who were kind enough to offer critical suggestions and publish them: *The Southern Review*, "Pastoral and Anti-Pastoral Attitudes in Seamus Heaney's Early Poems" (1987, 23:569–88) and "Crossing Divisions and Differences: Seamus Heaney's Prose Poems" (1989, 25:803–21); *Twentieth Century Literature*, "Seamus Heaney's Poetry of Meditation: *Door into the Dark*" (1987, 33:1–18) and "Poetymologies in Seamus Heaney's *Wintering Out*" (1989, 35:204–31); *Irish University Review*, "Ghostly Colloquies: Seamus Heaney's 'Station Island'" (1988, 18:233–50); *Contemporary Literature*, "History, Myth and Apocalypse:

ix

Seamus Heaney's *North*" (1989, 30:387–411); *Chicago Review,* "Seamus Heaney's Anxiety of Trust" (1989, 26:87–108); *Graham House Review,* "Heaney's Sweeney" (1990, 13:111–38); and the *Journal of Modern Literature,* "Heaney Among the Deconstructionists" (1990, 16:458–85). I must thank Catharine R. Stimpson for choosing my essay on Heaney's poetry of meditation as a co-winner of *Twentieth Century Literature's* annual prize for criticism, and for her introduction to it in that journal.

In preparing these essays for publication, Bonnie Chandler at William and Mary could not have been more industrious. Nigel Alderman read through the manuscript and pointed out various mistakes. David Morrill exercised his characteristic Holmesian scrutiny when asked to offer editorial suggestions and transform the notes. Jennie Summerall kindly photographed Seamus Heaney for the book jacket, and Bonnie Powell compiled an index. Martha Smith and the English Department at William and Mary helped me find funding for editing and indexing. Susannah Livingston proofread with a careful eye. To all these I am grateful, and I am especially indebted to David Morrill for his expertise and unflagging diligence.

Those who contributed to the final shape of my study are too numerous to name, but I would like to single out Jay Parini for his continual encouragement and friendship, Peter Bien for his early help with my work on James Joyce, and my colleagues at *Verse,* Robert Crawford and David Kinloch, who also provided support. My interest in Seamus Heaney and Irish literature received a boost from Richard Ellmann, my Oxford supervisor and friend, "a taskmaster of substance and style" as Heaney once put it. The élan and insightfulness of his writing and the kind but rigorous way he had of imparting his high standards are still sorely missed.

Williamsburg, Virginia   HENRY HART
January 1991

ACKNOWLEDGMENTS

Permission to quote from materials listed below is gratefully acknowledged.

Letters and unpublished poems by Seamus Heaney, by permission of Seamus Heaney.

"Seamus Heaney's Anxiety of Trust in *Field Work*," *Chicago Review* 36, nos. 3 and 4 (1990): 87–108.

Excerpts from *The Bog People*, by P. V. Glob (Ithaca: Cornell University Press, 1969).

Preoccupations, by Seamus Heaney (London: Faber and Faber Limited, 1980). Reprinted by permission of Faber and Faber Limited from *Preoccupations* by Seamus Heaney.

Excerpts from *The Bog People*, by P. V. Glob, 1969; *Celtic Revivals*, by Seamus Deane, 1985; *The Dying Gaul*, by David Jones, 1978; *History in English Words*, by Owen Barfield, 1924; *Seamus Heaney*, by Neil Corcoran, 1986; *Viewpoints*, by John Haffenden, 1981. Reprinted by permission of Faber and Faber Limited.

Excerpts from *Field Work*, by Seamus Heaney, copyright © 1976, 1979 by Seamus Heaney; *The Government of the Tongue*, by Seamus Heaney, copyright © 1989 by Seamus Heaney; *The Haw Lantern*, by Seamus Heaney, copyright © 1987 by Seamus Heaney; *Poems, 1965–1975*, by Seamus Heaney, copyright © 1966, 1969, 1972, 1980 by Seamus Heaney; *Preoccupations: Selected Prose, 1968–1978*, by Seamus Heaney, copyright © 1980 by Seamus Heaney; *Station Island*, by Seamus Heaney, copyright © 1985 by Seamus Heaney; *Sweeney Astray*, by Seamus Heaney, copyright © 1983 by Seamus Heaney. Reprinted by permission of Farrar, Straus and Giroux, Inc.

"Heaney's Sweeney," *The Graham House Review*, no. 13 (Spring 1990): 111–38.

"Ghostly Colloquies: Seamus Heaney's *Station Island*," *Irish University Review* 18 (1988): 233–50.

"Heaney Among the Deconstructionists," *Journal of Modern Literature* 16, no. 4 (Spring 1990): 458–85.

"Crossing Division and Differences: Seamus Heaney's Prose Poems" first appeared in *The Southern Review* 25, no. 4 (Oct. 1989), n.s., pp. 803–21; "Pastoral and Anti-Pastoral Attitudes in Seamus Heaney's Early Poems" first appeared in *The Southern Review* 23, no. 3 (July 1987), n.s., pp. 569–88.

"Poetymologies in Seamus Heaney's *Wintering Out*," *Twentieth Century Literature* 35 (1989): 204–31; "Seamus Heaney's Poetry of Meditation: *Door into the Dark*," *Twentieth Century Literature* 33 (1987): 1–18.

Excerpts from *Celtic Revivals*, by Seamus Deane (Winston-Salem: Wake Forest University Press, 1985).

"History, Myth and Apocalypse in Seamus Heaney's *North*," *Contemporary Literature* 30, no. 3 (1989): 387–411. By permission of The University of Wisconsin Press.

SEAMUS HEANEY
POET
OF CONTRARY
PROGRESSIONS

1

INTRODUCTION

FEW TWENTIETH-CENTURY POETS writing in English have been able to secure a wide audience among general readers and critics alike. After
W. B. Yeats, only Robert Frost achieved such bipartisan acclaim, although
for many years scholars denigrated Frost beside the intellectually more sophisticated modernists. In a culture where films, television shows, and com-
pact discs have usurped the monopoly on communication that books once
enjoyed, a popular poet is rare. Maintaining an "international reputation,"
as a writer in *The Observer* recently commented, "is a tricky business. . . . It
takes a special gift to win hearts on both sides of the Atlantic and no one
now possesses it quite like Seamus Heaney." With the publication of each
new volume, the critical consensus grows that Heaney is not only the most
gifted poet in Ireland and Britain, but also the most critically respected poet
writing in English today.

The anonymous *Observer* writer, echoing claims made by Robert
Lowell, Helen Vendler, and Harold Bloom, entitled his article "Poet Wearing the Mantle of Yeats" and mischievously drew attention to those among
the Irish who "suspect he's already a *better* poet than Yeats" (21 June 1987,
7). Mantles obfuscate as well as illuminate, and Yeats's mantle on Heaney is
both burden and honor. As Heaney's readers and critics proliferate, so do
his different mantles—his different masks and identities—and so do the
conflicting appraisals of his work. Those who suspect that Heaney's popular-
ity lies in the common demand for *one* Irish bard per generation argue that
he is a minor Dylan Thomas whose talent as a poetic "ornamentalist" with
"a fine way with language" (Alvarez 1980, 16) lacks substance. For others
he is a pastoralist whose homely portraits of rural Irish life attract both
curiosity and sympathy but are ultimately sentimental. Others believe his
appeal arises from his position as political spokesman for Northern Ireland's
perpetual Troubles, while those in the opposite camp claim that his poetry

1

amounts to a culpable escape from those Troubles. For some he writes a romantic poetry of transcendence, for others a classic one of principled social engagement. With regard to the Catholic religion in which he was reared, some say his poetry is still regressively steeped in sacrificial symbols and rituals; others declare that, like James Joyce, he has flown above the nets of religion for a more objective anthropological view. For those critics who demand allegories from their writers Heaney obliges by making his poems speak for religious, political, linguistic, sexual, and literary matters all at once. For those who believe allegory is mechanical and simplistic, bastardizing rather than legitimately representing history, Heaney is just the latest mythmaker in a long line of Irish mystifiers.

His complexity, understandably, leads to debate about what he stands for, what kind of poet he really is, and whether the ethical and aesthetic standards exemplified in his verse are meritorious or meretricious. He is so elusive, in fact, that while his wife can attest to his "magical ring of confidence" and his sense of security which, to her, is "like an egg contained within a shell, without any quality of otherness, without the sense of loss that this otherness brings" (Devlin 1983, 16–17), other less intimate observers declare that the personality behind the poems is wracked with anxiety, uncertainty, fear, anger, and painful self-consciousness. Heaney may not like wearing Yeats's mantle. Nevertheless, his poetry vacillates between antinomies as persistently as his precursor's. Like the Irish history that saturates it from beginning to end, his poetry is a battleground of competing affiliations. In a passage Heaney likes to quote from Yeats, and one that applies to much of his own work, his countryman remarked: "We make out of the quarrel with others, rhetoric, but of the quarrel with ourselves, poetry. Unlike the rhetoricians, who get a confident voice from remembering the crowd they have won or may win, we sing amid our uncertainty" (Yeats 1959, 331). Yet for Heaney poetry and rhetoric, art and politics, are entangled rather than distinct, merging and emerging as rhythmically as the uncertainty that underlies them.

At the root of his work is a multifaceted argument with himself, with others, with sectarian Northern Ireland, with his Anglo-Irish heritage, and with his Roman Catholic, nationalist upbringing on a farm in County Derry. As he follows Yeats in striving for "unity of being," mapping out the embattled factions in his nation and psyche, he is descriptive as well as prescriptive. He diagnoses Irish ills, suggests cures (like dismantling his country's archaic hierarchies so that different religious and political groups can engage creatively rather than murderously), then withdraws to let legislators and law enforcers put the plan into practice. He realizes his agenda may be utopian and that his personal renunciation of overt political action may be taken as a cop-out (at least by "the noisy set / Of bankers, school-masters, and clergymen / The martyrs call the world" in Yeats's "Adam's Curse" [1983, 80]). Nevertheless, he stands by the artist's right to choose one devotion over another. With Stephen Dedalus he will "forge the uncreated conscience of his race" (Joyce 1968, 253) in art rather than in government, although the blueprint for better governance will be scored into his poems for anybody to examine.

Behind Heaney's noble principles, however, is the worry that, as W. H. Auden proclaimed, "poetry makes nothing happen," that "it survives / In the valley of its making where executives / Would never want to tamper" (1971, 53), that art rather than reform only exacerbates the dominant authorities. So Heaney's poems, to borrow current critical terms, are assidu-ously self-reflexive, self-consuming, self-deconstructing. They search for im-ages and answers for Irish problems and submit them to intense critical scrutiny. What they set up they tend to knock down. Deploying a different metaphor, Heaney likes to quote Robert Frost on this process of composi-tion by decomposition: "like a piece of ice on a hot stove the poem must ride on its own melting." Similarly, "the poem . . . a linguistic exploration whose tracks melt as it maps its own progress" (Heaney 1980a, 80–81). The moral value of this poetry that vigilantly investigates cultural dilemmas but then dissolves its solutions and that deconstructs the ancient hierarchies and oedipal struggles between "patriarchal" British Protestants and "matri-archal" Irish Catholics bothers Heaney because it fails to articulate concrete political resolutions for Ireland. Of Yeats, Auden elegiacally commented in "In Memory of W. B. Yeats," "Mad Ireland hurt you into poetry" (1971, 53). Looking back on his career, which gained momentum during the Catholic civil rights movement in the sixties and the resurgence of I.R.A. attacks and Protestant counterattacks in the early seventies, Heaney inti-mates that if "Mad Ireland" had hurt him into politics he would feel less anxious. Politics, for better or for worse, makes things happen.

This kind of argument in which opposite views compel and repel Heaney with equal force begins with his first book, *Death of a Naturalist*. Here and in some of the uncollected poems printed when he was a student at Queen's University in Belfast he expresses a bittersweet nostalgia for his childhood on the farm in Derry. As in the pastoral tradition that stretches from Frost and Dylan Thomas (two of Heaney's early models) back to Virgil and Theocritus, Heaney depicts his rural, agrarian home ground as his golden age or Eden. As soon as pastoral enchantment wells up in him, however, he represses it with grim recognitions of farming in Ireland and the sectarian battles erupting or about to erupt just outside the farms' ditches and hedges. As he struggles to free himself from Mother Ireland's womblike pastures and reconcile himself with the historical facts of Father Britain's depredations, Heaney imagines himself as both an Adam falling from Eden into a knowledge of agonizing divisions and an oedipal child contending with both biological and cultural parents. His quest for fatherhood and poethood travels a dialectical path between pastoral and antipastoral traditions. Although he elegizes his early, innocent naturalism, which is traditional pastoralism thinly disguised, its death prepares the way for a more mature naturalism in tune with the struggles raging all around him.

Without the recognition of rural hardship, Heaney's poetry of agrarian ways would have floundered in the mists of another Celtic Twilight. Similarly, his meditational *via negativas* in *Door into the Dark* would have seemed solipsistic or narcissistic if they did not illuminate the psychological motives and consequences of meditation. While Heaney draws on the sort of Catholic meditation institutionalized by such divines as St. Ignatius Loyola and St. John of the Cross and updated for him by Evelyn Underhill and Thomas Merton, and while he sympathetically records sacred moments in the mystic's "dark night" (the altarlike anvil wreathed with sparks in "The Forge," the grass flaming in "In Gallarus Oratory"), his spiritual marriages are between imagination and unconscious rather than soul and Christ. His argumentative and iconoclastic way is to counter orthodox Catholic meditations by emphasizing their secular correlatives. As poetry replaces religion, Heaney demystifies the divine Word by transforming it into the poetic word. If Platonic and Judeo-Christian tradition has tended to denigrate writing as a cumbersome, improper medium for communicating sacred mysteries, Heaney, like his poststructuralist peers, contradicts that bias by deploying writing as a principal way to excavate the ground from which mysteries and prejudices have always burgeoned.

Realizing that pastoralism and mysticism have flourished primarily because of linguistic conventions and their power to evade or transcend the real world's troubles, Heaney in *Wintering Out* plunges even more methodically into language in order to expose its collusions with those troubles. In his poems on Northern Irish place names, etymology recapitulates history. An archaeologist of language, Heaney unearths signs of Scottish and English invasions lingering in the lexicon and pronunciation of his Irish compatriots. Focusing on British words transported to Ulster by colonizers and often fused with native Gaelic words, Heaney devises miniature allegories in which even the different syllables radiate political, religious, literary, and sexual significance. As he composed these poems, Heaney felt increasing pressure from the Catholic, nationalist community in his homeland to act as its propagandist. Yet his poems subvert partisan jingoism and strive to fashion in its place new emblems of sectarian cooperation.

As the bombs began to explode once again in the early seventies in Northern Ireland, Heaney responded with *North*, his most gruesome account of the tragic and mythical aspects of the sectarian hostilities. Some critics accused him of wallowing in rituals of sacrificial purgation and sexual renewal, as if he were emulating Yeats's more bellicose moods. Rather than clamber after the apocalyptic rapacity of Yeats's Zeus or Jehovah, Heaney typically identifies with and elegiacally mourns the victims of such myths. He repeatedly invokes ancient fertility cults and apocalyptic expectations to implicate them in the apocalyptic atrocities that have afflicted his country for centuries. Because Protestant and Catholic paramilitary groups shed blood in order to preserve their sacred ideals of Mother Ireland, she emerges more as a femme fatale or "terrible beauty" than as a benevolent fertility goddess. Heaney understands the devotion to the Mother among Catholics and the I.R.A., and sympathizes with their anger over her repeated desecration at the hands of Britain's Protestant Fathers. Still, he hopes for an oedipal resolution that is as political as it is psychological. To move toward civilized compromise, he suggests, both sides must realize that Ireland can be an old sow that eats her farrow, a tyrannical patriarch devouring sow and piglets alike, and also the androgynous, ecumenical humanist envisioned by Joyce in Leopold Bloom.

Heaney's year at Berkeley between 1970 and 1971 reinforced his liberal sentiments and loosened his early formalist constraints. In California he tried to incorporate the expansive American forms of Walt Whitman, Ezra Pound, William Carlos Williams, Robert Duncan, and Gary Snyder. If historically poetry has been an aristocratic art and prose a more democratic one, Heaney, following the experiments of the Americans, sought to yoke the two in a series of prose poems called *Stations*, which he published in pamphlet form in 1975. The title recalls the Stations of the Cross, but rather than focus on Christ's agonizing Passion and Crucifixion, Heaney dwells on personal and political crises. Again he secularizes the cross so that it refers to his own multifarious crossings—between Ireland and America, Ulster and the Republic, Protestantism and Catholicism, and even between prose and poetry. Although his sequence of prose poems can be read as a spiritual autobiography *in imitatione Christi*, it is more specifically a confessional narrative of a boy growing up in Northern Ireland after World War II and gradually recognizing that for centuries the Christian cross has inspired rancorous division rather than divine unity.

After the controversial move from Belfast to Glanmore in 1972, Heaney seemed prepared to shut his "door into the dark" and open "a door into the light" (Heaney 1979a, 20). In essays and interviews he spoke of trusting a more lucid, conversational voice and of trusting his new, more enlightened audience in the South (which was predominantly Catholic, unlike the pre-dominantly Protestant society in the North). Christopher Ricks in a pen-etrating review of *Field Work*, the book that grew out of this transition, rang the changes on this theme of trust. In poetry, politics, and marriage Heaney elevates trust to the status of faith. Still, his faith in a recently acquired freedom, voice, and audience in the South is nevertheless undermined at nearly every point by doubt and distrust. In the North he sought to tran-scend political responsibilities imposed on him; in the South he equates transcendence with political escapism. Accepting Dante and Robert Lowell as his models, he places his trust in art's ability to confront conflicts between freedom and responsibility, private craft and public involvement, but con-tinually chastises himself for evading commitments and failing to have more impact on the situation he left behind.

The medieval Gaelic poem, *Buile Suibhne*, which he translates as *Sweeney Astray* during this period, provides an ancient mask for his contemporary dilemma. Confronted by the horrors of the battle of Moira in Ulster (A.D. 637) and cursed because of his contempt for the invading Christian empire, Suibhne Geilt metamorphoses into a guilt-ridden bird and, like his Icarian heir, Stephen Dedalus, attempts to fly over nation, religion, and language and to survive by silence, exile, and cunning. He resembles the stock charac-ter of medieval iconography, the pagan wild man, although at the end he is converted by his friend, St. Moling, and comes to resemble that other stock figure of medieval Irish lore, the ascetic saint negotiating a penitential *peregrinatio* through the wilderness. For Heaney, Sweeney acts as a half-pagan, half-Christian persona that, especially in his "Sweeney Redivuus" poems, allows him to dramatize his own guilty feelings aroused by his flight from Ulster to the woods of Wicklow. But if Suibhne takes a penitential journey to atone for his murderous sins against insurgent Christians, Heaney's sin is that he *takes* a journey—that he abandons his embattled homeland. Once again he seizes on a character and narrative, implicates his own experi-ence in ancient paradigms, and then critically assails them.

The same ironic sense of sin and guilt predominate in that other long poem based on medieval precedents, "Station Island." In Dantesque tones and stanzas, Heaney records his early pilgrimages to the island in Lough Derg where St. Patrick supposedly initiated a three-day vigil of fasting, praying, and mortification. Imitating Dante's journey through the circles of hell and purgatory, Heaney traipses over circles of rocks on the island, communing with tutelary ghosts as he goes. In typical self-reflexive fashion, his pilgrimage engenders an argument about pilgrimages; he journeys to a holy island in order to purge the guilt and anxiety that such journeys create. As he fares forth, most of the prominent figures he summons from the dead

(Simon Sweeney, Patrick Kavanagh, William Carleton, Joyce) accuse him of groveling through old rituals that are masochistic, life-denying, meaningless, or simply distracting. They form a formidable opposition but really speak for Heaney's artistic conscience, which is painfully at odds with those two other internal gorgons, his political conscience and his religious conscience. Divided against himself, he once again launches an ambitious investigation into his ambivalent motives, assaulting his ideals and then shoring their fragments into a brilliant poem.

For a postcolonial poet who feels that the religious, political, and linguistic hierarchies imposed on his country by a foreign empire still watermark his psyche, deconstruction is as much a gut response as a well-thought-out strategy of exposure and demolition. In *The Haw Lantern*, Heaney mounts his most sustained attack on the binary oppositions that have stratified and oppressed his society in the past, tracing them, as Jacques Derrida and others have done, back to the Platonic and Judeo-Christian origins of Western civilization. Addressing such loaded terms as presence and absence, speech and writing, he deploys his deconstructive maneuvers along a *via negativa* that negates age-old prejudices in order to affirm the productive interplay of differences. In a country where one sectarian faction pretends to hold a monopoly on truth and justice and historically has chosen to kill those who oppose the "one true way," deconstruction is not simply an abstract hermeneutic strategy designed for clever critics. It has ethical relevance for the reorganization of all aspects of culture.

In *The Haw Lantern*, however, Heaney criticizes deconstruction, as others have done, for its reckless flirtation with nihilism and frivolous play. As he reinscribes absences with new presences and makes marginal cultures (like Northern Ireland's) central rather than peripheral, he also argues for reconstruction. The book, he proposes in terms borrowed from Mercea Eliade, charts the deconstruction of sacred by profane space. He uses an architectural metaphor of decentering to represent the cultural metamorphosis that he and his generation in Ireland witnessed: "I watched it happen in Irish homes when I first saw a house built where there was no chimney, and then you'd go into rooms without a grate—so no hearth, which in Latin means no focus. So the hearth going away means the house is unfocused. . . . it represents a reality: the unfocusing of space and the desacralizing of it" (1988b, 6). The generic deconstructionist applauds the unfocused, the decentered, and the indeterminate, concluding that all reading and writing is a ludic exercise of negative capability. Heaney responds by celebrating affirmative capability. He seeks "images of a definite space which is both empty and full of potential" (1988b, 6) and principled ways of tapping and governing that potential. His collection of essays, *The Govern-*

ment of the Tongue, elaborates on these poetic preoccupations, speaking eloquently of the always difficult balance between linguistic constraint and freedom, orderly space and unleashed potential, political dictate and private rebuke.

Heaney's former status as a "noncitizen" in Protestant-dominated Northern Ireland derived at least in part from his decision to choose writing as his mode of expression rather than the more customary political organ, speech. Domestic and social authorities repressed his will to speak out; poetry became the oracle for his impassioned sense of justice and injustice. His poetry notebook records a passage from the late French philosopher, Gaston Bachelard: "What is the source of our first suffering? It lies in the fact that we hesitated to speak. It was born in the moment when we accumulated silent things within us" (Clines 1983, 43). He told Francis Clines from the *New York Times*, "If I could make poetry that could touch into that kind of thing, that is what I would like to do" (Clines 1983, 43). Few other poets today articulate as self-consciously and judiciously the difficult issues of language and silence, and especially how they relate to poetic expression and political repression. In a century when major writers have espoused nazism, fascism, monarchism, and other antidemocratic creeds, Heaney's hesitancy to speak out politically seems noble rather than culpable. That his writing dramatizes bipartisan arguments in which historical differences continue to clash gives it an urgency that much contemporary poetry lacks and makes it even more worthy of attentive study.

2

PASTORAL AND ANTIPASTORAL
ATTITUDES

W HEN YEATS in "The Song of the Happy Shepherd" declared, "The woods of Arcady are dead / And over is their antique joy" (1983, 7), he was bemoaning the death of one version of pastoral. Rather than dismiss pastoral altogether, he would cultivate a version in which the Arcadian noon with its shepherds piping for lost friends and unrequited loves would be replaced by the fairies of the Celtic twilight. Seamus Heaney observed in "The Interesting Case of John Alphonsus Mulrennan," "The result was the birth of a new myth, a new version of pastoral, centred on the west of the country. Ireland was reconstituted as the land of the celtic twilight, where old men saw visions and young men dreamed dreams, in landscape dominated by Norman tower and Palladian mansion, where the speech of the beggarman and fisherman was as rich as the kernel of a nut, and the culture of the huntsman was supposedly as deep and cherished as Yeats's own" (1978a, 37). Following his predecessor, Heaney would also abandon one Arcadia for another. What he calls the "secret nests" (1980a, 17) in hay-rick and hedgerow on the farm in County Derry constitute the pastoral of his childhood. The celebration of rural securities collapses as he grows up and realizes the antipastoral nature of that landscape and the society that lives within it. The pastoral "nests" that persist do so in poems that dramatize the poet's struggle to see them for what they are. Heaney's diggings and plowings (his pastoral "field work") are conducted within the context of poetry itself. Swapping spade for pen, he continues to pry open the pastoral surface of his home ground to reveal the antipastoral elements beneath.

How Heaney fits into the pastoral tradition as a whole can be as perplexing to Heaney as to his critics. For Jay Parini he mines a seam that extends as far back as Theocritus and Virgil. "One should remember, of

9

course, that even Theocritus and Virgil did not write for country folk, to
put it mildly; rather, they evinced the atmosphere of rural life for the benefit
of cultivated city dwellers who could appreciate the subtle texture of meaning embedded in their eclogues. This is the pastoral tradition, and Heaney's
Death of a Naturalist (1966) fits into it" (1980, 101). The texture of
metaphor and allusion in Heaney's poetry may be difficult for rural folk to
understand, but it diverges sharply from the amorous melodrama of Daphnis
in Theocritus's Idylls and the high-pitched pining of Damon and his sundry
compatriots in Virgil's Eclogues. The founders of the pastoral tradition, in
fact, influenced Heaney's pastorals only tangentially, if at all. He admits, "I
think I read Vergil's pastoral poems, desultorily, half-reading, getting a sniff
of the atmosphere and a feel for the shapes and procedures, in a Penguin
translation, early on. Maybe when I was a sixth-former, maybe as an undergraduate. Theocritus, no. Not until much later, and then without passion,
though with satiated delighted curiosity" (letter to the author, 4 June 1987).
Clearly, part of Heaney's inability to recall exactly when he read his precursors is because of his aversion, or at least ambivalence, toward their work.

Heaney's attitude toward pastoral tradition expressed in his essay "In
the Country of Convention" shares some of the animus of Dr. Johnson's
attack on Milton's *Lycidas*. Johnson fulminated, "In this poem there is no
nature, for there is no truth. . . . Its form is that of the pastoral
[but] . . . whatever images it can supply, are long ago exhausted; and its
inherent improbability always forces dissatisfaction on the mind. . . . We know
that they never drove a field, and that they had no flocks to batten" (1973,
280). Focusing on the pastures of Northern Ireland, Heaney also dismisses
naïve glorifications of farming. Opposed to Theocritus and Virgil as pastoral
models, he finds them in more congenial figures closer to home. In an essay
on Patrick Kavanagh he praises the older poet's graphic and unsentimental
depiction of potato farming and famine in "The Great Hunger," which is
"a kind of elegy in a country farmyard, informed not by heraldic notions of
seasonal decline and mortal dust but by an intimacy with actual clay and a
desperate sense that life in the secluded spot is no book of pastoral hours
but an enervating round of labour and lethargy" (1980a, 122). In a review
of John Montague's *The Rough Field* he finds similar antipastoral sentiments
to praise. Montague's poem "is a version of pastoral," and in order to
remain faithful to contemporary realities it "concludes . . . with a car journey
out of the 'finally lost dream of man at home in a rural setting' " (1973a,
550).

Unimpressed by the idle, histrionic shepherds and melodramatic songs
of the classical pastoral, Heaney does not see the tradition as wholly defunct.
In a review of *The Penguin Book of Pastoral Verse*, "In the Country of

Convention," he concedes that the term *pastoral* "has been extended by usage until its original meaning has been largely eroded." Still, it points to rural beauty as distinct from "raggle-taggle farmland" (1980a, 173). With William Empson, Heaney believes that there are "versions of pastoral," one of them being his home ground. Names in the immediate area, such as Grove Hill and Back Park, "insist that this familiar locale is a version of pastoral. . . . Grove is a word I associated with translations of the classics" (quoted in Buttell 1975, 34). Unlike the editors of *The Penguin Book*, who maintain that the dialectic between pastoral and antipastoral has simply died out in twentieth-century poetry, Heaney insists that it continues in different form. The editors, inspired by Raymond Williams's *The Country and the City*, denigrate the classical pastoral from a Marxist perspective, claiming that it condones "a simplistic, unhistorical relationship between the ruling landowning class—the poet's patrons and often the poet himself—and the workers of the land," and therefore functions only "to mystify and to obscure the harshness of actual social and economic organizations" (Barrell and Bull 1975, 4). Heaney, by contrast, defends pastoral on aesthetic rather than political grounds, invoking "the satisfactions of aural and formal play out of which poems arise, whether they aspire to delineate or to obfuscate 'things as they are' " (1980a, 174).

Clearly Heaney is torn "between pastoral as realistic observation and pastoral as artificial mode" (1980a, 175), between the ethical imperative to report the harsh facts and the aesthetic need to transform facts into appealing fictions. He yearns to declare with John Keats, "Beauty is truth, truth beauty." His pastorals, however, show that truth and beauty are often violently at odds. In *Death of a Naturalist*, his poems often begin in rural splendor, only to fall into painful recognitions of enervating labor, decay, starvation, sexual turmoil, and fears of natural and political catastrophe. The pastoral "nests" referred to in his essay on Mossbawn, his family farm, offer only temporary sanctuary. The cultivated formal elegance of the poems themselves offers substitutes, while still bearing witness to the real world's pressures.

It is no surprise, then, that Heaney seizes upon the Genesis story as the kernel for his pastoral narratives. Mossbawn, where he spent much of his childhood, usually appears as his garden; the rats and frogs and fungus that evoke harrowing fears are avatars of Satan. Even his prose reminiscences of childhood follow the same narrative pattern of a falling away from Edenic pastures onto dangerous ground. "Those lush and definite fields gave way to scraggy marshland," he says in "Mossbawn." Around a "badger's hole, there hung a field of dangerous force" inhabited by demonic "creatures uncatalogued by any naturalist, but none the less real." He tells of stripping naked and plunging into a mosshole, "treading the liver-thick mud" and "coming out smeared and weedy and darkened . . . somehow initiated" (1980a, 18–19). He calls the initiation a betrothal, as if he were naked Adam "betrothing" himself to Eve after they plucked the apple, or an initiate in a vegetation ritual "betrothing" himself to the earth goddess. The act for the young Heaney is sexual, frightening, and titillating too, a stripping away of conventional artifices (clothes) for closer contact with the fecund earth. As Adam and Eve fell into a knowledge of divisions, Heaney falls into a knowledge of the political and religious conflicts of Northern Ireland. He recollects, "For if this was the country of community, it was also the realm of division [where] the lines of sectarian antagonism and affiliation followed the boundaries of the land" (1980a, 20). The pastoral serenity is ultimately broken up by historical conflicts and contemporary skirmishes, which lie underground. It is comparable to the "liver-thick mud," always ready to drag new victims down.

An obsession with Eden and a golden age of the past is, of course, one of pastoral's most distinguishing traits. Alexander Pope in his *Discourse on Pastoral Poetry* stated matter-of-factly, "Pastoral is an image of what they call the golden age" (quoted in Barrell and Bull 1975, 224). Milton employed pastoral motifs to describe Eden in *Paradise Lost*. Heaney recalls this in his review, adding, "Yet while the Genesis story gives shape to this persistent dream of paradise (and, by transference, utopia), it also acknowledges the world outside the garden as a place of thorns which man enters in sorrow, to earn his bread by the sweat of his brow" (1980a, 176). Nostalgia sanctions the conventional rendition of the past as a pastoral Eden. Nevertheless, such poems "misrepresent the quotidian actualities of the world man inhabits outside Eden, and in the end beget a form of anti-pastoral in which sweat and pain and deprivation are acknowledged" (1980a, 176). For Heaney, John Clare is the first poet devoted to an antipastoral mode in which imaginary swains are replaced by actual farmers sweating in the fields.

The compulsions behind pastoral and antipastoral are more archetypal, more entrenched in the psyche, and therefore more durable than the editors of *The Penguin Book* admit. "Surely the potent dreaming of a Golden Age or the counter-cultural celebration of simpler life styles or the nostalgic projection of the garden on childhood are still occasionally continuous with the tradition as it is presented here," Heaney declares, and cites poems by Edward Thomas, Edwin Muir, Hugh MacDiarmid, A. E. Housman, David Jones, Patrick Kavanagh, and John Montague as examples of the tradition's perseverance (1980a, 180). He could cite his own poems as well. His juvenilia attest that pastoral motifs captivated him from the start. In these uncollected pastiches of Keats, Gerard Manley Hopkins, and Dylan Thomas, he is not only searching for a voice, he is also trying to forge his own pastoral myth of a childhood Eden threatened by sundry afflictions. His first poems printed at Queen's University, Belfast, "all of them desperately imitative" (quoted in Broadbridge 1977, 22), he concedes, present autumnal scenes of harvest in which pastoral serenity is eclipsed by night and the mower's blade. In "Reaping in Heat" (1959c, 27), noon—that favorite time for the shepherd's piping—darkens forebodingly. In "October Thought" (1959b, 27), predatory mice attack barrels of the harvest corn. The singing poet in "Nostalgia in the Afternoon" (1959a, 17), having worked himself up into the "high intangible blueness" of heaven, where he grasps, alongside Percy Shelley's skylark, "a firm rounded moment, suspended in swaying space / Over sunny acres of hay," ultimately falls with night and crashes onto "black hard rocks."

In these early poems, the loss of security in the garden prompts in the poet a mood of wistful regret. An Arcadian twilight hovers over scenes of sunny labor and impassioned dreaming. Later, in *Death of a Naturalist*, the colors and sounds of this loss will become harsher, more apocalyptic. Instead of patronizing the singing hedge-crickets and whistling redbreasts of Keats's "soft-dying day," which Heaney echoes in the early poems, he writes of frogs farting and exploding like mud grenades. Heaney deploys the pastoral mode to document his own coming-of-age as a poet, his difficult dying away from an idealized mother (Mother Nature, Mother Ireland, and his actual mother) in order to gain the independence needed to write. He seeks to replace pleasure principle with reality principle. Yet he never really overcomes his primary ambivalence toward the original womblike garden. His poems strive for greater realism and at the same time cultivate the gritty world into a vestigial pastoral of seductive music and enchanting story.

As do most pastorals, Heaney's persistently overlap with the elegiac mode. Peter Sacks has shown in *The English Elegy* that "Eclogues are often about the very entry from nature to culture" (1983, 14), and from his psychoanalytical viewpoint this entails a symbolic castration or sacrifice, a rerouting of libidinal energies away from the erotic mother toward the subliminal substitutions of art or culture, and a battle with the repressive father in which the elegist overcomes his power by identifying with it, by becoming a "civilized" father himself. Heaney's "death of a naturalist," which makes possible his entry into culture, revolves around this oedipal passage from the mother love and self-love predominant in the child's narcissistic Eden to the older man's tough-minded attempts to negotiate with the realities of sectarian Northern Ireland. The journey proceeds from a pastoral unity to an elegiac comprehension of difference, division, and death, from a center of undifferentiated sexuality to the decentered underworld or unconscious where Irish desires and animosities continue to fester. "Mossbawn" charts Heaney's early pastoral narrative in prose. Here he comments, "I would begin with the Greek word *omphalos*, meaning the navel, and hence the stone that marked the centre of the world" (1980a, 17). Shortly afterward he connects this center with the community water pump, which "marked an original descent into earth" (1980a, 20). Later it would symbolically mark his fall into a knowledge of divisions raging in the political unconscious of the Irish psyche. His poems reveal that this omphalos is an original unity, womb and phallus combined, where feminine and masculine waters necessary for poetic and biological production mingle. After the child falls from this androgynous origin, he will try to redeem it in his allegorical art.

According to Heaney's sacrificial view, the naturalist must die for the artificer to live, and as for most pastoral elegists "the movement from loss to consolation . . . requires a deflection of desire, with the creation of a trope both for the lost object and for the original character of the desire itself" (Sacks 1983, 7). As for the oedipal child who loses the mother in the power struggle with the father, "the elegist's reward . . . involve[s] inherited legacies and consoling identifications with symbolic, even immortal, figures of power" (Sacks 1983, 8). According to Sacks, in pastoral myths and elegies these totemic figures can be feminine and masculine, their legacies of power matriarchal and patriarchal. "The figure of the fertility goddess, or of a female fertility token, bears a metaphorical relation to an individual woman's sexual impulse or powers as does the figure of Dionysus or Adonis or the phallus to those of a man" (1983, 13). Heaney's pastorals abound with phallic and feminine images of fertility. Usually the pen is his figure of power, the substitute for the spade wielded by his father and grandfathers (as in "Digging"). When Heaney figuratively dies from or kills off the paternal lineage of naturalists that haunts him, he raises his pen to reaffirm his solidarity with his biological fathers and newly adopted artistic fathers. Emulating Stephen Dedalus, he quests for artistic foster fathers but ultimately finds a mother, whose abundantly creative powers appear in mythopoetic form as the *telos* of his works. In step with other pastoral elegists, Heaney draws on pagan fertility cults and negotiates the paradoxical path of sacrifice whereby oedipal losses are matched by symbolic gains. His natural father and mother, as poems as different as "Follower" and "Clearances" attest, are superseded; in their place Heaney erects the memorials that are his poems. The natural sexual energies that produced him, and that he struggled with in order to mature, are identified with, internalized, and finally reproduced. The naturalist's death is only a temporary stage in nature's cycle of resurrections.

The oedipal foundations of Heaney's pastoral myth are complicated by his Catholicism and his Irishness. As his career progresses, he will dramatize his "family romance" more explicitly, so that the powerful, menacing father will be played by England, the seductive mother by Ireland. His early Catholicism, he states repeatedly, aligned him with the motherland. Ambivalence, as Freud proposed, rather than consistent partisanship typifies their relations. Devoted to the Mother, Heaney in his bog poems will deplore the I.R.A., whose devotion to Mother Ireland perpetuates bloody sacrifice and revenge. As Sacks points out, when elegy fails to deliver satisfactory consolation, revenge tragedy intervenes to fill the vacuum (and it is interesting to note that at Queen's University "the dramatic poetry of [Christopher] Marlowe and [John] Webster appealed" greatly to Heaney [Broadbridge 1977, 22]). Because England, the repressive Father in Heaney's political allegory, entered Northern Ireland in the early seventies to exert a civilizing force when Protestants were terrorizing Catholics, and because Heaney owes so much to the English literary tradition, his Anglophobia is tempered with Anglophilia. This oedipal ambivalence in the political arena is complemented by the symbols and rituals of Heaney's Catholicism. For Sacks, the communicant's identification with the sacrificed god through consumption of his flesh and blood is a ritual at-one-ment at the root of fertility cults and their later offspring, tragedies and pastoral elegies. Heaney acknowledges these roots in poems that also recoil from their barbarism.

The oedipal lineaments of Heaney's elegies appear in bold outline in later poems, "The Harvest Bow" and "Clearances" (where he speaks of going through a "*Sons and Lovers* phase" with his mother and then violently dismantling it). While his political and religious inheritance reinforced his ambivalent family dramas, his relations with his actual parents no doubt provided the original catalysts. In a *New York Times Magazine* article, Francis Clines revealed, "He is the product of parents whose education ended with grade school, unbookish people with differing approaches to the language, as Heaney describes it. 'There is the Heaney side, very intelligent with a belief in the authenticity of the unspoken,' he says, 'And my mother's side, the McCanns, very much devoted to argumentation, discourse; they're know-alls' " (1983, 104). The recent poem, "From the Land of the Unspoken," associates this repression of speech, this unwillingness to speak out politically, with the "silence, exile and cunning" of the writing life. And yet throughout his career Heaney battles against the political quietism inherited from his father for seeming to condone the atrocities of Northern Ireland. His mother is caught in the same dialectic, since her urge for argumentation, for debate with others (as Yeats stipulated) leads to rhetoric, not poetry. To become one of the fathers, one of the artificers, Heaney suggests repeatedly, he needs to repress speech and embrace its sublimated form in writing, and this entails a sacrifice of the mother inside him and the mother tongue she represents. His poetry from beginning to end delineates these tangled political, religious, literary, and linguistic lineages that he struggles to reconcile in an art that deliberately underscores the differences from which it is made.

Inheriting the oedipal plot encoded in the pastoral tradition, Heaney also inherited pastoral's rhetoric of shady fields and sighing trees. In love with the mellifluous sound of previous pastorals, he did little to transform them early on. Only gradually did they become part of an inheritance he tried to overthrow. The uncollected "Reaping in Heat" is partly about this need to mow down "the drowsiness" of a womblike pastoral Eden and all its seductive figures. (Later, in "Clearances," he will take a similar blade to the maternal tree.) "Reaping" imparts a melancholy tone to images of stubble fields and trilling birds (borrowed from "To Autumn," the first poem Heaney could recite from memory, and perhaps from Frost's "The Tuft of Flowers," by the poet who first "spoke" to Heaney). It elegizes pastoral and pasture alike:

> Lark's trills
> Shimmered
>> Down the thin burnt air. Lower
> And deeper and cooler sinks now
> The sycamore's shade, and naked sheaves
> Are whitening on the empty stubble.

"And gathering swallows twitter in the skies" could be appended to this without disturbing the poem's melody. The archaic inversions and pathetic fallacies of earlier lines,

> Came the rasp of steel on stone.
> For slashing the drowsiness,
>> the mower was whetting his scythe. . . .

> And the sycamores heaved a sleepless sigh,

fit neatly into a pastoral tradition that Heaney was slow to renounce.

His desire to slash through pastoral sonorities was partly instigated by Hopkins. Heaney's "October Thought" again requisitions motifs of swallows, willows, and twitterings from Keats, but the somniferous music is broken up everywhere by the clanging consonants that Hopkins adored:

Minute movement millionfold whispers twilight
Under heaven-hue plum-blue and gorse pricked gold,
And through the knuckle-gnarl of branches, poking the night
Comes the trickling tinkle of bells, well in the fold.

The pastoral sense of well-being, reinforced by images of heaven, gold, and sheep secure in the fold, contrasts sharply with the disturbing images of mice gnawing the harvested corn as if Father Time were sexually and mortally reaping Mother Nature's bounty. In "Nostalgia in the Afternoon," the pastoral interlude takes place in the past, in a synesthetic moment of ecstatic sounds and colors. Now T. S. Eliot and Dylan Thomas supplement Hopkins to provide the young poet with his alliterative sound effects, which he would later associate with the patriarchal powers of Anglo-Saxon as opposed to Gaelic Britain:

And I live times distilled from time past

Times when the cuckoo curled lobes of smooth music
Over sunny acres of hay coloured sound
And larks were spilling light pebbles of all
Sand falling, stumbling, tinkling,
Sound torn ragged and open with a corn-crake's
Jagged-edge noise,
Rasping backwards and forwards
As metal through gravel.

The poem, ironically, enacts its own failure. As time passes (sand falls through the hourglass), Eden vanishes, and the poem turns from "smooth music" into "jagged-edge noise." The involved conceits collapse from their own weight. The gush of nostalgia is finally stifling.

To succeed in constructing a new pastoral faithful to his ambivalent attitudes toward family and country, Heaney would first have to strip the historical model to its bones. His early uncollected "Pastoral" (1982b, 4) does just that. The poem depicts the death of pastoral and finds precedents for its iconoclastic attitudes in Lowell's "The Quaker Graveyard in Nantucket." Heaney echoes Lowell's lines: "Only bones abide / There, in the nowhere" (1944, 16) and "sea-gulls wail / for water" (17) while penitents, expressionless and heavy lidded "like cows" (19), trudge to the shrine at Walsingham. Heaney writes of "cows with eyes as round as bowls" who "chewed their rumbling cuds and stared / Into nowhere past gulls / That keened above the cows' green boneyard." The cows fail to notice the bones of their predecessors. Heaney and Lowell, on the other hand, examine their boneyards with scrupulous intensity, for they contain both ancestors and the pastoral conventions used to elegize them. The motif of birds keening, for example, could derive from Virgil's Fifth Eclogue, where all of nature joins in to keen for the departed Daphnis. "Pastoral" is a terse elegy in which the cows' boneyard functions as an emblem for the pastoral tradition itself, to which Heaney goes as a scavenger to gather old devices for his poem.

> White bones that roving dogs had gnawed,
> Lying scattered on the grazing
> Like prehistoric flint tools, showed
> The rock-bottom of living.
>
> From soup-pots and brown roasting-pans
> The sawed-up skeletons were cast
> For scavengers to suck and cleanse
> And drop there in the bleaching grass.

Encountering "the rock bottom of living," Heaney pares down his rhetoric correspondingly. The result is a skeletal poem (eventually cast aside—like one of the bones) whose example would lead to the grimly realistic pastorals of *Death of a Naturalist*.

Another poem published in a 1960 issue of *Gorgon*, a Queen's University literary magazine, forecasts Heaney's mature style; "Aran" again cuts the pastoral down to rock and bone, this time in an antipastoral description of rural life on the Aran Islands. John Synge's *Aran Islands*, which Heaney calls one of the "seminal texts" (1980a, 180) of modern pastoral, provides a precedent, as it does for the revised poem, "Synge on Aran," in *Death of a Naturalist*. Synge's clear, sympathetic prose recounts the desolate "small flat fields of naked rock" on the islands, the histrionic keening of women at funerals, the old Gaelic storytellers and their fairy tales, and the rugged lives of fishermen who seem oblivious to modern civilization. Synge draws the traditional pastoral distinction between the Edenic country and the despicable city when he travels to Galway. "The sort of yearning I feel towards those lonely rocks is indescribably acute. This town . . . seems in my present mood a tawdry medley of all that is crudest in modern life" (1935, 377). He returns to celebrate "the strange simplicity of the island life" where the girls resemble unfallen Eves ("The complete absence of shyness or self-consciousness gives them a peculiar charm" [1935, 382]) and the men resemble rugged Adams untainted by urban duplicities.

Heaney does not dwell on the pastoral charms as much as the

antipastoral brutality of these remote islands. He begins "Aran" with a grotesque, osteal simile: "The rock breaks out like bone from a skinned elbow." To those who expect cures, Heaney offers only gloomy prognoses.

> Here the people live the necessary life.
> They feed and worship, lancing the wizened veins
> Of scanty soil, trying to draw life from the stones.
> But as he digs, the islander's spade spangs off rock
> And stops.

No sycamores heave sleepless sighs here. No golden gorse whispers under heaven-hued skies.

> The knifing wind shivers, but no tree rustles
> No sedge whispers. . . .
>   The breakers constantly rush
> With a slow snow-smash explosion, and overhead
> A slush of grey cloud is forever melting.

The knives, slush, and exploding sea again recall Lowell's "Quaker Grave-yard in Nantucket" where "you could cut the brackish winds with a knife" and winds "rush / At the sea's throat and wring it in the slush" and a gaff bobs on "the greased wash exploding on a shoal-bell" (1944, 15, 20). Heaney must have known he failed to achieve Lowell's sinewy grace in "Aran." The later "Synge on Aran" sculpts the earlier poem into a well-honed artifact and reflects on the sculpting process as it is performed.

> Salt off the sea whets
> the blades of four winds.
> They peel acres
> of locked rock, pare down
> a rind of shrivelled ground;
> bull-noses are chiselled
> on cliffs.
>   Islanders too
> are for sculpting.

Creative inspiration (in inspiriting wind or "spiritus") is essentially a revisionary one, a compulsion to cut back or "pare down." The spade that earlier spanged off rock is now Synge's and Heaney's "hard pen / scraping in his head; / the nib filed on a salt wind / and dipped in the keening sea." The various blades (lances, knives, spades, chisels) are all metaphors for

Heaney's pen, which constructs by deconstructing, cutting away pastoral's decorative masks to produce poems as stubbornly enduring as the bull-noses on Aran's cliffs.

What does the sea keen for if not the pastoral condition in which poet and farmer can relax over "thir sweet Gardning labour" and savor, as Milton's Adam and Eve do, the lush "fruits which the compliant boughs / Yielded them, side-long as they sat recline / On the soft downy Bank damaskt with flow'rs" (*Paradise Lost*, Book 4, ll. 328–34)? On Aran, neither art nor potatoes come gratuitously. Heaney dismisses the pastoral motif of nature's spontaneous fecundity partly because of his experience as a poet. Along with Synge, Yeats taught him to distrust the mind's "spontaneous overflow" that led his earlier poems toward unbridled gushing. The essay, "The Makings of a Music," discusses the two different styles of composition exemplified by Wordsworth and Yeats, and in doing so traces Heaney's apprenticeship. Wordsworth, he observes, conceived "the poetic act as essentially an act of complaisance with natural impulses and tendencies," "as a wise passiveness, a surrender" (1980a, 71, 63), and Heaney associates it with the feminine part of his psyche. Yeats, on the other hand, contended that "composition was no recollection in tranquility . . . but a mastery, a handling, a struggle towards maximum articulation," something masculine in which thoughts "are hammered into unity" (1980a, 75). The two "Aran" poems demonstrate the benefits of regarding poetic composition as a violent hammering as opposed to a passive surrendering, ironically Anglicizing Yeats and Hibernizing Wordsworth. As a young poet, Heaney could draw shapes from the rock only after a deliberate assault, although later he would develop a trust in both masculine and feminine modes working simultaneously.

His early attempts to hammer Edenic memories of country life into rocklike artifacts were not always so keen-edged. In "Song of My Man-Alive," printed in 1961, he chose Dylan Thomas as his perilous guide, and specifically "Fern Hill," which transforms stock pastoral motifs in a startling way. The shepherd in Thomas's poem is himself—the herdsman "easy under the apple boughs." The Arcadian grove is the Welsh apple orchard. Adolescence is the poet's golden age, the farm his Eden where "Adam and Maiden" wake each morning with the dew. The Orphic child pipes to cows and daisies, and all of nature dutifully follows him and sings to his horn. Laying a wreath on the glorious, carefree days of his innocence, Thomas follows pastoral convention by suggesting an apotheosis through song. He sings "in his chains like the sea" and thereby transcends them, at least for the moment. Heaney tries to sing the same pastoral tune:

> At first, in oil-swirls of shadow, in whirlpools of sound,
> We were a giddy eddying; it was all tune-tumbling

>   Hill-happy and wine-wonderful,
>   The lithe liquid spurts
>   Of the dancing thrush-girls and hawk-boys spat round us,
>   Yet hooded in the soft music of your presence
>   I wandered away
>   and swam in the gush of my joy.

Womb and tomb images are borrowed from Thomas without being transformed. "It was life leaping wild in the womb / of my young spring / And
bursting headlong from the dead belly of twenty-one years." The golden
age for Heaney, as so often for Thomas, is characterized by a vegetative
unity with nature, an oedipal return to the maternal omphalos in which
lovers appear to be rooted at the center of the world, sharing the same sap:

>   We stood at the centre, our world
>   Rippled and rayed away from us, and golden life
>   Pumped through dark pulses
>   of trees and houses and clouds.

A crash inevitably follows the orgasmic surge, as if Father Time suddenly
severed the pastoral child from his Mother Earth. Heaney seems aware that
the poem has failed and looks toward a future when his music will be more
finely tuned:

>   I could wish
>   That the shrill skirl and mountain-power of the moment
>   which has passed would swell, swelter and crash
>   Into a life-time symphony,
>   Resonant through all days to come.

Heaney signs the poem "Incertus" (meaning uncertain) and is justifiably
unsure of his powers. Two years later he would begin composing those
poems included in *Death of a Naturalist*, which give to the "swelter and
crash" of his rural experience an assured, symphonic resonance.

The title poem of *Death of a Naturalist* exemplifies his new skill at
synthesizing disparate pastoral material. Here he counterpoises the theme of
Edenic childhood, where life is undisturbed by a knowledge of sex, violence, and death, against the theme of a fall into painful divisions. Still
impassioned, his music is now expertly modulated. To offset the traditional
melodies of pastoral elegy, naturalistic details strive for the antipastoral accents of John Clare, Patrick Kavanagh, and Ted Hughes. If this seems
contradictory, contradiction is the lifeblood of the poem. The title, to begin
with, is rife with ambiguities. The death is not a real death, only the

figurative death of Heaney's naturalism, which will reappear in multitudinous guises in following books. The poem dramatizes a metamorphosis or
rite of passage, as pastoral elegies often do, in which the poet sheds his naïve
childhood naturalism learned from tadpoles wriggling from spawn in collection jars and almost against his will recognizes what Yeats called "the
frogspawn of a blindman's ditch" where blind men batter blind men and
sexual love turns to brutal antagonism. Heaney's naturalism, paradoxically,
is no longer purely naturalistic; it has taken on some of the qualities of what
Thomas Carlyle called "natural supernaturalism." Supernatural and natural
terrors now haunt the pastoral child. His essay "Mossbawn" tells how the
bog contained "creatures uncatalogued by any naturalist" and intimates that
these supernatural creatures initiate the growing boy into a new knowledge
of reality. Heaney's poem could have been more accurately entitled "Death
of a Pastoralist," since it is the notion of a pastoral, childhood Eden that
actually dies. Whether as a literary naturalist preoccupied with the Irish poor
and the natural laws that govern them, or as a Darwinian naturalist studying
territorial imperatives and struggles for survival in Northern Ireland, Heaney's
naturalism persists, unabated, however tinctured it may be with supernatural
demons.

The fall from Eden onto demonized ground is both psychological and
political, the naturalist's dying inward into the ego and dying outward into
the *polis*. Although the bog usually represents both private and collective
unconscious for Heaney, in "Death of a Naturalist" a flax dam serves the
metaphoric purpose. On one level the poem simply depicts the country
activity of processing flax, which is then made into linen—a suitable subject
for an eclogue or bucolic. An uncollected poem published in the *Times
Literary Supplement* (*TLS*) only a few months after "Death of a Naturalist,"
entitled "Lint Water" (5 August 1965), goes into much greater detail in
describing how

> The flax was pulled by hand once it ripened,
> Bound into tall green pillars with rush bands
> And buried underwater, roots upward.
> When the dam was full they loaded stones and sods
> On top, then left the whole thing for three weeks
> To rot. . . .

Men stand in the water and throw the soggy flax onto dry grass with
pitchforks so that it dries before being bundled up and sent to the mill. The
"lint water" released from the dam is nauseous and poisonous, killing trout
in the stream. Heaney again fastens on the death and unpleasantness of the

labor as a precondition for transformation. The rotting, weighted-down flax stands symbolically for the repressed, vegetative sexuality and violence at the heart of his land. Heaney knows that health will come only from a purgative baptism in the gutter. The last image of the poem foreshadows his many other encounters with the unseemly underbelly of the bucolic scene in Northern Ireland along with his attempts to transform it. He states bluntly, "Putrid currents floated trout to the loch, / Their bellies white as linen tablecloths." The white textile, in the end, corresponds to the purified text, the tabula rasa. Nothing can be made whole, he would say with Yeats's Crazy Jane, "that has not been rent." Nothing can be written without erasure.

Traditional pastoral elegies align the death and rebirth of vegetation with the death and rebirth of the deceased (as Sacks states, "The immortality suggested by nature's self-regenerative power rests on a principle of recurrent fertility" that denies death's finality [1983, 26]). Heaney's "Death of a Naturalist" employs flax and frog spawn to trace the psychological gestation of the poet. The boy's instinctual life and the sexual and violent impulses in the society around him seem weighted down, repressed by religious codes, and as a result fester underground like the rotting flax. The toil and distress of the boy changing into man come later when Heaney recognizes the ignominy that has remained unconscious, battened down by a punishing conscience (the sun). His fable begins with a sense of burden:

> All year the flax-dam festered in the heart
> Of the townland; green and heavy headed
> Flax had rotted there, weighted down by huge sods.
> Daily it sweltered in the punishing sun.

Like the vegetation images in *The Waste Land,* the "heavy headed flax" has phallic and cultural implications. Sectarian prejudice also festers at the heart of Heaney's townland and will explode during the uprising of 1969, just as the "cocked" guns and "grenades" explode at the end of the poem. Heaney's point is that the repression of "heavy-headed" sexuality is merely destructive at this stage. Unable to initiate the transition to sublimated forms of cultural production and biological reproduction, Heaney's culture declines to impotence, stagnation, and simmering violence.

For Heaney as a child the ancient wound of sectarian strife is wrapped in a "gauze of sound"; it is sanitized, bandaged, covered up. In Northern Ireland, Heaney repeatedly points out, civilization's discontents mask their grievances with deceptive courtesies, and, when sublimation fails, volcanic passions erupt. Images of splendor—butterflies and dragonflies—flit like

Shelley's skylark over the festering dam. During this pastoral interlude, the spinsterish Miss Walls delivers a lecture couched in baby talk on the procreative abilities of the mammy frogs and daddy frogs. The otherworldly diction of the schoolroom alters dramatically by poem's end, when the slime kings—emblems of the world's gross physicality—invade the flax dam. Guardians of history's horde, they are grim reminders of ancient blood feuds that never die. As the candor of Heaney's rhetoric intensifies, he charts a therapeutic course away from romantic displacements toward a more clinical scrutiny of what is being repressed.

Most of the poems in *Death of a Naturalist* follow the narrative design of the title poem. They recollect moments of rural contentment and the conventional language that enshrines such contentment, and then shatter the conventions with graphic descriptions of the psychological and political turmoil beneath the charming surface of country life. The pastoral usually draws on an implicit sense of hierarchy, elevating shepherd over city dweller while maintaining urban sophistication in the face of rural gaucheness. Heaney wants to dismantle the hierarchy. He documents a democratic equilibrium between two classes that in traditional pastorals traded costumes but retained preestablished identities. Rather than harp on differences between metropolitan artist and rural craftsman, between sophisticated poet and illiterate potato farmer, he emphasizes the similarities that unite them. "The essential trick of the old pastoral, which was felt to imply a beautiful relation between rich and poor," William Empson declares in his study of the genre, "was to make simple people express strong feelings (felt as the most universal subject, something fundamentally true about everybody) in learned and fashionable language" (1935, 11). For Empson, proletarian literature, which allows workers the opportunity to express universal themes, is also a "version of pastoral," and for Heaney a preferable one, because the sense of egalitarianism shared by aristocrat and plebian in the pastorals of Theocritus, Virgil, and their many heirs is contrived. Heaney's versions of poetic and agricultural "fields" are bound by the same natural laws of decadence and rejuvenation, by the same urge to create, by the same laborious processes of cultivation. Urban and rural artisans encounter the same struggles between repression and expression. When George Puttenham in 1589 wrote that "the Poet devised the Eclogue . . . not of purpose to counterfeit or represent the rusticall manner of loves and communications; but under the vaile of homely persons and in rude speeches to insinuate and glance at greater matters" (quoted in Barrell and Bull 1975, 21), he was prophesying the pastoral style of Heaney.

To reveal what is fundamental and universal in human experience, even while restricting himself to his home ground, Heaney early on decided to make his poems mythic. He was following Patrick Kavanagh's dictum, "Parochialism is universal; it deals with the fundamentals" (Clines 1983, 104). His numerous retellings of the Genesis and Oedipus stories characterize sin and redemption in startling ways. "Death of a Naturalist" delineates evil designs and tragic heroes in the shape of slime kings—the frogs (close cousins to Milton's toad who whispers satanic dreams into Eve's ear). If the chorus in ancient Greek tragedy secured revenge by witnessing the oedipal murder of the king, Heaney fears a similar fate at the hands of the frogs. He says that "the air was thick with a bass chorus" and that "the great slime kings / Were gathered there for vengeance and I knew / That if I dipped my hand the spawn would clutch it." Heaney dies as a naturalist in order to be enthroned as a poet-king, but the frogs threaten his kingdom. As in Lowell's "For the Union Dead," "the dark downward and vegetating kingdom / of the fish and reptile" threatens to pull him down into pastoral's undifferentiated, prereflective womb and thus prevent his ascent as a politically engaged poet. In another Lowellish poem, "The Barn," rats play the role of tragic, parricidal heroes and gaze at Heaney with fierce, unblinking eyes. The barn itself assumes the dimensions of hell, where darkness is visible, fiery: "all summer . . . the zinc burned like an oven." The musty dark is a projection of Heaney's haunted conscience, just as the "mildewed day" in Lowell's "Mr. Edwards and the Spider" ("when the hay / Came creaking to the barn") is a projection of Lowell's. Speaking through Edwards, Lowell asks, "What are we in the hands of the great God?" and avers that we are nothing but frail spiders tossed into the "bowels of fierce fire." Experiencing his own dark moment, Heaney confesses,

> I was chaff
> To be pecked up when birds shot through the air-slits.
> I lay face-down to shun the fear above.
> The two-lugged sacks moved in like great blind rats.

The sacks of corn, reminiscent of the earlier jars of spawn that act as emblems of the vegetative body, its constricted sexuality and repressed aggression, are metamorphosed into something hideous by the guilty imagination. The "lugged" sacks (*lugge* from Middle English means ear) become huge rats as the conscience horrifies itself with phantoms created in its own image. With the force of the punishing sun and vengeful frogs, the poet attacks himself for imaginary crimes, and once again plays the role of a ratlike Oedipus blinded for his tragic flaws.

Rats scramble through Heaney's early poems, always instilling in the spectator a sense of sin and corruption. Like Joyce, Heaney had to come to terms with a Catholic heritage before he could "forge in the smithy of his soul" a new, affirming conscience. Early on both recoil from the body's and world's repugnance; later they joyously celebrate all organs of creation. In "An Advancement of Learning," a title taken from Francis Bacon's encyclopedic book debunking supernatural forms of knowledge and advocating an empirical approach to learning, Heaney rids his imagination of spurious fears by confronting the rats with the cold eye of a scientist. He is the naturalist again, examining "the tapered tail that followed him, / The raindrop eye, the old snout," and struggling to dispel supernatural bogeys. He stares down his evil phantom. "Forgetting how I used to panic / When his grey brothers scraped and fed / Behind the hen-coop in our yard," he then "advances" as the rat retreats up a sewer pipe.

Evil invades Eden once again in "Blackberry-Picking," a poem that may have found precedents in Frost's enchanting pastoral, "After Apple-Picking." Frost's modern-day Adam finds himself exiled from the paradisal apple orchard because of exhaustion and the painful knowledge that his labor and desire will never be perfectly fulfilled. Some of his apples will go "to the cider-apple heap / as of no worth" (Frost 1972, 69). Similarly, Heaney's berrypicker knows that the great harvest he desired will inevitably be ruined by a "rat-grey fungus." Heaney begins with a sacramental vision, both Christian and pagan, of communicants tasting the flesh and blood of the berries (crowned with thorns) and imagines they are ingesting the body of a seasonal vegetation god transubstantiated into wine.

> You ate that first one and its flesh was sweet
> Like thickened wine: summer's blood was in it
> Leaving stains upon the tongue and lust for
> Picking.

The stain of lust, as if harvesting nature's bounty were a desecration (as in Wordsworth's "Nutting" or Theodore Roethke's "Moss-Gathering"), becomes more overt later on when thorns prick the hands and palms grow "sticky as Bluebeard's." Like the flax in "Death of a Naturalist," the blackberries "fermented, the sweet flesh would turn sour." Bluebeard in the folktale murders wife after wife. The culprit here is not a homicidal misogynist so much as the body naturally declining toward corruption and death. Because of the inevitability of the "rat-grey fungus" on the blackberries the boy concludes, "Each year I hoped they'd keep, knew they would not."

Nearly all of Heaney's pastorals juxtapose the nostalgic hope for an Eden of permanent fruitfulness, where ripeness is all, against the antipastoral recognition of the laborer's toil and failure. Often the tension assumes

gothic proportions in a "family romance" where sexual violation and parri-
cide seem to be the rule and Satan, Oedipus, and Bluebeard the principal
agents of fate. In this perverse drama Heaney's country folk resemble Christian pastors who pit themselves against the world's weight—its fallenness or
sin—and strive to redeem what they can. Repeatedly they fall short of their
high expectations. If sin is "the specific gravity of human nature" as Karl
Barth once claimed (quoted by Hill 1984, 15), comparable to the gravitational force propelling all things toward earthly disintegration, Heaney's
pastorals are parables of the atonement which is "at-one-ment." In "Water-
fall," the comparison of human sin and natural "fall" is explicit. Heaney tells
how "water goes over / Like villains dropped screaming to justice," and
also how poetic vision can redeem the fall by accumulating details and
freezing them into a poem. "My eye rides over and downwards, falls with /
Hurtling tons that slabber and spill, / Falls yet records the tumult thus
standing still." Finally his cold eye is "at-one" with the fall of the villains. He
has attained a still-point by stoically confronting the turbulence around him
and reembodying it in words.

    Geoffrey Hill, remembering Karl Barth's definition of sin, once wrote,
"It is at the heart of this 'heaviness' that poetry must do its atoning work,
this heaviness which is simultaneously the 'density' of language and the
'specific gravity of human nature' " (1984, 15). Art is redemptive when it
"re-deems" or "re-values" the recalcitrant world by giving it new significance. For Hill, as for Heaney, the poet is a kind of alchemist turning lighter
elements into gold, whose solidity bears witness to the world's weight and
splendor. This is the gist of "Churning Day," although here the alchemist is
a rural butter maker. His "large pottery bombs" of fermenting milk are
heavy with the reek of sin. His task is to turn the lighter milk into the
weightier "gold flecks," as if he were purifying ore or conjuring up "the
golden life" of a pastoral past (as in "Song of My Man-Alive"). The poem
describes how the "yellow curd . . . weighting the churned up white, /
heavy and rich . . . like gilded gravel" was beaten into shape in birchwood
bowls. The final product, the artifact, is butter. Heaney is interested in the
effect it has on the household, how it communicates (like a communion
wafer) a sense of "gravid ease." The word *gravid* is weighted with significance. It derives from the Latin *gravis*, meaning heavy, and *gravidus*, meaning pregnant. A sense of grace pervades the house, conjoined with a sense
of gravity, of the heavy weight of the world that submits to human shape
only after strenuous labor. The making of a child, the making of butter, the
making of a culture, or the making of a poem are one for Heaney. Anxiety is
purged in the pain of labor, although the splendor of the final artifact never
occludes the memory of its arduous process. By weighting his lines with an

etymological density and with the heavy "plash and gurgle," "pat and slap" of all worldly makings, Heaney achieves his at-one-ment, his temporary catharsis.

Perhaps the best example of Heaney's synthesis of pastoral and antipastoral motifs is "At a Potato Digging," where the "gravid" earth is both pregnant womb and rotting grave, a mound of fallen refuse and the compost heap for new life. The poem is a pastoral elegy for the famine victims of 1845 that places the human deaths into the larger context of nature's ineluctable, regenerative rhythm. It commemorates the toil and death of past farmers. Those who remember the "seasonal altar of the sod" and the "passion" of victims before them, paradoxically turn out to be sacrificial victims themselves. "Processional stooping through the turf" that "recurs mindlessly as autumn" ritually mimes the season's cycle. "Centuries / of fear and homage to the famine god" motivate the repetitive act of humility. Potatoes rather than communion wafers invoke for the poet sorrowful and terrifying scenes of crucifixion, the "live skulls, blind-eyed, balanced on / wild higgledy skeletons." The rural communicants "stoop" in humble supplication primarily because they have been beaten down by years of duress. Their communion at the end is as secular as it is sacred, pagan as it is Christian, and impelled by a recognition of nature's cruelty as well as by a religious desire to appease nature's wrath and bless its fruitfulness.

> Dead beat, they flop
> Down in the ditch and take their fill,
> Thankfully breaking timeless fasts;
> Then stretched on the faithless ground, spill
> Libations of cold tea, scatter crusts.

Employing elegiac and religious gestures to indicate that the potato diggers will go on "Tomorrow to fresh Woods, and Pastures new" (Milton [1637] 1983, 11) to ply their trade, Heaney is also underscoring the barrenness of such gestures. Tea and crusts parody the Eucharistic wine and bread. They mean nothing, either as manure or symbolic sacrifices to the "faithless ground." The pathos is reminiscent of Stephen Duck's "Thresher's Labour."

> With Heat and Labour tir'd, our Scythes we quit,
> Search out a shady Tree and down we sit:
> From Scrip and Bottle hope new Strength to gain;
> But Scrip and Bottle too are try'd in vain.

Heaney quotes Duck in his article on pastoral conventions and identifies him as "a voice protesting on behalf of the agricultural labourer, who no longer appears as jocund swain or abstract Industry but as a hard-driven human being" (1980a, 179–80). While Duck gravitated toward stock pastoral allusions and clichés, Heaney deploys an antipastoral diction that is as terse and earthy as the workers it memorializes.

For Heaney's pastoral lovers and farmers, a terrifying, inexplicable fate resides just beyond the pasture's walls and is always ready to invade. This is why in "Scaffolding," when the two lovers peer from their newly constructed walls, they declare, "Never fear. We may let the scaffolds fall / Confident that we have built our wall." Such wishful thinking, as it turns out, is a flimsy barrier against the fear that predominates in Heaney's early poems. To Robert Frost's narrator in "Mending Wall," who mocks his curmudgeonly neighbor for distrusting the notion of a society without walls, Heaney would retort that good walls not only make good neighbors, they make good lovers. Both poets speak for the romantic idealist and his pragmatic opponent. Heaney again echoes Frost in "Storm on the Island." In "Storm Fear" and "Old Man's Winter Night," Frost uses the image of a house to represent a limit, a psychological boundary, beyond which affliction and chaos reign. In Heaney's poem, which aims for Frost's colloquial fluency, two lovers retreat behind the walls of their house on an island where they are afflicted with almost military ferocity by a sense of chaos and nothingness. The poem is as antipastoral as Heaney's early "Aran," and is a sequel to it. The lack of pastoral fields first strikes the poet as terrifying, then as somehow appealing. "This wizened earth has never troubled us / With hay, so, as you see, there are no stacks / Or stooks that can be lost." They have nothing to do and nothing to lose; they also have nothing to gain. They remain as "unaided" by religious, political, or psychological supports as Frost's couple in "Storm Fear."

> We just sit tight while wind dives
> And strafes invisibly. Space is a salvo,
> We are bombarded by the empty air.
> Strange, it is a huge nothing that we fear.

The end is ambiguous. With "nothing to fear except fear itself," their imaginations are their real threat, not the dive bombers, bombs, and machine guns fabricated out of ordinary wind.

Heaney has followed what was once called the *rota Vergiliana* (Virgil's cycle) at his own pace and along his own route. He began his career writing pastorals and proceeded to tackle the epic (in diminutive form) in the mythical and historical accounts of "heroic" journeys in *North* and *Station Island*. Although pastorals traditionally depict shepherd boys at noon reclining by their flocks in the shade of olive groves, waging song contests in which, with the accompaniment of oaten flute, they commemorate lost friends and unrequited loves, Heaney depicts real friends and real lovers in the fields and houses of his rural background. Traditional pastorals juxtapose Edenic farms with cities rife with political corruption and war; Heaney shows that the worker can find hell and heaven, war and peace, and all sorts of psychological turmoil in his own "townland." *Death of a Naturalist* yearns for the unfallen condition of the child in the country, swaddled in a gauze of sunlight, but nearly every poem reveals him breaking from his maternal cocoon into the frightening patriarchal world outside. As the boy matures, he falls into a disturbing consciousness of sin, public and private, natural and supernatural, and finally struggles to construct a poetry that will bear witness to it.

Pastorals, like the troubles of Northern Ireland, have Christian roots. God is often construed as a shepherd, his intermediaries as pastors, his church as a flock gathered into a fold. The blood of the lamb is redemptive; the Apocalypse is a grand reaping. In Heaney's pastorals, however, Christian concepts provide little balm. Because of sectarianism, uprootings persist; apocalypse promises future blood feuds, not new Jerusalems. John Aikin once wrote in his "Essay on Ballads and Pastoral Song" that "pastoral poetry is a native of happier climates, where the fact of nature, and the manners of the people are widely different from those of our northern regions. What is reality on the soft Arcadian and Sicilian plains, is all fiction here" (1772, quoted in Barrell and Bull 1975, 383). Although an Arcadian twilight hovers over some of Heaney's poems, the bulk of them take place in the glare of painful northern realities.

Entangled in the antipastoral, oedipal nature of Irish religion and politics, Heaney in his first book struggles to achieve a mature as opposed to a narcissistic view. "As a child, they could not keep me from wells," he confesses in "Personal Helicon," the last poem in *Death of a Naturalist*. The muse's well is a tunnel into himself, a place for solipsistic soul-searching, for egoistic savoring of personal sins. The well water in which he sees his reflection marks his initiation into a knowledge of the "other"—the otherworld or unconscious—which for Freudian revisionists is often identified as the repressed text of one's culture. As William Richardson explains: "This fabric includes the cultural myths of his race, his ethnic style, his social traditions, the particularity of his ancestral lineage, the personal and social milieu of his immediate family . . . in short, the universal 'discourse' that has preceded him and into which he has been born" (1983, 60). In Heaney's allegorical account, this determining other is matriarchal and patriarchal, the cultural discourse of Mother Ireland and Father England combined. These different and endlessly embattled parents fashion the mirror in which Heaney learns who he is, and what he learns is not flattering. The well of introspection, he declares, "was scaresome for there, out of ferns and tall / Foxgloves, a rat slapped across my reflection."

What he examines is an "aquarium" of roots and rot, a synecdoche of that heavy, fallen world buried beneath the Eden of flax fields and butterflies. It is the antipastoral sump, the festering private and political unconscious, the history of agricultural depredations and cultural violence beneath the pastoral heaven. Heaney concludes, "Now, to pry into roots, to finger slime, / To stare, big-eyed Narcissus, into some spring / Is beneath all adult dignity." The voyeuristic obsession with the self, like Frost's inward gaze in "For Once, Then, Something," focusing on "me myself in the summer heaven, godlike" (Frost 1972, 225), is partly renounced. Heaney's pastoral dialectic moves from a childhood Eden of repressed awareness to its antithesis, a self-conscious, narcissistic relishing of antipastoral slime and desolation, and finally to a candid appraisal of "things as they are" beyond the pasture's walls. The first poems can be naïve, both in craft and passion, the later, such as "The Early Purges," morbid in their infatuation with grotesque detail. His mature style, eminently represented in *Death of a Naturalist* and in the books that follow, orchestrates a synthesis between rustic beauty and the harsh exigencies of farming. Writing poetry, which Heaney repeatedly compares to plows versing and reversing through fields and spades digging through historical soil, becomes a curative pastoral activity in itself. Heaney's unsentimental way of equating rural laborer and cultivated poet, which directly opposes the traditional way of dressing up city boys in swain's garb and transporting them to Arcadia to sing of ideal loves, reveals not so much the death of naturalism or realism as their healthy resurrection. If the unconscious is structured like a language, as Lacan claims, then Heaney's project will be to make the linguistic unconscious speak more candidly of its hierarchical structures. For Heaney, language's "binary oppositions" will take on greater complexity as he allows family differences and sectarian differences a chance to speak through him. His pastorals represent the first step in a scrupulously self-critical career that invokes traditional discourses in order to break through their mystifying values and assumptions.

3

THE POETRY OF MEDITATION

IMAGES OF DARK AND LIGHT APPEAR so frequently in poetic tradition that, when summoned for contemporary use, they run the risk of being immediately obsolescent. Each poet must dust off the old clichés and glaze them with new varnish. For Seamus Heaney, who is more attached to tradition than most, darkness and light dramatize his most pressing concerns. In *Death of a Naturalist*, as Dick Davis points out, "Darkness is associated with an uncontrollable fecundity, a pullulation of alien, secret, absorbing life" (1982, 29). Darkness is persistently linked to Heaney's adolescent fears of sex and death, light to their possible transcendence.

Even though many critics refuse to accept Heaney's second book, *Door into the Dark*, as an "advance on its predecessor" (Morrison 1982, 33), it certainly reveals a significant psychological advance. Rather than run from the dark, as he tended to do before, Heaney now faces up to it with grim determination or actively seeks it out. He mines the metaphor of a "door into the dark" so extensively that many of the new poems can be read allegorically. Still preoccupied with country matters—with farming, fishing, thatching, forging—he casts his rural personae in roles that dramatize the oppositions dueling in his imagination. Dark and light are now associated with speech and writing, forgetting and remembering, expiration and inspiration, blindness and insight, destruction and creation. The poems are intensely self-reflexive as they investigate their own perplexed making. Although Blake Morrison claims that "*Door into the Dark* is more promise than fulfillment, more hovering on the threshold than a decisive arrival" (1982, 33), Heaney's narrators restlessly cross back and forth over thresholds. As in traditional Christian meditations, their crossings from confusion to revelation, from mute blindness to luminous communion with the divine, are overshadowed by the cross itself.

For a poet who attended a Catholic school as a young man (St. Colomb's College in Londonderry from 1951 to 1957), the *Spiritual Exercises* of St. Ignatius Loyola, as well as of his compatriots St. Theresa of Avilla and St. John of the Cross, must have presented obvious parallels to his poetic practices. James Joyce, whose role as a mentor Heaney acknowledges at the end of "Station Island," may have suggested some of these parallels. Stephen Dedalus in *A Portrait of the Artist* finds Loyola's "composition of place" in the hellfire sermon so imaginatively effective that its central dictum "to imagine with the senses of the mind . . . the material character" (Joyce 1968, 127) of all things and events, when filtered through Aquinas, becomes his fundamental aesthetic principle. In *The Poetry of Meditation* (1954), Louis Martz demonstrated how Renaissance poets often derived narrative models from Loyola's pattern of composition of place, self-analysis, and colloquy and dwelled on the psychological processes behind them: memory, reason, and will. Heaney's meditations usually focus on scenes of artistic as opposed to Christian passion; still, they employ traditional meditational techniques in doing so. Their compositions of rustic artificers, who sacrifice financial contentment and bodily vigor in their devotion to outmoded crafts, act as reflectors in which Heaney analyzes his own procedures. His soul-searching is often as self-incriminating as was his well-gazing in "Personal Helicon," although now his investigations are more social than private. Rather than carry on a colloquy with the godhead or his sublimated mirror-image, normally he bears silent witness to craftsmen of his own ilk. Like Joyce, he finds in the divine author of creation a metaphor for the authorial imagination, praising and accusing it accordingly. Poetry, which for Heaney includes all makings, is a substitute religion that he never wholeheartedly reveres because it also mystifies the word. As his meditating narrators withdraw from the world into a pregnant, darkened silence, he often accuses them of narcissism, of stubbornly denying society's pressing concerns. If in the womb of the imagination both secular and holy words are made flesh, as Dedalus attests, the desire to regress can be infantile and defeating.

Heaney's emblematic "door into the dark" has numerous religious and literary precedents. It may come from the Bible's "I am the door: by me if any man shall enter in, he shall be saved" (John 10:9), where Christ is promising salvation for all. St. Theresa uses the metaphor in the initial stages of her meditational treatise, *The Interior Castle*, declaring that "the door by which to enter this castle is prayer and meditation" (1958, 19). It is implicit in St. John of the Cross's meditation, *The Dark Night*, in which the soul passes through a door in a darkened "house of the senses" to venture into a night infused with divine illumination. St. John explains, "When this house of the senses was stilled (that is, mortified), its passions quenched, and its appetites calmed and put to sleep through this happy night of the purgation of the senses, the soul went out in order to begin its journey along the road of the spirit, which is that of proficients and which by another terminology is referred to as the illuminative way or the way of infused contemplation" (1973, 327). Poems form the kernels of St. John's meditations, and Heaney translates one of these ("Song of the Soul that Rejoices in Knowing God through Faith") in "Station Island," comparing its theme of the dark night to St. Patrick's Purgatory on Lough Derg. In his second book the "dark night" is a metaphor for the imagination, which burns most intensely when darkened to the world.

Heaney mythologizes his door to make it archetypal. It may echo the "spiritual windows and doorways" in *The Cloud of Unknowing* (1961, 52), the anonymous medieval book on mysticism that holds that the doors of worldly perception must be closed so that the meditator can approach God's light. According to Benedict Kiely in "A Raid into Dark Corners," Heaney's poetics are based on "the cloud of unknowing [and] . . . what Patrick Kavanagh . . . called the fog, 'the fecund fog of unconsciousness.' Kavanagh said that we have to shut our eyes to see our way to heaven. 'What is faith, indeed, but a trust in the fog; who is God but the King of the Dark?' " Kiely traces Heaney's poetic mysticism to Catholic roots. From what Heaney calls the "negative dark that presides in the Irish Christian consciousness . . . the gloom, the constriction, the sense of guilt, the self-abasement," comes his poetic contention: "I think this notion of the dark centre, the blurred and irrational storehouse of insight and instincts, the hidden core of the self—this notion is the foundation of what viewpoint I might articulate for myself as a poet" (Kiely 1970, 10). Joseph Conrad's "door of darkness" and "door opening into a darkness" in *Heart of Darkness* (1989, 25, 36), Robert Frost's poem, "The Door in the Dark," and the illuminating, purgatorial darknesses in Yeats's "Byzantium" and Eliot's *Four Quartets* perhaps gave further support to Heaney's metaphor.

A letter from Heaney reveals that "all of the great spiritual writers were constantly being applied, in digested, pre-packaged form, by preachers at retreats, and were generally in the Catholic air I breathed at boarding school." He acknowledges his familiarity with St. John of the Cross, St. Theresa, Loyola's *Spiritual Exercises;* as a student at Queen's he read Evelyn Underhill's *Mysticism,* which thoroughly discusses the sort of Catholic meditation instilled in him as a young man. Most importantly, Heaney admits, "I read, as an undergraduate, in a pious spirit, *Seeds of Contemplation* by Thomas Merton" (letter to the author, 4 June 1987). In what Merton concedes is "nothing more than a collection of notes and personal reflections" on the interior life, Heaney found a contemporary and vigorous account of "Catholic tradition about the self-discipline of Christian asceticism" (Merton 1972, vii–ix). Furthermore, Merton declares that "those who have made the acquaintance of St. John of the Cross will find that much that is said about contemplative prayer follows lines laid down by the Spanish Carmelite. And so this book makes no claim to be revolutionary or even especially original" (ix). Throughout *Seeds of Contemplation*, as in St. John's work, the author affirms the purgatorial journey through darkness that culminates in transcendent illumination, the paradoxical death that is "the entrance into higher life" (2). "Contemplation is always beyond our own knowledge, beyond dialogue, beyond our own self," he proclaims. It even goes "beyond art, beyond poetry" in order to achieve "spontaneous awe at the sacredness of life" that proceeds "from an invisible, transcendent and infinitely abundant source" (1). The darkness needed to eclipse the stubborn egotism and worldliness of the meditator runs like a leitmotif through Merton's work, and he employs images of doors and thresholds to indicate the arduous crossing from worldly attachments to reverence of God. "Yet you find that you can rest in this darkness and this unfathomable peace without trouble and anxiety," he counsels late in his disquisition, "even when the imagination and the mind remain in some way active outside the doors of it" (177). Elsewhere he uses a darkened church, just as St. Theresa uses the darkness of an interior castle, to illustrate the soul's deliberate renunciation of the ordinary lights of reason and social convention along the mystical way.

To transform the past, Heaney stakes out territory that is unmistakably his own even while occupying the eminent domain of others. His emphasis on ascetic withdrawal into the dark, for example, downplays the traditional mystic's grim desire for mortification. Although St. John and St. Theresa relish God's "delicious wounds of love," and Loyola advises the retreatant to end his first week by chastising "the body by inflicting actual pain on it . . . by wearing hairshirts or cods or iron chains, by scourging or beating" (Ignatius Loyola 1963, 36), Heaney usually retreats from temporary distractions and confusions in a less melodramatic way—by walking, driving his car, or, like Kavanagh, by simply shutting his eyes. His meditations bear the influence of Merton's enlightened pacifism, social commitment, and affirmation of love that were so important to Heaney's generation of the sixties.

Still, Heaney is more iconoclastic than Merton. He embraces the mystic's sensory deprivation and intense concentration for secular and poetic purposes. St. Theresa summed up the contemplative's 'rite of passage' in the Fifth Mansion of *The Interior Castle*. "God deprives the soul of all its senses so that He may the better imprint in it true wisdom: it neither sees, hears, nor understands anything while it lasts" (1958, 55). For the traditional Christian like Merton (at least he professed orthodoxy), the purgative way culminates in unity with God through grace and love. When Heaney recollects Catholic spiritual exercises, he does so to better focus on their hallowed assumptions, which now seem hollow, and attacks their methods even as he employs them. He aims for transcendent clarity to obtain a better view of the ground he is trying, often foolishly, to transcend. When he quests for unity with a mysterious creative source, usually he finds it in a peat bog, in his own head, or in his wife. Rather than climb a ladder to heaven, Heaney opens his front door and discovers avatars of the Creator in the blacksmiths and thatchers working nearby.

Perhaps the best example of Heaney's unconventional meditative style can be found in "The Forge," a sonnet whose first line provides the title of his second book. To distance himself from Yeats, who celebrated golden smithies of the Byzantine empire, and Joyce, whose smithy was an adolescent aesthete dreaming of forging art but never quite managing to, Heaney greets a brawny artisan who, "leather-aproned, hairs in his nose," hammers out horseshoes. Heaney approaches this "maker" or "artist-god" in a traditional meditative way, by entering a dark "cloud of unknowing." He declares, "All I know is a door into the dark." The door is knowable but the dark beyond blinds him to a creative process that is ultimately unknowable. Heaney intimates correspondences between his blacksmith and God, then retracts them. The blacksmith may be one of God's intermediaries, a priest transubstantiating the materials of common experience into holy artifacts; at the end he is fundamentally a common laborer beating "real iron out."

Profane denotations undercut their sacred connotations. The blacksmith's anvil resembles Heaney's mysterious omphalos at the center of space and time. Heaney says, "The anvil must be somewhere in the centre." It is "horned as a unicorn," a product of fairy tale and legend, as well as an eternal, "immoveable . . . altar" where the blacksmith "expends himself in shape and music." Against this mythical background, he attends to secular makings rather than sacred ones, artifice rather than sacrifice, horseshoes rather than communion wafers. God's spirit in the last lines is no holy wind or breath inspiriting the soul of a communicant. It is simply the air pumped from the bellows into the forge's coals. If the blacksmith is an archetype (a type of Hephaestus), he is also a common man on the verge of obsolescence, sadly at odds with the modern day world of traffic outside his door. Cars have made horses nearly redundant, yet he continues to recollect better days and bang out shoes with heroic, if not pigheaded, devotion:

He leans out on the jamb, recalls a clatter
Of hoofs where traffic is flashing in rows;
Then grunts and goes in, with a slam and flick
To beat real iron out, to work the bellows.

Heaney admires his artificer. Nevertheless, he refuses to gaze at him through the mystic's mystifying spectacles. By the end of the poem he has grounded the blacksmith firmly in the social and economic community that determines and indeed threatens his existence.

Both Heaney and blacksmith follow the meditational paradigm of renunciation and reunion. Heaney withdraws from the noisy bustle of traffic and the decaying yard of rust outside to glimpse the work inside; the blacksmith leans out from the jamb and then returns to his forge. For Heaney, the outside world is governed by a grim, incontrovertible law of entropy and corruption, the inside world by a passionate, irrational will to creation: "Outside, old axles and iron hoops rusting; / Inside, the hammered anvil's short-pitched ring, / The unpredictable fantail of sparks." Outside things fall apart; inside, "somewhere in the centre," they are held together and hammered into unity.

"The Forge" illustrates the preliterate, instinctual, unconscious urges and binary oppositions Heaney finds at the center of all creation. As in Wordsworth's poetry, "what we are presented with is a version of composition as listening, as a wise passiveness, a surrender to energies that spring within the centre of the mind" (1980a, 63). In "The Forge," Heaney listens passively to the "short-pitched ring" of the anvil "in the centre" of the shop. He follows Yeats too, for whom "composition was no recollection in tranquility, not a delivery of the dark embryo, but a mastery, a handling, a struggle towards maximum articulation. . . . Thoughts do not ooze out and into one another, they are hammered into unity" (1980a, 75). Heaney's smith recollects the old equestrian days only to repudiate nostalgic musing at the end and hammer "real iron" in a fury of labor.

Blake Morrison contends that "what links the various traders, labourers and craftsmen who fill his first two books is that, unlike him, they are lacking in speech" and that Heaney, embarrassed by the linguistic sophistication provided by a university education, "found himself in the position of valuing silence above speech, of defending the shy and awkward against the confident and accomplished, of feeling language to be a kind of betrayal. . . . The community Heaney came from, and with which he wanted his poetry to express solidarity, was one on which the pressure of silence weighed heavily" (1982, 20, 23). In Catholic Northern Ireland, speaking your mind can be a dangerous business. For social and political reasons

Heaney elevates his mother's dictum, "Whatever you say, say nothing," into a poetic principle. He celebrates silence to underscore solidarity with his Irish Catholic ancestors and peers and more than anyone else, his father, a cattle dealer as devoted as the blacksmith to "the authenticity of the unspoken" (Clines 1983, 104). Silence is also part of the knowing "ignorance" and self-inflicted "blindness" of meditation. "You must become an ignorant man again," Stevens said in his long meditation, "Notes Toward a Supreme Fiction," "and see the sun again with an ignorant eye." In "The Forge," when the smithy ignores the fleeting present and focuses in silence on a radiant, sempiternal source (the forge of blazing coals), Heaney follows suit. Expiration—his figurative dying away from the environment—necessarily entails a repression of speech which, with luck, makes way for linguistic inspiration and the sublimation that is writing. Heaney and his compatriots may keep quiet to avoid sectarian recrimination; they also keep quiet to meditate and write.

Oppositions such as speech and writing, fact and fiction, intellect and intuition, work and play, father and mother, and hierarchies that have valued one over the other receive a new ordering from Heaney. If a logocentric preference for the spoken has devalued the written in Western thought, as Derrida insists, Heaney tends to celebrate the concrete accomplishment of writing over the evanescence of speech. While traditional Christian meditations culminate in colloquies "in which the soul speaks intimately with God and expresses its affections, resolutions, thanksgivings, and petitions" (Martz 1954, 27), Heaney's meditations on the artist-god concludes with speechless, writerly acts. His blacksmith, for example, merely "grunts"—he never speaks. Deconstructing the hierarchies instituted by Platonic and Christian tradition, Heaney also goes against an Irish grain. Hugh Kenner points out in *A Colder Eye* that "Irish writers have always been naggingly aware that Irishmen do not as a rule buy books, have never bought them, have even inherited a tradition whereby to write when you might be talking is an unnatural act. . . . And sensing that written words can even be *dangerous,* the Republic employs pretty active censors, who in addition to keeping out *Playboy,* contraceptive advice, and tons of quick-turnover porn, have interfered with some poets and with nearly every major prose writer" (1983, 16). Heaney protests the view that writing is "unnatural" as well as Socrates' view that it is a superfluous supplement, a "semblance of truth" causing forgetfulness and deception. And in this instance, as in the oedipal pastorals of *Death of a Naturalist,* he counters his own urge to return to a mother "devoted to argumentation, discourse" so that he can find a father—a model for the silent, cunning artificer he would strive to become. Writing, he will affirm, like sex, derives from a natural urge to reproduce life out of life. And its considered messages may contain more pungent truths than the less premeditated utterances of speech.

In "The Peninsula," Heaney specifically addresses the traditional opposition of speech and writing and casts his investigation in the form of a meditation. The poem recounts a passage into a "dark night" that blinds the poet to an unremarkable present so that, like the blacksmith, he can recall the past in graphic detail. Writing here is not an unnecessary appendage to, or a repression of, speech; it is a natural complement of speech:

> When you have nothing more to say, just drive
> For a day all round the peninsula.
> The sky is tall as over a runway,
> The land without marks so you will not arrive
>
> But pass through, though always skirting landfall.

At the start, the landscape appears to be a text that has been erased of all 'marks' of speech and writing. The emptying is a necessary purgation. In time, it will make space for a new 'annunciation,' a new influx of words. The 'negative way' has its dangers (landfalls, darkness), as the mystics warned, but Heaney's journey ends with renewed inspiration for writing. Reality is eclipsed, then recalled by the mind as it finds what will suffice for its poem.

> At dusk, horizons drink down sea and hill,
> The ploughed field swallows the whitewashed gable
> And you're in the dark again. Now recall
>
> The glazed foreshore and silhouetted log,
> That rock where breakers shredded into rags,
> The leggy birds stilted on their own legs,
> Islands riding themselves out into the fog.

The birds and islands are emblems of the poet who is also doubled back on himself, who meditates on the writerly imagination by means of the imagination. When the meditation concludes, perception is clarified. Things are seen in their *quidditas,* their unique thingness, radiantly and cleanly defined. Previously unfocused, the speechless poet is now prepared to uncode the landscape and translate what he reads into writing. Heaney admonishes,

> drive back home, still with nothing to say
> Except that now you will uncode all landscapes
> By this: things founded clean on their own shapes,
> Water and ground in their extremity.

Rather than write an imagist poem Heaney writes a poem about how imagist poems get written.

An intriguing essay on Andrew Marvell's use of the "self-inwoven simile or . . . short-circuited comparison" by Christopher Ricks highlights the meditative drama of "The Peninsula" and shows how Heaney draws on the earlier poet's legacy. "The reflexive image," Ricks claims, "simultaneously acknowledges . . . opposing forces and yearns to reconcile them" and may refer to the "art of poetry . . . , philosophical problems of perception and imagination" (1984, 54–55) as well as the raging factions in Marvell's England and Heaney's Northern Ireland. Although Heaney's 'self-inwoven' meditations become more overtly political in later books, in *Door into the Dark* they aim primarily at reconciling oppositions in the poetic imagination. The symbolic "birds stilted on their own legs" and "islands riding themselves out into the fog" provide images for the self-conscious poet. They also dramatize the paradox of creation, which is partly controlled and partly uncontrollable. Recalling Frost's poetic ice riding on its own melting, Heaney's islands ride on a conscious and unconscious flow.

"The Peninsula," in its 'self-inwoven' way, criticizes meditative tradition even as it follows its basic structures. Its sentiments resemble those of Roland Barthes, who complained in his essay on Ignatius Loyola that too often commentators of *The Spiritual Exercises* succumb to "the old modern myth according to which language is merely the docile and *insignificant* instrument for the serious things that occur in the spirit, the heart or the soul" (1976, 39). Heaney and Barthes deem language all-important and all-encompassing. In *The Spiritual Exercises* themselves, Barthes notes, "there is the awareness of human aphasia: the orator and the exercitant, at the beginning, flounder in the profound deficiency of speech, as though they had nothing to say and that a strenuous effort were necessary to assist them in finding a language" (45). He concludes, "The invention of a language, this then is the object of the *Exercises*" (48). This is the object of "The Peninsula" as well, where the silent driver quests for linguistic renewal, a new encoding rooted in the material world. Loyola has a more transcendent goal. He develops a language of prayers that, paradoxically, subvert human language as they prepare the meditator for an otherworldly sign. Loyola strives for 'indifference,' the opposite of language, which is a system of differences. God the Maker is God the Marker. He signifies the way for the meditator searching election and vocation. "The exercitant's role is not to choose, i.e., to mark, but quite the contrary to offer for the divine mark a perfectly equal alternative. The exercitant must strive not to choose; the aim of his discourse is to bring the two terms of the alternative to a homogenous state. . . . This paradigmatic equality is the famous Ignatian *indiffer-*

ence which has so outraged the Jesuit's foes: to will nothing oneself, to be as disposable as a corpse" (Barthes 1976, 72–73). Heaney's meditation moves in an opposite direction. He passes through linguistic indifferences (the unmarked landscape and his own silence) to a situation where differences are marked, distinct shapes uncoded, and not by God but by himself.

Heaney's parable of reading and writing could have been suggested by Joyce's *Ulysses* where Stephen takes an epistemological stroll along Sandymount strand ("water and ground in their extremity"). Stephen reads the "signatures of all things" (1961, 37), wondering whether the world is an apparition of words in his head or composed of actual objects that might hurt if he knocked his head against them. Both Dedalus and Heaney conclude that the world has a degree of independent existence, that the writer's duty is to manipulate codes of realism in order to deliver a facsimile of "things founded clean on their own shapes."

Heaney is prescriptive (he asserts, "you *will* uncode all landscapes") and is also diagnostic, analyzing how the meditative mind capitulates to 'codes' or 'transcendental signifiers' that mystify as they pretend to mediate reality. Heaney would have learned from Underhill that mystics of the *via negativa*, following the example of Dionysus the Aeropagite, assert only signs or signatures of God can be known and that God's book (the created universe) conceals as much as it reveals. Heaney diagnoses this linguistic mystification in the poem, "In Gallarus Oratory," a title combining notions of speech (oratory) and religious withdrawal (an oratory is a small chapel for special prayers). As in "The Forge" and "The Peninsula" Heaney renounces speech as he enters the sacred dark of the early Christian oratory (in Gallarus on the Dingle peninsula). His composition of place and self-analysis lead him toward those monks in the past whose rapport with God he respects but cannot quite share. His oratorical poems, so conscious of their rhetoric and fictive status, resemble the oratorical prayers of the monks in their passion but not in their goals. Drawn to the old chapel, like Philip Larkin in "Church-Going," he also intimates that the earlier communicants were both literally and figuratively "in the dark." All the images contribute to a sense of claustrophobic oppressiveness. The community's awareness of sin and fallenness is so strong it resembles a gravitational force pulling them down and burying them in a grave or "barrow." Roland Barth would say they resemble corpses. Heaney's meditative door opens on "a core of old dark walled up with stone / A yard thick" through which the monks, not unlike Robert Frost's "old-stone savage" in "Mending Wall" who "moves in darkness . . . / Not of woods only and the shade of trees" (1972, 34), enter a dark night that Heaney records with ambivalence. "When you're in it alone / You might have dropped, a reduced creature / To the heart of the globe." What for Heaney is a hypothetical situation, for the earlier monks was a dire exigency. Their sense of fallenness was irrevocable. "No worshipper / Would leap up to his God off this floor." The "heart" and "core" of this place at first seem radically different from the creative altar at the center of the blacksmith shop.

Heaney begins the sestet of his sonnet with the traditional meditative turn from dark trials to uplifting illuminations, from morbid concentration on evil to a vision of God's grace. The "dead" Christians awaken, resurrected from their graves (ironically, like pagan Vikings who were once buried in barrows).

> Founded there like heroes in a barrow
> They sought themselves in the eye of their King
> Under the black weight of their own breathing.
> And how he smiled on them as out they came,
> The sea a censer, and the grass a flame.

Obediently scouring their souls, the monks seem pressured into doing so by "their King." They burrow inward because they have nowhere else to go. When they emerge after systematically deranging their senses, as Arthur Rimbaud would say, they uncode all landscapes in a delusively sacramental as opposed to a realistic way. For a Catholic from Northern Ireland, "King" is hardly an innocent word. If for the monks it signifies an angry, jealous God, for Heaney it also implies the brutality of an imperialist master.

At the center of the Gallarus chapel is the oratorical scene in which spiritual words are delivered up to God, who in turn inspirits the communicants with holy words and a mystic vision of censers and flames. In this logocentric arena Heaney does not offer the traditional Catholic response. He does not pray or speak; he observes and writes. He may be recollecting the instructions of Loyola. "Every time I breathe in, I should pray mentally, saying one word of the 'Our Father' . . . so that only one word is uttered between each breath and the next" (Ignatius Loyola 1963, 85). He also mocks his heavy breathers by making them seem uncontrollably narcissistic. The communicants, "under the black weight of their own breathing," pray in a gothic atmosphere worthy of the stultifying enclosures of Edgar Allen Poe. Their sublime visions of censers and flames may be hallucinations bred out of repression.

A nonbeliever, Heaney still expresses empathy for the Gallarus monks. This is clearly evident in a prose account of a trip he made to Gallarus Oratory in 1967, which he appended to an article on early Irish nature poetry. The repressions and oppressions of Christianity he experienced produced a "small epiphany."

> Inside, in the dark of the stone, it feels as if you are sustaining a great pressure, bowing under like the generations of monks who must have bowed down in meditation and reparation on that floor. I felt the weight of Christianity in all its rebuking aspects, its calls of self-denial and self-abnegation, its humbling of the proud flesh and insolent spirit. But coming out of the cold heart of the stone, into the sunlight and the dazzle of grass and sea, I felt a lift in my heart, a surge towards happiness that must have been experienced over and over again by those monks as they crossed that same threshold centuries ago. This surge towards praise, this sudden apprehension of the world as light, as illumination, this is what remains central to our first nature poetry and makes it a unique inheritance. (1980a, 189)

For Thomas Weiskel, this sublime crossing of the threshold, "in which a burden . . . is lifted and there is an influx of power" (1976, 11), is essentially oedipal. The "King" imposes his repressive power in the oratory. The meditators, by identifying with the divine patriarch, avoid obliteration by becoming empowered patriarchs themselves. "The sublime moment releases the ego from guilt through an identification with the power by which (in melancholy) it had formerly been punished. . . . The affective coincidence of ego and super-ego appears to be the foundation of mystic ecstasy—an absorption into a greater power at once beyond and within" (97). Corroborating Barthes, Weiskel points out that the sublime moment comes when ordinary discourse breaks down ("this will be the working definition of the sublime—it is that moment when the relation between the signifier and signified breaks down and is replaced by an indeterminate relation" [ix]) and when the meditator, suspended in linguistic indifference, waits for a new sign. Humbly sacrificing his worldly speech and writing he prays to be 'written' or 'spoken' by a supernatural power.

Heaney investigates the psychological and political power relations in the religious heritage to which he still feels partly enthralled. As a result, his poems resemble a workshop littered with old icons and "trial pieces" constructed to replace them. His narratives, which are full of grammatical negatives, usually negate past myths to make way for saner, more realistic alternatives. His meditations, in line with their classical paradigms, move toward love with increasing frequency but celebrate its worldly more than its apocalyptic forms. "Girls Bathing, Galway 1965" begins negatively.

> No milk-limbed Venus ever rose
> Miraculous on this western shore.
> A pirate queen in battle clothes
> Is our sterner myth.

After the first negation, Heaney draws attention to the way his mind doubles back on itself, washing away the past images after it casts them up for contemplation. "The breakers pour / Themselves into themselves, the years / Shuttle through space invisibly." The apocalyptic sea changes them too, mixing tales of Christian judgments with tales of Irish pirates.

> The queen's clothes melt into the sea
>
> And generations sighing in
> The salt suds where the wave has crashed
> Labour in fear of flesh and sin
> For the time has been accomplished.

Heaney brilliantly invokes expectations of Christian apocalypse only to assert the living reality that such myths deny. In contradistinction to St. John on Patmos, who envisioned a sea offering up the dead for judgment, Heaney imagines the sea offering up ordinary girls in bathing suits.

> As through the shallows in swimsuits,
> Bare-legged, smooth-shouldered and long-backed
> They wade ashore with skips and shouts.
> So Venus comes, matter-of-fact.

To Christian mystics who abase themselves before patriarchal powers and clamor for spiritual marriages with God, and classical mythmakers who dream of beautiful women born out of sea foam like Venus, Heaney offers a flesh-and-blood beauty, countering the phantasmal fathers and etherealized women of old.

In tracing the arduous process by which the mind purges its images to create them anew, Heaney's meditations resemble what Mercia Eliade called "the eternal return." They seek to abolish temporal history (Father Time) in order to recover the timeless void (the Eternal Mother) out of which new order or 'cosmos' burgeons. For cultures that regard action as a ritualistic repetition of archetypes, Eliade claims:

> 1. Every creation repeats the pre-eminent cosmogonic act, the Creation of the world.

2. Consequently, whatever is founded has its foundation at the center of the world (since, as we know, the Creation itself took place from the center.) (1954, 18)

For Joyce, the artist repeats the cosmogonic act in the womb of the imagination, so that "the mystery of esthetic like that of material creation is accomplished" (1968, 215). Heaney's imagination is similarly ritualistic, gravitating toward "centers" in order to repeat profane as well as sacred acts of creation that, he often painfully confesses, are wedded to destructions. In "The Salmon Fisher to the Salmon," a poem reminiscent of Robert Lowell's metaphysical fishing poems, the poet is the Fisher King, both victimized fish and Christlike, 're-creational' fisherman. Heaney, *in imitatione Christi*, follows the fish as it withdraws from the sea toward an interior space, a contemplative center. Here destruction is united with its opposite.

> you flail
> Inland again, your exile in the sea
> Unconditionally cancelled by the pull
> Of your home water's gravity
>
> And I stand in the centre, casting.

At the "centre" a created and captivating lure unites fisher and wounded fish. "I go, like you, by gleam and drag / And will strike when you strike, to kill. / We're both annihilated on the fly." At-one-ment with God's crucified body (Christ's symbol was the fish) is the sacred analogue that Heaney repeats in the common experience of fishing. The lure unifies opposed forces. So does the poem, which is a love song to the fish as much as an elegy for its annihilation.

Heaney may have found support for his views on circularity and recurrence in Ralph Waldo Emerson, who states in his essay "Circles," "The eye is the first circle; the horizon which it forms is the second; and throughout nature this primary figure is repeated without end. It is the highest emblem in the cipher of the world. St. Augustine described the nature of God as a circle whose centre was everywhere and its circumference nowhere" (1940, 279). Heaney, likewise, finds circles everywhere. "The Plantation," for example, maps an eternal cycle of creation and destruction that at first bewilders him. After he withdraws from the disturbing present—the "hum of the traffic"—his meditation as before strives to locate emblems for its own doubling back, its own circularity. The plantation provides a historical emblem too; the cycle of invasion and domination has recurred so many times in Ireland that Heaney regards it as archetypal. His act of communion invokes master and slave, victim and victimizer, man and woman, English landlord (Munster was divided into hierarchical plantations in the 1580s) and Irish tenant. Heaney dramatizes the combination of psychological and historical antinomies with a familiar, haunting fairy tale.

> You had to come back
> To learn how to lose yourself,
> To be pilot and stray—witch,
> Hansel and Gretel in one.

When he begins his investigations, "any point in that wood / Was a centre." Now he is lost, traveling in circles, like the "toadstools and stumps / Always repeating" themselves. A meditative darkness ("the black char of a fire") marks his exclusion from society, yet reveals those who have made similar journeys before. "Someone had always been there / Though always you were alone." As in "The Salmon Fisher to the Salmon," Heaney finally reveals his dual role as destroyer and creator, which unites him culpably to a process he would rather repudiate. He must play the reclusive witch, sacrificing childlike enthusiasms in order to redeem them in poems.

The last poem in *Door into the Dark* finds a new and startling image for the contemplative mind and its sacrifices in that most common of Irish landscapes: the bog. Earlier he approached a door in a blacksmith's shop or oratory; here he is drawn to the bottomless "wet centre" of a tarn. His concentration is Emersonian. A "transparent eyeball" focuses in ever-intensifying circles on a mysterious center.

> We have no prairies
> To slice a big sun at evening—
> Everywhere the eye concedes to
> Encroaching horizon
>
> Is wooed into the cyclops' eye
> Of a tarn.

Concealing the sunlit world outside and paradoxically penetrating the "dark night" inside, Heaney's eye glimpses its own reflection in the tarn where images are received, broken down, preserved, and exhumed. The ground, like the mystic consciousness 'wounded' by love, opens itself to all. It is "kind, black butter / Melting and opening underfoot, / Missing its last definition / By millions of years." Its *caritas* seems ineffable and unknowable, archetypal rather than historical. He concludes,

Our pioneers keep striking
Inwards and downwards,

Every layer they strip
Seems camped on before.
The bogholes might be Atlantic seepage.
The wet centre is bottomless.

Common acts in the present again echo sacred ones of the past. His pioneers are turf diggers who double as spiritual questors. They ritually reenact the "eternal return" in their search for a mysterious, cosmogonic source.

The contrast between the expansive prairie and the vertical descent into the bog intimates a conflict in Heaney's mystic stance. Heaney, like many Irish before him, is attracted by the "mystic" democracy of America (the country of prairies and pioneers), whose apotheosis is Walt Whitman's cosmic embrace of all created things. He is also irrevocably European as he plumbs tradition's hoard. He goes outward to encounter the reality of experience and also downward, an archaeologist retrieving reliquary forms. Closer to Joyce and Yeats than to Whitman, Emerson, and William Carlos Williams (whom, especially in *Wintering Out*, he tried to imitate), he struggles to find in central institutions, such as the Catholic church and its spiritual exercises, rituals, and symbols, a faith he has lost and rediscovered in *poesis*. Whitman's apocalyptic rejection of European traditions tempts him. So does the American penchant for leveling hierarchies, decentering centralized institutions, and questing for democratic ideals in transcendent spaces. Heaney's sensibility, however, is as inextricably rooted in traditional poetic forms as in the political and religious institutions of Ireland. He wields the iconoclast's axe for the sake of ambivalent reconstruction, not of outright demolition. His emphasis on order and pattern is doggedly formalist, even though he overhauls old forms to make them consistent with contemporary experience.

With some justification, critics suspect Heaney's formalism to be part of a larger conservatism and accuse him of stubbornly refusing to modernize himself. His unsettled attitudes with regard to both past and present, however, seem particularly modern. A. Alvarez, for example, chastises Heaney for repudiating Modernism's "literary declaration of Independence" (however antiquated it may be in the eighties) and claims, "If Heaney really is the best we can do, then the whole troubled, exploratory thrust of modern poetry has been a diversion from the right true way" (1980, 16–17). On the other hand, Heaney's skepticism of "right true ways" and of the sensibility that tenders such illusions makes him more modern than his detractors. His meditative style *is* troubled and exploratory. If it is not specifically informed by structuralist and poststructuralist debate, as Blake Morrison occasionally worries, it certainly shares its principle concerns. Obsessed with such hierarchical oppositions as writing and speech, forgetting and remembering, blindness and insight, profane and sacred love, marginal and central institutions, Heaney typically reveals a dialectical relation where oppressively one-sided relations were or are the rule. His doors into the dark open onto a present inextricably wedded, for better or worse, to the past. In "Literary History and Literary Modernity," an essay in *Blindness and Insight*, Paul de Man points out, "As soon as modernism becomes conscious of its own strategies . . . it discovers itself to be a generative power that not only engenders history, but is part of a generative scheme that extends far back into the past" (1983, 150). Heaney's premeditated forgettings and renunciations in *Door into the Dark* aim to purge earlier anxieties and the hierarchical structures that provoked them. "Make it new," for Heaney as for Pound, also means "make it old." De Man writes, "When [writers] assert their own modernity, they are bound to discover their dependence on similar assertions made by their literary predecessors, their claim to being a new beginning turns out to be the repetition of a claim that has always been made" (161). Heaney's meditations, which scrutinize their own procedures and compare them to all makings, find precedents in a tradition of Catholic meditation. By substantially revising that tradition, Heaney gives to the old forms a new complexity and an attractive, personal finish.

4

POETYMOLOGIES

W HEN SEAMUS HEANEY remarked to Elgy Gillespie of the *Irish Times*,
"I've been writing poems lately that grow out of words and ways
of talking" (Heaney 1972c, 10), he revealed that his attentiveness to language had taken a new philological turn. His first two books, *Death of a
Naturalist* and *Door into the Dark*, as critics were quick to notice, resonated
with heavily stressed vowels and consonants and depicted Irish landscapes in
images as sensuous as they were harsh. *Wintering Out*, published in 1972
(the year Heaney spoke to Gillespie), began to sketch Irish wordscapes in
which even the vowels and consonants conveyed mythic significance. What
is startling about Heaney's wordscapes is the deft, unobtrusive way they
delineate allegories of his Northern Irish heritage. From the phonetic and
lexical features of individual words he creates moving dramas in which
religious, political, literary, and sexual differences clash and fuse.

Heaney's leaps from an early, gritty pastoralism, which countered stock
images of Arcadian groves and teary-eyed shepherds playing on oaten flutes
with tales of actual farming, to a meditative style that countered traditional
Catholic meditations with secular alternatives and then to a linguistic poetry
whose characters and plots derived from little-known words, left many of his
critics baffled. An anonymous reviewer in the *Times Literary Supplement*
echoed the sentiments of many by complaining that the new poems failed
to confront the resurgence of violence in Northern Ireland. "No one was
plucking up" cobbles "to throw them at anyone," the reviewer stated,
implying that Heaney had to be poetry's Sam Peckinpah to be taken seri-
ously. He concluded, "*Wintering Out* gives the slightly unsatisfactory im-
pression of being a transitional book, skirting round themes he is reluctant
to tackle head on" (15 December 1972, 1524). Stephen Spender in *The
New York Review of Books* suggested that it was Heaney's intoxication with
words that blinded him "to a much wider subject matter." Compared to

49

Joyce, "he is still at the *Dubliners* stage of his development" (1973, 13), that is, at square one.

Seamus Deane, in many ways Heaney's most insightful critic, was one of the only reviewers of *Wintering Out* to explain Heaney's impasse, and to point out that Heaney was painfully aware of it. To turn poetry into a bullhorn for political policies would ruin its lyric impulse, he suggested, but poetic rhetoric that excludes current affairs smacks of irresponsibility, of a willful indifference to the community's needs. Regarding Heaney's sins of omission and commission, Deane commented, "The poems express no politics and indeed they flee conceptual formulations with an almost indecent success. Instead they interrogate the quality of the relationship between the poet and his mixed political and literary traditions. The answer is always the same. Relationship is unavoidable, but commitment, relationship gone vulgar, is a limiting risk. Nevertheless commitment is demanded during a crisis." To articulate a moral response to the origins and outbursts of sectarian conflict in Ireland was not enough. Deane concluded, "He is called upon to assume responsibility. In doing so, he does not satisfy his critics, for whom his commitment is not of the sort they want; nor does he satisfy himself, for, in attempting to do 'the whole job of culture,' he may forget to live" (1976, 203).

"Living" as a Catholic in Belfast sometimes means fighting and dying for minority rights. Heaney actively participated in the civil rights marches in 1968 and a few weeks later declared angrily in *The Listener*, "the Catholic minority in Northern Ireland at large, if it is to retain any self-respect, will have to risk the charge of wrecking the new moderation and seek justice more vociferously" (1968, 522). Two years later he surprised some and infuriated others when he decided to leave Belfast. In 1970 he took a temporary position at Berkeley, and after returning in 1971 to Northern Ireland and the Provisional I.R.A.'s new bombing campaign, he moved permanently to the South. The critical consensus was that Heaney's *Wintering Out*, published the year of his departure, was a cop-out as well. His preoccupation with language and poetic craft was simply the literary analogue of his political betrayal.

Heaney was certainly aware of his divided allegiances. To Robert Druce he confessed, "I'm always thinking to myself—'when people are killing one another, what are *you* doing?'. . . And I came to this notion that, in a time of politics or violence, it wasn't the artist's function just to be liberal and deplore it, but if you believed in one set of values over the other, to maintain those values in some way. You needn't necessarily maintain that belief by writing political poetry or writing deploring the army. . . . But I think you can write about, or out of a sensibility or a set of images which imply a set of values" (Heaney 1979b, 27). What critics of *Wintering Out* objected to was the way Heaney intimated his politics. Why not declaim them? Heaney approached Ulster's turmoil from his own oblique angle, a technique every writer employs when facing a well-worn subject. Literary strategies, for better or worse, often preclude political ones. Blake Morrison pointed out, "What *Wintering Out* does is to explore the deeper structures of present hostilities, the way in which divisions of Protestant and Catholic communities are embedded in language and topography" (1982, 39). Heaney's tacit values are those of a physician who seeks a cure for a chronic disease. Despite Gavin Ewart's accusation that Heaney advocates "the ordinary, unscientific view" ("He isn't in there, whirling, with the atoms" [1972–73, 133]), Heaney's eye is trained with scientific deliberation on the X ray of his broken inheritance—the spoken and written language of Ulster.

According to Heaney's vision, science and myth conjoin. Sparring with Edmund Spenser, whose imperialistic schemes were built into *The Faerie Queene* and whose vicious plans to garrison and starve Ireland into submission were articulated in *A View of the Present State of Ireland* (a book alluded to in both *Wintering Out* and *North*), Heaney devises subtle, miniature allegories in which the antinomies within words assume bodily forms and act out political, religious, poetic, and sexual battles that have sundered Ireland for centuries. Vowels are Irish, nationalist, Catholic, and female; they stand for a Gaelic literary tradition and for the mythic body and soil of Mother Ireland. Consonants are English, Anglo- or Scots-Irish, unionist, Protestant, and masculine; they embody an Anglo-Saxon literary tradition and a rapacious, patriarchal England bent on imperial dominance.

When Heaney alludes to Spenser at the end of "Bog Oak" he is rebutting the allegorical techniques of the earlier poet as well as his invidious politics; he is also announcing his own guilty sense of collusion in dreamy attempts to impose myths, allegorical or otherwise, onto a culture's living body. His tone suggests a sad recognition of complicity more than an angry denunciation.

> Perhaps I just make out
> Edmund Spenser
> dreaming of sunlight
> encroached upon by
>
> geniuses who creep
> 'out of every corner
> of the woodes and glennes'
> towards watercress and carrion.

The vision of the dreaming poet haunted by ghosts of his political sins, whose sunlit reveries have turned to accusing nightmares, recurs in Heaney's poetry.

Spenser and Heaney join hands only for a moment. Heaney obviously finds little use for *The Faerie Queene*'s knights "pricking on the plain / Y-clad in mighty arms" (*FQ*, 1.1.1). He aims for an allegorical marriage between Protestants and Catholics in Ireland, not, as did Spenser, between English institutions and their imperial destiny. While *The Faerie Queene* musters all sorts of arcane ceremonies in order to consecrate its sacred sense of marriage between Una and the Redcross Knight (the lighting of sacred lamps "for feare of evill fates," sprinkling of "all the posts with wine," and perfuming the house "with frankensense divine" [*FQ*, 1.12.37–38]) for Heaney the vocables of everyday Anglo-Irish speech suffice as tokens of a more compelling marriage.

Spenser's *A View of the Present State of Ireland* acts as the more potent catalyst for Heaney's allegorical poems. Irenius and Eudoxus (Ireland and 'good judgment'), the two figures who carry on a dialogue in *A View*, represent different sides of Spenser's personality, just as the Gaelic and Anglo-Saxon phonemes represent two sides of Heaney's. Heaney would agree with Eudoxus's belief that we should approach Irish problems as "wise physicians which first require that the malady be known thoroughly and discovered, [and] afterwards do teach how to cure and redress it" (Spenser [1596] 1970, 3). Heaney's alter egos agonizingly attempt to re-dress old wounds. Spenser's twins, by contrast, chat urbanely about the most efficient way to bring Ireland to its knees. Curing, for them, means killing, and their targets are Irish words, Irish customs, and the Irish rebels who seek to perpetuate them. Linguistic imperialism is no figment of a paranoid psyche; it is a principle of Elizabethan colonialism explicitly out-lined by Eudoxus, who speaks for both Spenser and his Anglican cohorts. "It seemeth strange to me that the English should take more delight to speak that language [Irish] than their own, whereas they should (methinks) rather take scorn to acquaint their tongues thereto, for it hath been ever the use of the conqueror to despise the language of the conquered, and to force him by all means to learn his" (67).

To eradicate the corrupting Irish influence among the English immi-grants, Irenius finally dreams up his "modest proposal," which Heaney refers to at the end of "Bog Oak." By starving the natives into cannibalism so that "they would quickly consume themselves and devour one another," the English can subjugate the notion as well as avoid the high cost of a protracted military campaign. Irenius offers historical precedents (the "late wars in Munster") as evidence that his gruesome plan can work. Heaney quotes from his argument.

> Out of every corner of the woods and glens they came creeping forth upon their hands, for their legs could not bear them. They looked anatomies of death, they spake like ghosts crying out of their graves, they did eat of the dead carrions, happy were they could find them, yea and one another soon after in so much as the very carcasses they spared not to scrape out of their graves, and if they found a plot of water cress or shamrocks, there they flocked as to a feast for the time, yet not able long to continue therewithal, that in short space there were none almost left and a most populous and plentiful country suddenly left void of man or beast. (Spenser [1596] 1970, 104)

Fabricating Spenser into a monument of poetic guilt, Heaney makes sure to distinguish his sins from his precursor's. By choosing art over political engagement Heaney may be allowing the old plantation mentality, which Spenser directly fostered as secretary to Lord Grey, a right-of-way. His art still repudiates Spenser's politics with the powers available to it. It advocates unity and reconciliation on Irish soil and speaks eloquently against bloodshed to all who will listen.

Heaney's allegorical wordscapes have a political message even though it may not be the sort that makes politicians stand up and vote. As Neil Corcoran observes, a poem like "Broagh" delivers "an implicit emblem for some new political community . . .; it acts as a linguistic paradigm of a reconciliation beyond sectarian division" (1986, 90). Most of the poems that explore the etymological roots of words tell one story and one history too. The central narrative has the charm of a fairy tale and the candor of a documentary. It proposes an original unity where one language (Gaelic) was spoken. The language, Heaney presumes, was feminine, a natural, spontaneous efflorescence of the Irish earth. During the Renaissance the phallocentric, imperialistic language of England, clanging with Anglo-Saxon armor, invaded, raped, and conquered. Consonants were grafted onto vowels. Having fallen from power, feminine Ireland rose up only to be beaten down. The history of rebellion, dating to Norman invasions in the Middle Ages, is embedded in the language, a fossil record. Heaney rereads and rewrites the record of ancient antagonism, fashioning new emblems of adversity as well as new emblems of cooperation. The word redeems in Heaney's "catholic" poetics, not by ignoring or overhauling the past but by witnessing its injustices and offering judicious alternatives.

54

SEAMUS HEANEY

Heaney has often been accused of distorting history with myth (especially by Edna Longley and Ciaran Carson), and in his philological poems he surely gives a highly stylized and condensed version of Anglo-Irish history. From a poet who once said about his childhood in Northern Ireland, "I think Catholicism meant *everything* to me . . . because it was my whole life" (1979b, 30), one might expect a vision of history refracted through the lens of Christian typology. Even though Heaney's version of linguistic history presupposes an Eden, a vulnerable, innocent Eve, a Satanic, patriarchal intruder, a fall into conflict, and a redemption through the 'word,' it also self-reflexively attacks myth and reorders its classic priorities. As in the pagan, matriarchal myths Robert Graves examines in *The White Goddess*, a book that reinforced Heaney's mariolatry, the allegorical woman comes first in Heaney's narrative. She is no biblical Eve consigned to secondary status. If she is militarily and economically weaker than England, she is so because of the exigencies of history, not the prejudices of Heaney. She does not fall of her own free will, as Milton would have it; she falls because of multiple acts of patriarchal aggression. Redemption, as Adrienne Rich might assert, is "the dream of a common language." Its embodiment is not the Christ-Word dead on the cross so much as secular words living on communal tongues, uniting "crossed" factions traditionally opposed in inarticulate combat.

To claim that Heaney employs gender stereotypes and myths in an unreflective, patriarchal way grossly simplifies his mythic method. Following Wallace Stevens and James Joyce, Heaney is the most self-conscious of mythmakers. His poems dissect "supreme fictions" in order to forge them anew. Deploying myths that express personal and cultural fixations presents no philosophical difficulties for Heaney, because he consistently addresses them as fictions. In his interview with John Haffenden he remarks, "I'm not what you call a pious Catholic . . . [but] I've never felt any need to rebel or do a casting-off of God or anything like that, because I think in this day anthropologists and mythologists have taught us a lot, to live with our myths" (Haffenden 1981, 60). To another interviewer he said, "I think we have become more aware . . . of the deep value of some kind of belief, of some kind of ritual. Of their value as fictions, if you like, or as structures. And I suppose I am grateful for the whole burden of Catholicism in that way" (1979b, 30). While Catholicism is his seminal myth, the lineaments of his ultimate myth approximate what Joyce in *Finnegans Wake* called the "monomyth," a story in which all myths fit into one organic, catholic whole.

Joyce's intense sensitivity to the political and religious connotations of words, and his way of mythologizing them, provide Heaney with valuable directives. Joyce also scores the soft, lambent vowel-flow of Irish into the monologues of his archetypal women, Molly Bloom and Anna Livia Plurabelle, and the harsher, consonantal hammer strokes of English into his archetypal men, Leopold Bloom and Humphrey Chimpden Earwicker. Heaney composes similarly, but on a less grandiose scale. Heaney remarks that Joyce "could invest the very names of punctuation marks with historical riddles when he addressed his people as 'Laities and gentes, full-stoppers and semi-colonials' " and that his mythic method "melted time and place into a plasm of rhythms and word-roots, puns and tunes, a slide-show of Freudian slips for the Jungian type-setter" (1984a, 16). With Joyce in his wake, Heaney's allegories of vowels and consonants seem traditionally Irish rather than eccentrically English. Both authors treat Ireland's Anglo-Gaelic language as a labyrinth of history's tortuous process. They fly over it primarily to gain a more panoramic perspective of the vestiges of a colonial past scarred on its walls.

Heaney knows, if for no other reason than because he has read Joyce, that philology and myth have walked in tandem throughout Western tradition. Up until two hundred years ago, scholars of language tended to conjure up etymological scenarios as magicians pulled rabbits out of hats. For Socrates, etymology was part fantasy, part comedy, and part history. Medieval etymologists, working from a less enlightened Christian view than Heaney's, speculated that a universal language existed in Eden. The collapse of the Tower of Babel reduced this primordial harmony to a discordant babble. St. Isidore of Seville, whose twenty-volume *Etymologies* was the most authoritative source of the discipline during the Middle Ages, spoke for a consensus when he declared in the early 600s, "The different languages are a result of the Tower of Babel, and before that, there was a single language, Hebrew" (quoted in Dineen 1967, 148). When Adam named the animals in Eden, according to medieval sages he did so in the divinely inspired language of the Old Testament fathers.

Philology became more scientific in the eighteenth century, although etymologists still searched for mythic universals beneath language's puzzling surface. The famous linguist, Horne Tooke, exercised his scholarly imagination with great ingenuity in order to prove all parts of speech were originally signs for concrete things. Beneath the obfuscations of abstract words lay a prelapsarian Eden of earthly clarities. Etymology was his archaeological tool with which he could dig to the bottom of even the most tangled metaphysical problem. He ended up, ironically, promoting his own brand of what he derisively called "etymological metaphysics." Giambattista Vico, also writing during the eighteenth century (he would later provide Joyce with a cyclical model of culture for *Finnegans Wake*), formulated a similar metaphysics. "The philosophers and philologians ought all, we claim, to have begun their treatment of the origin of language and letters from the following principles: that the first men conceived the ideas of things through imaginative characters [gods]; that, being mute, these men expressed themselves by actions and objects which have natural relations to these ideas" (1982, 234). This natural "theological" language that expressed no ideas but in things, he concludes, was the universal language of Atlantis. The first language users, like Joyce's stuttering Earwicker, were both tongue-tied giants and imagist poets whose speech came gradually from imitating Jove's thunder, and whose words for objects were the names of gods.

Around the turn of the eighteenth century, William Jones and Friedrich Schlegel renounced the etymological myths of their predecessors and applied painstaking scholarship to the linguistic problems of the past. Through his study of Latin, Greek, and Sanskrit, Jones hypothesized "that no philologer could examine them all three, without believing them to have sprung from some common source, which, perhaps, no longer exists" (quoted in Aarsleff 1983, 133). The mythical Atlantis—the original tongue behind all Indo-European languages—finally had been discovered "scientifically." Despite repeated attempts to locate it geographically and historically, it remained elusive. While Heaney's poetic etymologies are tied closely to actual geographical places and historical events, they fit into this wider context of philological myth and conjecture. He can be as fanciful as Vico, whose sentiments about poetic language he echoes vis-à-vis Joyce, or as meticulously scholarly as William Jones. In each case he presupposes a lost Edenic source, an original unity, from which language has fallen. To reveal the historical disasters coming after the fall he examines their repercussions coded in the words themselves.

In his discussion of toponymy (the study of place names), the linguist Mario Pei shows how "in Europe and Asia . . . almost every place name contains a record of migrations and conquests, far-flung trading posts and garrison towns. . . . Changes in place names frequently reflect historical transfers of power and political events as well as nationalistic aspirations and ambitions" (1949, 60, 65). Heaney, as his meditations on local Northern Irish place names attest, would agree. Words such as Toome, Broagh, Anahorish, and Mossbawn trace Ulster's heritage of invasions precipitated by the military and commercial interests of Scottish and English planters and countered by Irish patriots. With Vico and Tooke, Heaney etymologizes to reveal a sense of the actual places and objects the names have veiled. He redeems the clichés, and in tones of nostalgia and despair documents the sacred places that have been desecrated.

His etymological quests often find fulfillment, oddly enough, in a renunciation of words, in a silent communion with the fecund, healing earth. Like Stevens in "Credences of Summer," he too wants to "see the very thing and nothing else / . . . Without evasion by a single metaphor" (Stevens 1972, 288). In later poems, as "etymologist of roots and graftings," Heaney admonishes,

> Come back past
> philology and kennings,
> re-enter memory
> where the bone's lair
>
> is a love-nest
> in the grass.

The word *mystery*, as Heaney would probably know, derives from the Greek *mu-sterion*, "to initiate and keep silent." Ancient mystery cults—those at Eleusis celebrating Demeter or those in Iron Age Denmark commemorating Nerthus—form the narrative spine of many of Heaney's poems. Whether he is digging up root crops or etymological roots, his purpose is the same: to reestablish contact with the mysterious, productive, preliterate energies of earth. Again he echoes Vico who, in his discussion of how the Latin *mutus* (mute) was derived from the Greek *mythos*, postulated a protolanguage with which the first theological poets contacted the mysteries. "Thus, in the mute era was born the mental language which, in a golden passage, Strabo says existed before vocal or articulated language: whence *lógos* signifies both 'idea' and 'word.' And it was appropriate that divine providence should order it thus in such religious times, in view of the eternal property that it is of greater importance to religion that one should meditate it than that one should speak of it" (1982, 221). In his paradoxical process of conjuring and then abjuring philology and Anglo-Saxon devices (kennings, alliterations), Heaney stands in mute recognition before the Gaelic "love-nest," remembering the sacred fertility goddess of Ireland inherent in the silent emblem in the grass.

Heaney's etymological poems are rituals that recreate the bond between word and root, place name and sacred earth. *Etymologist*, in fact, means a "studier of roots." Latin Stoics such as Varro during the first century A.D. claimed that by discovering the original forms of words, called *etyma* or "roots," the precise correspondence between reality and language could be ascertained. Greek Stoics, by contrast, envisioned the *logos* (both word and reason) rooted in the divine mind or *nous*. In his *History in English Words*, a book Heaney perused during his university days, Owen Barfield explains that the Greeks "were the first to make the progressive

incarnation of thought in audible sound a part of the creative working of
God in the world; and it is to them accordingly, with their deep sense of the
divine significance of words and their origin, that we owe the word *etymology*, the first half of which is composed of a poetical Greek adjective meaning 'true' " (1924, 113). For Heaney the sacred *nous* is less highfalutin. It is
the vaginal "love-nest," the earth's procreative oracle, as well as any imagination that repeats in the finite mind the original act of creation, as Coleridge
and Joyce believed. To Heaney's naturalistic mind, nature is both original
poet and divine inspirer. The human imagination reads the sounds and
images in her divine book and transliterates them into intelligible symbols.

"The Backward Look," a poem in the middle of *Wintering Out*
whose title comes from Eliot's "the backward look behind the assurance /
Of recorded history, the backward half-look / Over the shoulder, towards
the primitive terror" ("The Dry Salvages," in Eliot 1969, 187), looks back
to the sort of primitive poetic sensibility Vico believed the first humans
possessed as they attempted to translate nature's signs into their own tongue.
The poem begins like Yeats's "Leda and the Swan," with a sudden beating
of wings, but the mysterious silence, the *mu-sterion* ("as if a language
failed"), initiates a mundane, poetic annunciation rather than an apocalyptically historical one. Yeats's divine swan is reduced to a common snipe. Still,
it has a significant linguistic message for the transcribing poet:

> A snipe's bleat is fleeing
> its nesting ground
> into dialects,
> into variants,
>
> transliterations whirr
> on the nature reserves—
> little goat of the air,
> of the evening,
>
> *little goat of the frost.*

For the poetic naturalist, as for Vico's onomatopoeic Adam, nature is a
living text to emulate. If one looks and listens, "it is his tail-feathers /
drumming elegies / in the slipstream / of wild goose / and yellow bittern."
Heaney's exploration into the origins of poetic language ends, surprisingly,
as Shelley's "Ode to a Skylark" ends, with the bird transcending words and
cognition altogether. This may be a mute obeisance to a sacred source (the
"nesting ground" again) or a simple acknowledgment that linguists are

mystified by language's origins. His concluding twilit scene offers an oblique self-portrait. Heaney is a composite archaeologist, etymologist, turf cutter, and initiate into mysteries. He records the Irish bird music,

> disappearing among
> gleanings and leavings
> in the combs
> of a fieldworker's archive.

The generative source of language may be absent. But like the original vegetation and sunshine that produced the peat, or the original flutter of inspiration that produced the poem, its traces remain in mute lexicons and in the archival poem itself.

Encoded in Heaney's poem on the poetic origins of language is the history of a specific language's decline. With characteristic economy and skill, he writes an elegy for Gaelic, pointing to the Battle of the Boyne as a fateful turning point and modern sectarian violence as one of the consequences of Gaelic's suppression. Much of the poem's message derives from the philological work of John Braidwood. Referring to the early influence of Owen Barfield and Braidwood, Heaney comments, "I did own Barfield, but the more important imprinting was a first arts course in the history of the English language, given by Prof. John Braidwood at Queens University. That covered the ground from Anglo-Saxon up to Ulster English, and wakened something in me" (letter to the author, 4 June 1987). On 23 April 1969, shortly before Heaney left Queen's, Braidwood delivered a lecture that contained the material that would reappear in "The Backward Look" (as well as in "Traditions," "Serenades," and "Broagh"). John Braidwood explains, "Some of the most imaginative bird names are translation loans from Irish—*Little Goat of the Evening* [gabhairín oidhche] or *Air Goat* [mionnan aeir] for the snipe, from its plaintive call (in Munster it is called *gonreen-roe* [gabhairín reo, little goat of the frost])" (1969, 26). Braidwood shows how the three main dialects in Ulster conform to a pattern of invasion by land-hungry Scottish and English pioneers, and how "dialect, or local accent, is the mark of our history on our tongues" (4), causing sympathy or suspicion depending on the allegiances of those addressed.

Heaney's politicized account imagines the British snipe "fleeing / its nesting ground," its indigenous Irish, English, or Scottish roots, and scattering "imaginative bird names" among different dialects that no longer recall their original Gaelic forms. The Gaelic names have been "modernized"; their roots lie in obscure archives where only students and scholars tread. The bird's plaintive cry elegizes the "wild geese," the term for those Irish patriots who, when defeated by William III at the Battle of the Boyne and given the choice of taking an oath of allegiance to the king, joining the English army, or sailing to France where James had exiled himself, decided to flee to Europe. With the renewal of English dominance in Ireland came renewed efforts to silence the indigenous tongue. Two centuries later, the Gaelic League (founded in 1893) would attempt to resurrect the language, and the Irish Republican Brotherhood, forefathers of the I.R.A., would add military muscle (ultimately in the form of the Easter Rising of 1916) to their program. Language and politics have been inextricably entangled in Ireland for centuries. By mapping the snipe's linguistic flight from its original ground in England through Irish *aeir* to the "sniper's eyrie / over twilit earthworks / and wall-steads," Heaney traces the plight of his colonial culture. An eyrie or aerie is either the high nest of a bird of prey (hawk or eagle), its predatory brood, or any high dwelling spot. Heaney's "sniper" is not so much a snipe hunter as a nationalist or unionist preying on enemies below with a rifle. Heaney refrains from taking specific sectarian sides here. Instead he simply bears witness to the terrifying offspring of old crimes and implicates their "high" idealism in the atrocities they engender, as Eliot did with similar images of birdlike bombers in "Little Gidding" and Geoffrey Hill did with his machine-gunning birds "feathering blood along the shore" in "Genesis."

Heaney exhumes the split roots of current words and catalogs ways they have been used, abused, and all but obliterated. He also pays tribute to an oral tradition now eclipsed by print, and the bardic pscyhe that once regarded words as poetic vehicles of mysterious portent. Owen Barfield writes, "Speech was a more miraculous and rhythmical thing to the Achaians than it is to us today, and whether or not the Gaelic *bard* is cognate with the Greek 'phrazein,' to 'speak,' there is no doubt that 'epos,' the 'word,' had its other meaning of 'poem' " (1924, 31). He could be speaking for Heaney, who often declares words *are* poems, and their written form a substitute for a speech that, for policital and psychological reasons, has been repressed. Like Richard Trench, Heaney believes "many a single word . . . is itself a concentrated poem, having stores of poetical thought and imagery laid up in it" (quoted in Aarsleff 1983, 243), and with Emerson he would agree that words are fossil poems. His linguistic attitudes, however, have more ancient Gaelic and Anglo-Saxon sources. He writes in "The Sense of Place," "I might have begun the exploration much further back, of course, because in Irish poetry there is a whole genre of writing called *dinnseanchas*, poems and tales which relate the original meanings of place names and constitute a form of mythological etymology" (1980a, 131). Etymology, in Heaney's hands, lays bare the poetic fossil within the linguistic ore.

His mythical approach to words parallels, and is often equivalent to, his attitude toward the landscapes the words depict. He concurs with John Montague that "the Irish landscape . . . is a manuscript which we have lost the skill to read" (1980a, 132), and that poets need to reread it so that the old mystical bond between sacred word and sacred place is reaffirmed. For the primitive mind, Heaney declares with obvious nostalgia, the "sensing of place . . . was more or less sacred. The landscape was sacramental, instinct with signs, implying a system of reality beyond the visible realities (1980a, 132). Taking up the banner of Yeats, Heaney defies the central, rationalist, technological infrastructure of today and practically deifies yesterday's "foundation for a marvellous or a magical view of the world, a foundation that sustained a . . . structure of love and superstition and half-pagan, half-Christian thought and practice" (1980a, 133). Although this reverence may be another anachronistic attempt to resurrect the fairies of the Celtic Twilight (or the Ulster Twilight, as Heaney playfully calls it), Heaney's commitment to the sacred past seems more down-to-earth than Yeats's. He summons archaeologists and professors of philology to corroborate his myths, and leaves Madame Blavatsky and Mohini Chatterjee to his predecessor.

Myth and history are asymptotic for Heaney, and because historical conflicts between Ireland and England date back even further than the Anglo-Saxons (as the Roman Empire declined the Gaels were the notorious invaders, imposing Gaelic on western parts of Roman Britain and dragging off slaves, among them the future St. Patrick), it makes sense to draw on both Gaelic and Anglo-Saxon traditions to dramatize these ancient feuds. Writing the etymological poems "Anahorish," "Toome," and "Broagh," Heaney said, convinced him "that one could be faithful to the nature of the English language—for in some senses these poems are erotic mouth-music by and out of the anglo-saxon tongue—and, at the same time, be faithful to one's own non-English origin, for me that is County Derry" (quoted in Corcoran 1986, 87). In his linguistic myth, sexual politics, as Yeats tirelessly demonstrated, acts as a metaphor for national and international politics. Out of the disastrous and fecund unions between Ireland and Britain Heaney aims to make "'vocables': vowels and consonants turning into a harmony of some kind" (Heaney 1973b, 629), so that political ideology resonates from the very linguistic sounds that express it.

Sectarian discord and rapprochement are implicit, for example, in the poem "Anahorish," where Heaney etymologizes in order to rediscover the lost Eden of his childhood. Anahorish, a small townland in County Derry near where Heaney grew up, was also the name of a mixed Catholic and Protestant primary school that he attended between 1945 and 1951. After the 1956–62 I.R.A. campaign in Northern Ireland and the resurgence of Catholic and Protestant battles in the late sixties, his recollection and repetition of the word "Anahorish" is as much a wistful lament for, as a happy communion with, past moments of peace. His "place of clear water," which is what Anahorish (anach fhíor uisce) means in Gaelic, precipitates a meditation comparing his early haunt typologically to both Ararat, "the first hill in the world," and Eden flowing with rivers, "where springs washed into / the shiny grass." Here linguistic differences, and their political and religious correlatives, are unified under the same roof. When Heaney anatomizes "Anahorish" phonologically—"soft gradiant / of consonant, vowel-meadow"—he underscores that here, as in Blake's Eden, oppositions interpenetrate creatively (Adam's phallic 'gradiant' is embedded in Eve's 'meadow'). He redeems the place name's Gaelic meaning only to acknowledge through archaeological puns on "barrows" (wheelbarrows as well as mounds erected over Viking graves) and "mound-dwellers" (fieldworkers as well as prehistoric Scandinavian "mound people"—such as those described in P. V. Glob's *The Mound People*) that this original paradise is dead and buried. Only the "after-image" lingers on. The paradisal "first hill" has metamorphosed into a Golgotha of ruins. "Dunghills" at the poem's end suggest decay, just as "winter evenings," "mist," and "ice" denote the eclipse of a once vibrant life. The mound-dwellers seem to persist in an eerie, posthumous twilight, a landscape of memory as obscure as the place name intoned to resurrect it. Cousin to the dead spirits, Heaney returns to elegize vanished felicities (Anahorish School was actually demolished after Heaney left it).

A similar progression from intoned word to detritus occurs in "Toome," the name of a small townland in County Derry near Mossbawn, the farm where Heaney grew up. It is also one of the oldest inhabited areas of Ireland, the site of major archaeological finds, where prehistoric relics mingle with the musket balls of Wolfe Tone's United Irishmen, the revolutionary (and ecumenical) ancestors of the I.R.A. who fought government troops in the Rebellion of 1798. "Toome" functions as a talisman, a secret password uttered at an oracular passageway into the underworld. Heaney's clever conceit unites sibylline cave and oracular mouth. As so often in his poetry a force no less powerful than dynamite is needed to resurrect speech from "the slab of the tongue." The chanted "*Toome, Toome*" mimics the booms or "soft blastings" that break the tomblike silence so that the mind can utter its findings. Complementing the Sibyl who once gazed into the future and told Aeneas in a cave at Cumae that terrible destruction would precede the founding of Rome, Heaney's sibylline archaeologist gazes backward and confirms that destruction is the inevitable consequence of all imperial quests and conquests.

> I push into a souterrain
> prospecting what [is] new
> in a hundred centuries'
>
> loam, flints, musket-balls,
> fragmented ware,
> torcs and fish-bones.

Rebel musket flints lie beside Stone Age flints and Viking torcs. The souterrains (the ancient underground chambers first built in Ireland during the late Bronze Age (1000–500 B.C.), which were also "constructed during the Early Christian period and may have been used, if not actually constructed, in Medieval times" [O'Riordain 1942, 33]), harmonize strangely with Wolfe Tone's Irishmen, who were forced "underground" in 1794, and the I.R.A., who rekindled their "underground" campaign in 1970 (two years before the poem was written). In *Antiquities of the Irish Countryside*, a book that provided Heaney with much of the archaeological information found in *Wintering Out* and later volumes, Sean O'Riordain confirms that "some ancient souterrains were used as hiding places or deposits for 'dumps' of arms during the recent periods of fighting in Ireland" (34), that is, before 1942, the date of the book's publication.

It is typical of Heaney to employ words as mantras to open historical vistas and then pass beyond them into wordless astonishment. He copies Joyce's Humphrey Chimpden Earwicker, who plunges into a similar cave full of "kraals of slitsucked marrogbones" at the beginning of *Finnegans Wake* (1939, 16), and in a hilariously incoherent dialogue between Mutt and Jute explores his, and Ireland's, embattled heritage. Heaney at the end of "Toome" descends again into stonelike silence, resembling Mutt, who asks Jute at the end of their deaf-mute dialogue, "Ore you astoneaged, jute you?" and Jute, the foreign invader, who replies, "Oye am thonthorstrok, thing mud" (18), aligning himself with Scandinavian gods and political organizations as well as Vico's theological poets who arose from the mud and imitated thunder in their speech. Heaney is also "astonied" by history's ineffable origins and outrageous events. His plunge into "alluvial mud that shelves / suddenly under / bogwater and tributaries" culminates in a communion with an old Celtic goddess, who represents both the mystery of all being and the particularly nightmarish aspect of Irish history.

Initiated into the mysteries of the underworld, Heaney keeps quiet. He surprisingly portrays himself as a Medusa; "elvers trail my hair," he declares. The image may have come from Anne Ross's *Pagan Celtic Britain*, which he had read before writing the poem and which argues that Medusa heads were originally solar symbols for the early Celts. Later the heads became associated with evil-averting guardians and healing springs. Heaney transforms the Medusa into a symbol for Mother Ireland, whose "terrible beauty" can turn even the most well-intentioned hearts to sacrificial stone, as well as heal them. For him the most fecund ditch of all is the "alluvial mud" that betokens a time before all human habitation and slaughter. Having mined "a hundred centuries' / loam" (Ireland has been inhabited for only the last sixty-four centuries), Heaney disinters a primordial intelligence of earth, a *genius loci*, a goddess who engenders Irish life and preserves it when it falls. Head cults were endemic in pagan Ireland. "The Celts seem truly to have venerated a 'god head,' and they imbued the 'tête coupée' with all the qualities and powers most admired and desired by them—fertility, prophecy, hospitality, wisdom and healing" (Ross 1967, 126). Humbled and perplexed into meditative silence, Heaney for a moment assumes the mask of the androgynous 'god head.'

Dreaming of a common language that, as in "Anahorish," reconciles potentially murderous oppositions, or as in "Toome," traces historical alliances between Irish Protestant and Irish Catholic (e.g., Wolfe Tone's United Irishmen), Heaney consistently elegizes such ideal marriages from the position of a man engulfed by the recent Troubles. His point of view is catholic in the secular sense; it is all-encompassing. In his revealing essay, "Place, Pastness, Poems: A Triptych," right after praising "Wolfe Tone, our enlightenment revolutionary and founding father of Irish Republicanism" (1985–86, 35), he suggests how his archaeological interests derive from similar urges to unite differences in an enlightened catholic myth. " 'My neighbor,' the catechism declared, 'is all mankind.' So I think of my mesolithic Ulster neighbor, and of his flint flakes, flint spears and arrowheads which were found in abundance at New Ferry on the River Bann. . . . I do not say that a sense of the mesolithic ancestor could solve the religio-political conflicts of the Bann Valley but I do say that it could significantly widen the terms of the answer which each side could give to the question, 'who do you think you are' " (37). Later, discussing how Symbolist theory awakened in him the notion that historical events were inextricably grafted onto the actual words that described them, again he dwells on unities. "The idea that each vocable, each phonetic signal, contains a transmission from some ur-speech and at the same time is wafted to us across centuries of speaking and writing, that the auditory imagination unites the most ancient and most civilized mentalities, this has been one of the most influential refinements of

Broagh

poetic theory during the last century" (38–39). His allegories of unity, division, and reconciliation take their impetus from this refinement.

"Broagh" again dissects a word in order to map the fate of Protestant and Catholic divisions in Northern Ireland. With Elgy Gillespie Heaney discussed the place name's title. "Protestant and Catholic can say it perfectly in this part of the world. Yet the Protestant won't be entranced by its Gaelic music. He'll think of the *gh* sound perhaps, as in Scottish" (1972c, 10). The word, in fact, is already an anglicization of the Gaelic *bruach*, and as John Wilson Foster points out, "the velar fricative *gh* (pronounced ch [x]) was [not simply] a native Irish rather than English sound that was adopted by the Scots planters, but in fact it was also an English sound that disappeared early in the Modern English Period" (1974, 48). Nevertheless, Heaney remarks, "The English can't altogether manage that last *gh* sound, that guttural slither. . . . If I can write the right poem about Broagh it might be a miniscule definition, getting in affection, elegy, exclusiveness. . . . I mean it might touch intimately, though not spectacularly, the nerve of history and culture" (1972c, 10).

With a glance at Eliot, who employed archaic Sanskrit words in *The Waste Land* to commemorate Western culture's dying roots, Heaney uses etymology to chart historical uprootings of a specifically Irish culture. Neil Corcoran has shown that one can detect in "rigs" (Scottish for furrows), "docken" (Scottish for docks), and "boortrees" (old Scottish for elders) invasions by seventeenth-century Scottish planters and the subsequent dispossession and oppression of native Catholics. "The long rigs / ending in broad docken" gesture emblematically to a prelapsarian fertility. The garden in the second stanza whose cultivated soil has been bruised, cut, and scarred, attests to the falls and redemptions of Heaney's culture.

> The garden mould
> bruised easily, the shower
> gathering in your heelmark
> was the black O
>
> in *Broagh,*
> its low tattoo
> among the windy boortrees
> and rhubarb-blades
>
> ended almost
> suddenly, like the last
> *gh* the strangers found
> difficult to manage.

The strangers are undoubtedly English or Scottish, although they could be any foreigners. In the garden of language, where the original significances of words (like their original stamps or prints) inevitably get soiled and worn smooth, the poet must play redeemer. Purifying the language, like restoring Eden, may be a futile task, but every new poet enters the garden to try.

Skeptical of his own mythologizing, Heaney thinks of Irish earth and culture as a giant body whose language reveals symptoms of real historical contusions. "In handling the English language," Geoffrey Hill once said, "the poet makes an act of recognition that etymology is history. The history of creation and the debasement of words is a paradigm of the loss of the kingdom of innocence and original justice" (Haffenden 1981, 88). Heaney also bears witness to the idea, however illusory, of an original state of innocence and justice, to an ur-speech that connotes cultural harmony, which has been consistently shattered. When Heaney in "Englands of the Mind" claims that Hill possesses "something of Stephen Dedalus's hyperconsciousness of words as physical sensations, as sounds to be plumbed, as weights on the tongue" (1980a, 160), he may also be recalling Hill's contention that the poet must address the gravitational 'weight' of language—its heaviness, its perpetual tendency to fall into imperfection and decay—and strive for at-one-ment between the poem and the words that threaten to undermine it. "Broagh" displays language as a tattooed body, stained and mortal as the humans who create and trample it, and thereby atones for its fallen components.

From seemingly innocent words Heaney can detect a whole array of political and religious affiliations and afflictions. If a man says " 'He's very staunch,'" according to Heaney, "you can be sure your man is a true-blue, sash-wearing, Newsletter-reading, grass roots Unionist" (1972c, 10). "The Wool Trade" employs a new metaphor for the deceptive innocuousness of the English language and the historical injustices woven into it. It begins with an epigraph from Joyce's *Portrait of the Artist*, where Stephen makes his famous pronouncement on the language of his English Jesuit instructor: "How different are the words *home, Christ, ale, master*, on his lips and on mine!" which comes from the longer passage, "The language in which we are speaking is his before it is mine. . . . I cannot speak or write these words without unrest of spirit. His language, so familiar and so foreign, will always be for me an acquired speech. I have not made or accepted its words. My voice holds them at bay. My soul frets in the shadow of his language" (Joyce 1968, 189). For Dedalus, a nightmarish history lurks in the shadow of his master's speech. English is his hairshirt, and he will evolve ever more elaborate ways to wriggle free of it. For Heaney in "The Wool Trade" it is a kind of hairshirt too, made out of "tweed, / A stiff cloth with flecks of blood."

He traces his jacket's strands back to British and Irish entanglements, to the time of the Penal Laws, which excluded Catholics from parliamentary, military, legal, and academic positions, and even from buying land or owning a horse worth more than five pounds. During the year these laws were passed (1699), England also prohibited the export of woolens to any country except England. By protecting its own foreign markets from competition it virtually destroyed the Irish wool trade and precluded industrial growth by dissuading investment. To sell wool to countries in Europe, Ireland had to resort to smuggling. As England's injustices intensified, some writers reacted with vehemence. Jonathan Swift bitterly observed, "Ireland would never be happy till a law were made for burning everything that came from England, except their people and their coals . . . nor am I yet for lessening the number of those exceptions" (quoted in Rowe 1975, 129). Heaney's attack is more oblique. He could be referring to the smuggling wool merchants in his portrait of "square-set men in tunics / who plied soft names like Bruges / / In their talk, merchants / Back from the Netherlands." The soft Dutch place name suggests alliances with Gaelic Ireland as opposed to the hard, consonantal English. When the man of presumably Protestant and English descent (actually a man from southwest England involved in the Shroud Festival, 1968–69, whom Heaney recollects as Paige Smith) utters the phrase, "the wool trade," Heaney experiences a shock of Irish recognition, and recoils from the memory of English imperiousness. The Englishman's phrase is a fleece, raw material for the Irish poet "to shear, to bale and bleach and card" in linguistic meditation. It is "raw" and "confused" because the speaker is not self-conscious enough to realize the historical perversities it contains.

The text and textile Heaney weaves is "unwound from the spools" of the other man's vowels as he steals back his Gaelic inheritance. With the vowels, however, come Anglo-Saxon consonants that conjure up memories of bloodshed. His emotional apostrophe at the end expresses both shock and elegiac despair that all acts of union between Ireland and England have been soaked in blood.

> O all the hamlets where
> Hills and flocks and streams conspired
>
> To a language of waterwheels,
> A lost syntax of looms and spindles,
>
> How they hang
> Fading, in the gallery of the tongue!

The way "The Wool Trade" analyzes the words, sounds, and procedures inherent in its own making is typical of Heaney's more general self-consciousness as a member of the Catholic minority in Northern Ireland and an 'inner émigré' in the Republic. As a writer, he explained to an American reporter for *The Boston Phoenix,* he never feels at home. "Everybody's in exile to start with, everybody who writes. Especially if you're in the minority, you're in two places at once at the very beginning. . . . I never had a feeling of comfortable consonance between myself and a place. The travel reinforces a condition that would be there anyway" (RD 1987, sec. 3.3). An inveterate exile, Heaney follows Dedalus in mastering the language once meant to enslave him and in declaring his independence from all masters, whether political or literary. Of Joyce, Heaney remarked, "His achievement reminds me that English is by now not so much an imperial humiliation as a native weapon" (1978a, 40). He too turns the language of his ancestral foes against them, and against himself as well. His impassioned involvement with maternal Irish and paternal English, as in the earlier pastoral and meditative poems, is oedipal. Naturally attracted to his mother tongue, he fights off the patriarchal tongue that threatens to curtail it, then resolves the power struggle by mastering English. In effect, he becomes one of the masters, one of the fathers, but one devoted to incorporating differences in a civil, androgynous way.

Despite his good intentions, Heaney still bristles against the 'civilized,' 'masterly' English that masks ancient and modern antagonisms. "The Wool Trade" was originally entitled "Tweed," an apt emblem for the deceptive decorum of scholarly masters. The etymology of *tweed* characteristically reveals historical entanglements. The word has Scottish and English origins; it came from Scotland and insinuated itself into English through a misreading of *tweel,* a Scottish form of *twill.* Twilled woolen cloth, which is still chiefly made in southern Scotland, in Heaney's hands unravels into a testament of multiple mistakes and crimes. Although the emperor's clothes are all too visible on Heaney, by unstitching and restitching them he transforms what could be an unconscionable straitjacket into a conscious symbol of historical constrictions. His 'twilling' of etymology, history, and myth is ultimately an elegy for an imagined "kingdom of innocence and original justice," whose bloody end is dyed in the very wool used to sew it up.

Heaney's metaphors for the linguistic invasion foisted by Scotland and England upon Ireland are legion. Typically he imagines Ireland as innocent maiden sexually compromised by imperial insurgents. When he begins "Traditions" with "our guttural muse / was bulled long ago / by the alliterative tradition," Anglo-Saxon assumes the dimensions of a mythical bull, as Zeus often did, that despoils the feminine Gaelic muse. Differentiating himself from Yeats, who dramatized a similar coupling in "Leda and the Swan," Heaney recounts the plunder and decline of Gaelic with more anger and sardonic fatalism than tragic joy. When he declares "custom, that 'most / sovereign mistress,' / beds us down into / the British isles," he is not only recalling the Duke's description of opinion as a "sovereign mistress of effects" in *Othello* (1.3.226) and Othello's acceptance of "tyrant custom," which has turned his lover's bed into "the flinty and steel couch of war" (1.3.231). He also recalls the fact that after the initial bulling and bullying, the tyrant language—English—has been accepted as an accustomed institution. The fusion of sexual and military politics in *Othello* provided Heaney with an illustration of custom's ambiguous power. In the scene he refers to, Othello and Desdemona have just explained their love to the girl's irate father, Brabantio, who disapproves of his daughter's liaison with the Moor. As soon as domestic troubles are smoothed over, Othello agrees to abandon his new wife to wage war against the Turks, which, according to "opinion" and "custom," he is eminently qualified to do. "Traditions" picks up this tale of turmoil in domestic and foreign affairs and shows how Irish traditions also precipitate wars and afflict the possibilities for peaceful 'marriages' between opposed racial, religious, and national groups.

When Heaney declares, "We are to be proud / of our Elizabethan English," his sarcasm recalls traditional Irish conflicts as well as lessons learned in John Braidwood's philology course at Queen's. In his explanation of the colonial lag—the "post-colonial survivals of mother-country culture"—Braidwood points out, "It is this colonial lag which has led more than one devout Ulsterman to proclaim that 'pure' Elizabethan English can be heard in Ulster to this day." "Pure Elizabethan" is a jingoistic illusion. Braidwood claims that "there never was such a thing as 'pure' Elizabethan English; Queen Elizabeth would probably have sounded Cockney to our ears" (1969, 23). Elizabeth, the "sovereign mistress" mythically extolled by Spenser as the Faerie Queene, with regard to Ireland was hardly pure and fair. The Act of Supremacy made her dictatorial head of the Irish church; her Act of Uniformity enforced English by means of the church onto a largely uncomprehending and resentful Gaelic population. Spenser helped implement her peremptory orders, and he duly surfaces at the end of Heaney's poem in the phrase "anatomies of death" (from *A View of the Present State of Ireland*). If Spenser had his way, Irish patriots would be crushed until they spoke "like ghosts crying out of their graves" (104). According to Heaney's scheme, "MacMorris gallivanting / round the Globe" (a character in Shakespeare's *Henry V*) begins a complex but affirmative quest for cultural identity with his question, "What ish my nation?" (*Henry V*, 3.2.136), although his answer in the play is anything but complimentary:

Ireland "Ish a villain and a bastard, and a knave, and a rascal" (3.2.137).
That other Odyssean questor, Leopold Bloom, appears at the end of "Traditions" to reaffirm his, as well as his country's, divided past. He seeks to
rectify its confusions with his blunt, unembarrassed statement of his citizenship in " 'Ireland' . . . / 'I was born here. Ireland.' " When Heaney alludes
to the "consonants of lowlanders / shuttling obstinately / between bawn
and mossland" he recalls his own divisions between traditions of English
colonists (whose fortified farmhouses were 'bawns') and Scottish planters
(who called bogland 'mossland'). Like his family's first farm, Mossbawn, his
poetry is situated, sometimes comically, sometimes tragically, on the militarized boundary between native and foreign domains.

His poetry is also divided between traditional feminine and masculine
ways of engaging with the world. Critics may complain that the allegorical
attribution of "feminine" qualities to Ireland and "masculine" qualities to
England appears antifeminist and unhistorical (Queen Elizabeth and Marg-
aret Thatcher, after all, *are* women). Still, Heaney's attack on the age-old
hierarchies, once he pins them down, is feminist in sentiment. If language is
a repository of petrified sexual and political discriminations, a bog full of
preserved artifacts, Heaney is conservative only insofar as he is preoccupied
with investigating the reliquary forms for the injustices they contain. His
linguistic myths, in fact, are usually antimythological; what he resurrects
with one hand he deconstructs with the other. If Catholic Ireland is Virgin
Mary and Gaelic muse, soft and pliable before the onslaught of England's
Protestant, patriarchal Jehovah or bullish Zeus, Heaney's goal is to feminize
England and masculinize Ireland. With Jung, his mentor in these matters,
he espouses "a symbolic resolution of opposing truths" (1984a, 7), both in
his poetics and his politics.

How he plans to accomplish this resolution, and whether he even
intends to make his mythopoetic scenarios concretely political, has often
aroused acrimonious debate. "The Other Side" casts his Protestant neighbor as an archetypal patriarch, one of the fiery Calvinist offspring of Moses
(he shares the animus of Heaney's earlier "Docker") who, having declared
himself "elect" and his tribe the "chosen people," dictates commandments
from on high and then turns away "towards his promised furrows." After
struggling to absorb "each patriarchal dictum," Heaney assumes the role of
matriarchal and mariolatrous Catholic, wondering whether he should talk
about such inanities as "the weather / / or the price of grass seed" to
defuse the potentially explosive situation. Or should he just "slip away" into
artistic "silence, exile and cunning?" At the poem's end his various options
are quietly suspended. He refrains from forcefully laying down political
directives for himself or for anyone else.

A more politically aggressive poem in *Wintering Out* is the aptly titled "A New Song." Reminiscent of the earlier place name poems, it records a multifaceted epiphany suggested by Derrygarve, the name of a river flowing out of the Moyola River (close to Heaney's early home, Mossbawn). The allegorical waters are sacred, feminine, Irish; they contain and dispense sustenance to a land subverted and broken up by patriarchal British planters. On a linguistic level, the rivers represent the fluent Gaelic speakers of the past (their stones are "black molars" in their mouths), whose vowels have been dammed up by foreign consonants. The Irish voice is pure, virginal; Derrygarve is a "smooth libation" poured by the "vestal daughter." The river is reminiscent of the girl Heaney meets as well as of the flowing name she pronounces. The poem is a marriage song between himself and the river girl that, in this case, turns out to be combative. It admonishes the Irish to rise up, flood, and "embrace" their adversaries in order to repossess pilfered ground.

> But now our river tongues must rise
> From licking deep in native haunts
> To flood, with vowelling embrace,
> Demesnes staked out in consonants.

Heaney's essay "1972" sketches the relevant geography. "I was symbolically placed between the marks of English influence and the lure of the native experience, between the 'demesne' and 'the bog.' The demesne was Moyola Park, an estate now occupied by Lord Moyola . . . ex-Unionist Prime Minister of Northern Ireland. The bog was a wide apron of swamp on the west bank of the River Bann" (1980a, 35). Heaney finishes by addressing further emblems of British dominance: townlands, plantations, fortified "bawns," and "bleaching greens" used by planters in their flax and linen work.

> And Castledawson we'll enlist
> And Upperlands, each planted bawn—
> Like bleaching-greens resumed by grass—
> A vocable, as rath and bullaun.

To "enlist" these names and from them form a unified phalanx indicates Heaney's desire to fight for unities on Irish soil. The greening of Northern Ireland is a 'resumption' of an original green once bleached by intruders. Because "the demesne was walled, wooded, beyond our ken" and the bawns "dropped on the country like the jaws of a man-trap," his 'new song' wants the walls down and the traps opened. "My hope is that the poems will be vocables adequate to my whole experience" (1980a, 35, 36, 37), he declares. At the end of his poem, however, his vocables are distinctly Irish; *rath* is a Gaelic hill-fort, *bullaun* a ritual Gaelic basin stone. His etymological tale of two cultures grants a privileged place to the embattled native Irish. He acknowledges the rights of the heirs of Protestant conquerors, challenging them to practice a similar openness toward the native Irish.

Heaney tempers his philological myths with a conscience attuned to the lessons of history. Nevertheless an underlying myth persistently asserts itself. The sacred water of the bullaun, the pure rivers, the spontaneous fertility of the earth goddess, the liquid vowels, are all associated with an Eden in which Irish is the lingua franca. His allegorical narrative retelling the biblical story of fall and redemption presumes that Gaelic is the original Edenic tongue corrupted by a rapacious English invader and, thus, can be misleading. In his interesting "New Look at the Language Question," Tom Paulin argues that "in Ireland, the English language has been traditionally regarded as an imposed colonial tongue and Irish as the autochthonous language of the island." In the nineteenth century, when English became equated with freedom and a lucrative future in America, and Gaelic with obstacles to progress, traditional views toward Gaelic changed. Irish "parents encouraged their children to learn English as this would help them make new lives in America," and English was enthroned as the "autochthonous language," not because of "any law or official regulation" but because of a "social self-generated movement of collective behaviour among the people." Later, with the founding of the Gaelic League and the Easter Rebellion, Irish "was reinstated as the national language" (1986, 10). The myth of the originality of Irish and the sins committed against it, as Paulin demonstrates, has a history of its own.

Political history, in fact, debunks the myth of an original, innocent Gaelic by revealing that the Gaels played postlapsarian oppressor too. Around 700 B.C. Celts, or *Galli*, as the Romans called them, speaking a language close to modern Irish, invaded and conquered central Europe. Empowered by well-made iron weapons, they expanded into Asia Minor, into western Europe, and finally into Britain and Ireland. When the Romans invaded Britain, Agricola (alluded to in Heaney's *North*) gazed over at Ireland from Scotland, convinced he could break the island's resistance with a single legion. In the end he stayed away. Seizing this as their opportunity, the Gaels crossed the Irish sea, harrassed the declining Romans, and imposed their authority and language on Britain's coast. Heaney's allegory might be constructed differently to account for these historical facts. Poetic license allows him to select the history and myths that express most emphatically his dilemmas as a Catholic brought up amid the sectarian frictions of Northern Ireland and oedipally torn between biological and literary parents. The story, however, should not be confused with the history.

Mythopoetic poets are usually autobiographers in disguise, yet Heaney is not simply promoting Catholic and nationalist ideologies by linking his Irish roots with a prelapsarian Eden. He dwells on those place names and archaeological names with English, Scottish, and Irish origins, records a pastoral Gaelic past that perhaps never existed, and laments social and personal falls that certainly did. While British planter plays antithesis to Irish native, Heaney always aims for a dialectical synthesis. His allegorical symbols and etymological myths are meant to highlight the present Troubles against a more fertile, unified background. His ideal ground may be one of time's fictions, bred out of nostalgia and political idealism. Heaney readily admits that the narratives he fashions have a figurative if not a literal truth. With consummate lyrical skill, he fashions preferable alternatives, albeit schematic and fictive ones, to the bloody cycles of antagonism that have afflicted Irish history from the start.

5

HISTORY, MYTH, AND APOCALYPSE

A DECADE BEFORE HE DIED Yeats wrote a friend with the mischievous gusto that typified his later years. "I am still of the opinion that only two topics can be of the least interest to a serious and studious mind—sex and the dead" (1955, 730). For Yeats history had turned Ireland into a holy land comparable to Greece, where spirits of the dead inhabited every hill and rath. The dead, according to the poet's arrogant view, lived only for those capable of imagining them, and Yeats excoriated the democratic, commercial, commonsensical "mob" that failed to appreciate his phantasmal necropolis. Only through a violent sexual annunciation like the one foisted by Zeus upon Leda, he believed, could the inert masses awaken to a proper recognition of the heroic dead. "Sexuality and death posed against the mob and democracy" was Yeats's plan for revolution as well as revelation, Seamus Deane has written (1985a, 143). If apocalypse was to occur, Yeats's ideal aristocrat and peasant—his custodians of culture—would first have to pitch the modern set into the "fecund ditch" where blind men battered blind men and mad women copulated with beggars.

Death, sex, and a gruesome fusion of the two find a new and startling expression in Seamus Heaney's *North*, a book that marks another stage in Heaney's long, fertile contest with Yeats. Heaney descends into history's mire to offer up the dead to be judged for their deeds and the deeds done against them. He lingers with erotic fondness on victims of ritual killings, knowing all the while that their deaths were inspired, ironically, by myths of sexual fertility. His intentions are apocalyptic; "description is revelation!" he exclaims at the beginning of "Fosterage" (*apokalupsis* in Greek means a revelation, an uncovering). With John of Patmos, he yearns for a last judgment in which history's graveyard avails itself for enlightenment and redemption. He examines "dead relations" at funerals, dead Vikings lying in the "belly of stone ships," Irish famine victims, sacrificial corpses preserved

74

in Irish and Danish bogs, casualties of sectarian feuds in Northern Ireland and concludes that Mother Ireland is more a femme fatale seducing her devotees to violent death than a holy land populated by sacred ghosts. *Wintering Out* dramatized the resolution of the oedipal conflict between the Northern Irish son and his mythical Anglo-Irish parents primarily in terms of language. There the regressive urge to merge with the edenic Irish Mother was ultimately redirected toward the mature poet's goal of unifying English and Irish factions. Now he shifts his focus from the psychological and mythic compulsions behind linguistic history to those behind political history. He scrutinizes the mortuary of the past, interrogating the myths that motivate or sanction those acts that fill its halls with corpses. Yeats in his bellicose moods extolled apocalyptic myths of sacrificial purgation and sexual renewal; Heaney continually dwells on the innocents who are compromised by such myths. He communes with history's defeated and banished: with Antaeus killed by the "hero" Hercules, with Sitting Bull forced to flee to Canada after Custer's last stand, with the Irish maid raped by Sir Walter Raleigh, and with the bog people ritually murdered to appease "the powers that ruled man's destinies" (Glob 1969, 20) in ancient agrarian societies. To his Catholic temperament these are the martyrs bearing witness to history's perpetual tragedy. Against Yeats's tragic joy Heaney poses examples of vicious sacrifice, of violence provoking more violence, and delivers a protest that wavers between moral outrage and stoical resignation. According to Seamus Deane, Yeats's "idea of Revolution . . . was history illuminated by a brilliant temperament" (1985a, 46), by an apocalyptic space invader like Zeus, who descended periodically to bring light to "savages" and extend civilization to the dark corners of the earth. "His so-called fascism is, in fact, an almost pure specimen of the colonialist mentality" (146), he writes. Heaney's idea of apocalypse, by contrast, is steeped in the anticolonial and antiimperialist allegiances of his Irish Catholic inheritance.

Although Heaney and Yeats "see things double—doubled in history, world history, personal history" (Yeats in Whitaker 1964, 298), Heaney sees and expresses this double vision without insisting that it be implemented politically. His apocalypse is tempered by lessons of romantic revolutionaries and modernist reactionaries of the past, by their botched political dreams and doomed political acts. When he asserts he is "torpid in politics" (1982a, 409), it is not laziness he is confessing so much as a principled determination to curb a naturally romantic bent. He struggles to renounce the spontaneous, instinctive reactions of a mind watermarked by Catholic nationalism. His revelations, as a result, are customarily descriptive instead of prescriptive, emotionally rather than legislatively involved in the political turmoil of Ireland. Thomas Whitaker, in his discussion of Yeats's "Dialogue with History," illuminates the private ramifications of apocalypse that seem more pertinent to Heaney than to Yeats. "The poet in quest of the apocalypse must accept . . . history's dark forces and . . . the correlated forces within his own being" (1964, 36). Early on Yeats discovered "that the apocalypse—an image of wholeness transcending the fragmented world and self—could be nothing other than a full rendering of the opposites within that world and that self. Hence his alchemical path, his way of being wise as a serpent and harmless as a dove, led not to the cancelling out of right and wrong but to the agony and exhilaration of self-knowledge" (54). When Yeats translated his apocalypse of the "rough beast" and patriarchal artisan into political terms, his dovishness turned foolishly and ferociously hawklike. Heaney wrestles with the call to become more politically engaged and ultimately resists it for the safer, more private ardors of poetry.

The painfulness of his vacillations between art and politics is high-lighted in his pamphlet on Northern Irish poets, *Place and Displacement*. Wordsworth, whose belief in the apocalyptic possibilities of the French Revolution jarred painfully against his patriotic love for England, is Heaney's model of the poet torn by opposing affiliations. Wordsworth's long poem, *The Prelude*, Heaney argues, resembles contemporary Northern Irish poetry because it is "the symbolic resolution of a lived conflict" between political ideals and recalcitrant local facts. Of Wordsworth he comments, "His political, utopian aspirations deracinate him from the beloved actuality of his surroundings so that his instinctive being and his appetitive intelligence are knocked out of alignment. He feels like a traitor among those he knows and loves. To be true to one part of himself, he must betray another part. The inner state of man is thus shaken and the shock waves in the consciousness reflect the upheavals in the surrounding world" (1984a, 3). According to Heaney, Northern Irish poets deal in Jungian fashion with similar antinomies in their political and artistic commitments. Faced with "an insoluble conflict" between ideal and exigency, they solve it "by 'outgrowing' it, by developing a 'new level of consciousness' " (1984a, 1). The passage Heaney refers to comes from a discussion by Jung of one of his patients, but could just as easily apply to Heaney's notions of apocalypse, which are less a recipe for a new heaven and new earth or for a transcendence of historical strife than a stark, realistic revelation of conflicts in culture and mind that the poet knows he must face.

Heaney's use of myth, whether of apocalypse or sacrifice, has elicited praise and scorn, the latter usually coming from critics in Northern Ireland. In *The Honest Ulsterman*, Ciaran Carson led the attack by accusing Heaney of abandoning his "gift of precision" and accepting the crown of "laureate of violence—a mythmaker, an anthropologist of ritual killing, an apologist for 'the situation,' in the last resort, a mystifier." Heaney's mythopoesis, in his view, "has degenerated into a messy historical and religious surmise—a kind of Golden Bough activity" (1975, 183–86). The underlying assumption held by Heaney's more strident critics was that his poetry should be a transparent window on the Irish turmoil around it. Language being what it is, his poems could never attain such perfect objectivity. He began a review, "Irish Eyes," in 1967 with the blunt avowal, "To make a book . . . about any place is to re-create it; to mythologise or distort; to interpret or mistake" (1967, 851). Language and the devices of poetry inevitably alter the things they seek to reveal. Recognizing this, Heaney's Modernist forbears tried to communicate a more complete picture of things as they are by providing multiple points of view. Their "mythic method," as Carson seems to forget, brought past and present into ironic, illuminating conjunction. Their myths implied that a single, unmediated perspective free of distortion was impossible. By conflating the vestiges of ancient legends and rituals with the disorder of contemporary experience, as Heaney does, the Modernists did not apologize for disorder so much as diagnose it with whatever "gifts of precision" they had.

The most noticeable way Heaney provides multiperspective "views / On the Irish thing" is by splitting the book between the early, dense, meticulously crafted poems, which are rich in myth and history, and the final section of discursive, proselike commentaries, which document the poet's experience in the North with autobiographical candor. The structure with its contrasting styles resembles the pattern of Norman Mailer's *Armies of the Night*, written only a few years before, which also focuses on political troubles from two distinct vantage points. By combining fictional and documentary perspectives, as Heaney combines poetic and proselike ones, Mailer vows to give a clearer, more comprehensive view than the journalists. "So the Novelist working in secret collaboration with the Historian has perhaps tried to build with his novel a tower fully equipped with telescopes to study—at the greatest advantage—our own horizon. Of course, the tower is crooked, and telescopes warped, but the instruments of all sciences—history so much as physics—are always constructed in small or large error" (Mailer 1968, 245). Heaney's apocalypse raises the historical dead and then judges them from different perspectives, all the while, like Mailer, investigating his 'visionary' apparatus with self-conscious scrutiny.

Many of the poems, in fact, are parables of bifurcated perception. "Hercules and Antaeus," Heaney explains to Seamus Deane, traces a contest in which rational perception finally conquers and illuminates the dark instinctual outlook of the tribe. "Hercules represents the balanced rational light," he says. "Antaeus represents the pieties of illiterate fidelity" (Heaney

1977, 63). Nevertheless, "with every increase in the degree of consciousness," as Kierkegaard pointed out, "the intensity of despair increases" (1941, 175). Stripping whatever obfuscates the grim remains of history and elevating them, like Antaeus, into the light of reason, Heaney's poems modulate into elegiac gloom. Ruthless analysis paralyzes the will; conscience, by invading the creative darknesses of the mind, can render them impotent. Triumphs and defeats see-saw according to perspective.

What is so disturbing about the poems in *North*, and what especially disturbs Heaney's critics, is the implication that, as Yeats's Crazy Jane tells the bishop, "fair and foul are near of kin / And fair needs foul" (1983, 259), that the battling factions of Northern Ireland are perversely symbiotic. To Heaney's detractors, he seems to justify atrocities any humane person would condemn. They overlook his engagement in a perplexed debate over the proper way to approach and mourn atrocities in art. At times he admonishes himself to "cast a cold eye / On life, on death" ("Under Ben Bulben," Yeats 1983, 328) or, recasting Yeats's icy stoicism into a more vivid metaphor, to "keep your eye clear / as the bleb of the icicle." To reveal the past coolly and precisely he borrows tools from archaeologist, linguist, and political scientist. In other instances his detached, analytical "bleb" melts away, and warmer lyrical impulses predominate. Averse to merely recording the way art feeds off catastrophe and redemption feeds off sin, he expresses empathy for both sinner and sinned against. He laments the fate of Antaeus, lovingly addresses victims of prehistoric fertility cults, elegizes murdered Catholics, but also finds himself paradoxically admiring the heroic traditions of the Herculean victors, even though they belong to English colonizer, Viking conqueror, or Norse raider. Alluding to Heaney's statement, "I think that my own poetry is a kind of slow, obstinate, papish burn," Edna Longley claims that there is a profoundly Catholic slant to *North* (1982, 70). The poems, she argues, are for the most part rituals commemorating acts of immolation and martyrdom and the "savage tribal loyalties" behind them. To say that Heaney "excludes the inter-sectarian issue, warfare *between* tribes" (78) is to miss the book's message. His Catholic confessions expose allegiances to both tribes. Emulating Robert Lowell's "Confessional" poems, he embraces a divided heritage and articulates his guilty role within it.

The "bleb of the icicle" is a brilliant emblem for Heaney's troubled stance in *North*. Like the water bead, Heaney hangs suspended between the frozen icicle of the North and the warmer air of the South. He turns, often purgatorially, at the midpoint between Irish and English literary traditions, Catholic and Protestant camps, Mediterranean and Norse mythologies. The "bleb" is not only the blob that drips from the icicle's tip; it is also the air bubble encased in ice. In both cases, it is 'clear' as well as convex and distorting, just as the languages of myth, history, and poetry (and the physical eye itself) refract what they reveal. "The function of language in much modern poetry, and in much poetry admired by moderns, is to talk about itself to itself. The poem is a complex word, a linguistic exploration whose tracks melt as it maps its own progress," Heaney claims (1980a, 81), recalling Empson's *The Structure of Complex Words*, which explores the emotive and cognitive refractions of words, as well as Robert Frost's assertion that the poem must compose itself out of "its own melting" (quoted by Heaney 1980a, 80). The title poem, "North," brilliantly illustrates this process in which the poem scrutinizes and erases the apocalyptic ideas that attract it. To alter the metaphor, the emotive myths of the Anglo-Saxons, Vikings, Norsemen, and Northern Irish provide the fuel that the poem methodically burns up as it progresses. The poem, as Stanley Fish would say, is a "self-consuming artifact." It does not wallow in cultic mystiques and sloppy surmises, as Longley and Carson contend. In fact the poem acknowledges the slipperiness and obliqueness of 'mythical' language and tries to resist it at every turn.

The poet's actual return to a particular beach on the Atlantic coast typifies the poem's many other returns. The voices of dead northerners, for example, return from the sea, "lifted again / in violence and epiphany," just as St. John's apocalyptic sea returns the dead to be judged. Heaney cancels the biblical supposition of a timeless new heaven and new earth by reaffirming the old world and old hell of history. History rumbles on to the cacophonous din of Thor's hammer blows and toward a last judgment that is pagan and secular. Thor, rather than Christ, judges the dead for their deeds. Heaney may recall a similar iconoclastic vision at the end of Sylvia Plath's "Blackberrying," where she looks "out on nothing, nothing but a great space" of ocean waves "like silversmiths / Beating and beating at an intractable metal." Heaney declares,

> I returned to a long strand,
> the hammered shod of a bay,
> and found only the secular
> powers of the Atlantic thundering.

If Auden succumbed to the pagan 'magic' of Iceland and its sagas, Heaney alludes to the sagas only to dismiss their deceptive romanticism. His apocalypse strives to purge the 'heroic' dross from the hard historical facts.

I faced the unmagical
invitations of Iceland,
the pathetic colonies
of Greenland, and suddenly

those fabulous raiders,
those lying in Orkney and Dublin.

Half-enchanted by the heroic dead, he delineates a *via negativa* in which
their "ocean-deafened," Sirenlike voices fade away so that their real voices
can be heard. Their "warning" is the "epiphany" that reveals the mystique
that later generations have bestowed upon them and exposes their rapacious, bloodthirsty lives for what they were. *Njal's Saga*, which Heaney
refers to in "Funeral Rites" and no doubt is remembering here, as one
writer put it, recounts "the years of savage internal strife, murderous in-
trigues, and ruthless self-seeking power-politics that led, in 1262, to the loss
of the independence that her [Iceland's] pioneers had created" (Magnusson
and Palsson 1960, 10). From the *Saga*'s anonymous author, writing
around 1280 of the chronic feuding among Iceland's Norsemen, Heaney
garners sobering lessons for his own bellicose culture seven hundred years
later.

Bearing in mind the *Saga*'s preoccupation with marriages that go
wrong (between Unn and Hrut, Thorvald and Hallgerd, Gunnar and
Hallgerd, to name a few), murders that burgeon from broken alliances, and
grimly comic attempts to appease them at the *althing* (the judicial and leg-
islative parliament of the Icelanders), and the ultimate entropy of the principal blood feud between Kari and Flosi (who killed Njal), Heaney renounces
its epic pretentions. 'Heroic' journeys, like those by the Vikings and
Norsemen, or those by the English and Scots in their conquest of Ireland,
for Heaney are essentially brutal ventures initiated for territorial and economic gain. Heaney returns to myths and histories of primitive cultures that
resemble his, stripping the old gods of their grandiose cloaks and implicat-
ing them in the worldly affairs from which they arose. He could be speaking
of either ancient Icelanders or modern Irelanders when he observes,

Thor's hammer swung
to geography and trade,
thick-witted couplings and revenges,

the hatreds and behindbacks
of the althing, lies and women,
exhaustions nominated peace,
memory incubating the spilled blood.

If Heaney is thinking of Bernadette Devlin and other women in the civil rights battles of the late sixties and early seventies, they are surely tame compared to their Icelandic precursors like Hallgerd, who ordered her first husband's head split open with an axe, mustered death squads to pillage and murder her foes, and colluded with Gunnar's attackers in his fatal last stand.

Returning to his northern hoard of internecine squabbles, Heaney understandably turns away from politics toward poetics. He continues to trace a *via negativa* through a dark night in order to explore the visionary "gleam" of his "furrowed brain." His meditation charts the "mind in the act of finding / What will suffice" ("Of Modern Poetry," Stevens 1972, 174), erasing fabulous tales of the past in order to propose saner, more cogent alternatives. He may be referring to Wallace Stevens's "Auroras of Autumn," which also bids farewell to mythic embellishments, when he tells himself, "Expect aurora borealis / in the long foray / but no cascade of light." Stevens writes of desolate, wintry, clear-sighted vision too, and it is to Stevens Heaney refers in his discussion of poetry mapping its progress with its melt, and being "ineluctably itself and not some other thing" (1980a, 81). Although Heaney's poem recalls Stevens's aesthetic of negations, Heaney is much more the Anglo-Saxon scop burrowing into the alliterative treasure trove than the fluent, bittersweet, iambic philosopher. When Stevens declares, "We were as Danes in Denmark all day long" in "Auroras" (1972, 315), his tone is playfully ahistorical. Heaney tends to be more sombre and earnest, as if weighted down by the actual detritus of Danish tragedies. For Heaney the ancient mythic principles—honor, fate, revenge, fame—that once sustained Iceland's and Ireland's 'heroic' cultures have melted away. When he tells himself at the end, "trust the feel of what nubbed treasure / your hands have known," he is returning to his former persona, Incertus. He feels in the dark for what he cannot see for certain and stares through the melt or bubble of the icicle at old values that have evaporated into air.

The urge to reveal past and present confusions in an apocalyptic "cascade of light" derives from the rational humanist inheritance Heaney finds partly eclipsed both in himself and in his 'northern' culture. The distant, insubstantial glimmerings of the night's aurora, like Wordsworth's diminishing "visionary gleam," is all he expects and all he really trusts. His poems entertain notions of full, luminous revelations, conceding after a struggle that such revelations are undesirable and probably impossible. "There is always the question in everybody's mind," he tells Seamus Deane, "whether the rationalist and humanist domain which produced what we call civilization in the west should be allowed full command in the psyche, speech and utterance of Ulster" (Heaney 1977, 63). But when Deane attacks Conor Cruise O'Brien for obstinately applying a rational light to the irrational acts

of Ulster, Heaney backs O'Brien for "the clarity [and] validity of his position." Like O'Brien who rebukes "all easy thoughts about the Protestant
community in the North" (64) and insists on evaluating both sides clearly
and critically, Heaney strives for an impartial view of ancient and contemporary history as well. In the end, he embraces a complex dialectic. His
apocalyptic desire for both rational and intuitive judgments seems as antithetical as the Protestant and Catholic opposition itself.

His archaeological and philological investigations are all part of his
humanistic attempt to promote dialogue between Ireland's warring factions.
In "Belderg," the name of an excavated Norse settlement in County Mayo,
he speaks to the archaeologist, Seamus Caulfield, who owns the bog in
which he exhumed quernstones (round, socketed, mortarlike stones for
grinding wheat). The archaeologist explaining the local relics of Iron Age,
Stone Age, and Bronze Age cultures ("His home accrued growth rings /
Of iron, flint and bronze") is his alter ego. Heaney is also the etymologist
explaining 'growth rings' of Scottish, English, and Irish words grafted into
the name of his family's first farm, Mossbawn. *Moss*, he says in an essay, is "a
Scots word probably carried to Ulster by the Planters, and *bawn*, the name
the English colonists gave to their fortified farmhouses. Mossbawn, the
planter's house on the bog. Yet . . . we pronounced it Moss bann, and *ban* is
the Gaelic word for white. . . . In the syllables of my home I see a metaphor
of the split culture of Ulster" (1980a, 35). Heaney's companion at Belderg
makes the 'growth rings' in his geneological tree even more problematic
when he suggests that *moss* derives from "older strains of Norse." This
precipitates the painful, cosmic revelation at the end, in which Heaney
envisions himself as no longer possessing an identity, but ground and mixed
up in the warring factions of all history. As was true for Joyce's Finnegan, all
times circulate through his baffled and baffling psyche. He is Yggdrasil, the
ash tree of Norse legend, whose branches and roots extend through the
whole universe, as well as a universal body, "a world-tree of balanced stones,
/ Querns piled like vertebrae, / The marrow crushed to grounds." Neil
Corcoran deems this an image of the "terror and savagery" that is the
"sustaining power" (1986, 108) of the Viking world. It is just as plausibly
an image of Heaney's own self-reflexive consciousness, which, turning on
his ties with historical opponents, grinds itself down with anxious questioning, like "grist to an ancient mill."

The grinding is strangely affirmative. Painful as it is, it atones for
history's nightmare by setting its cycles at one with the mind's purgatorial
turnings and returnings. The poem, in fact, is as much about Heaney's
divided inheritance as the contradictory, restorative way Heaney perceives
that inheritance. His focus progresses from innocent enchantment with

heroic figures of the past (represented by those buried in the Norse tombs at Belderg) to a disturbing knowledge of the crimes of those heroes and ends with a redemptive avowal of complicity in their 'heroic' crimes. This is the twisted backbone of Heaney's confessional tale. The quernstones themselves become the objective correlative for Heaney's 'I' and 'eye.' They first appear as "one-eyed and benign," dreaming romantically of prehistoric Ireland. The archaeological turfcutter strips off the "blanket bog" of the sleeping poet and, at the same time, opens his eyelids to history: "to lift the lid of the peat / And find this pupil dreaming / Of neolithic wheat!" As he perceives his cherished dreams and myths of fertility transmogrified into murderous political sacrifices, his painful revelation of history commences. He declares, "The soft-piled centuries / Fell open like a glib." *Glib*, as Shakespeare uses it in *The Winter's Tale* (2.1.148), means castrated (and castration was not an unusual practice in fertility rituals, as Robert Graves and James Frazer inform us). In addition, Heaney is probably remembering Spenser's *A View of the Present State of Ireland*, where he records how Irish criminals wore glibs—thick masses of matted hair thrown over their faces—so they could go about their business in disguise. Heaney exclaims that the criminal past is "repeated before our eyes," although near the poem's end he implies that he has transcended its cycle. "I passed through the eye of the quern," he says, as if, in line with the biblical parable, he has passed through the needle's eye into heaven. He admits that heaven is "in my mind's eye" and that history will never stop grinding away, despite St. John's apocalyptic predictions. Nevertheless, the passage from a sentimental, sleepy vision of the past to an acutely vigilant one is a triumph. It represents what Heaney called in his discussion of Jung and Wordsworth "that evolution of a higher consciousness in response to an apparently intolerable conflict" (1984a, 1).

The transcendence afforded by simple, clear-sighted expressions of political blunders, atrocities, and anxieties is always tentative in Heaney's *North*. In "Funeral Rites" he declares, "we pine for ceremony, / customary rhythms," but pining does not entail fulfillment. He can only imagine a massive, nonsectarian funeral cortege to "the great chambers of the Boyne," in which both sides bury their hatchets with their dead, knowing all the while that the feuds of neolithic times endure like the stones of passage graves at Newgrange that commemorate them. The Orange Day marches every 12 July, celebrating the defeat of Catholic James II by Protestant William III, are also "customary rhythms" associated with the Boyne. Ritual still-points and timeless moments in history's "long foray" are as evanescent as the northern lights or the four lights flickering in Gunnar's tomb. As Peter Sacks observes, Heaney's poem figures into a modern tradition of elegy in which "the mourned subjects . . . include not only the deceased but also the vanished rituals of grief and consolation themselves" (1983, 299–300). As elegy fails to palliate, revenge tragedy provides a violent alternative. "When no consoling substitution is available even in language, the griever will be unable to avoid responses such as melancholy or revenge" (63). What Thomas Kyd states in *The Spanish Tragedy* applies equally to the Irish tragedy: "where words prevail not, violence prevails" (2.1.110). When language and culture break down, the oedipal resolution of "the work of mourning" collapses as well. Chaos follows. The sons once again clamber to murder the fathers (the British) and wed themselves to the mother (Ireland) through blood sacrifice.

Despite his elegiac skepticism, Heaney tries desperately to offer at least a glimpse of consolation. He ends his poem with a scene similar to the one at the end of Yeats's "Lapis Lazuli," where the Chinamen, having climbed to their transcendental height on the mountain, overlook the tragic cycles of world history with gay and glittering eyes. Heaney's setting, however, is Iceland, and Gunnar looks at the moon with a contentment that must be as fleeting as that ancient symbol of cycles itself.

> Men said that he was chanting
> verses about honour
> and that four lights burned
>
> in corners of the chamber:
> which opened then, as he turned
> with a joyful face
> to look at the moon.

This telescopes two incidents in the middle of *Njal's Saga* where, after Gunnar is buried, a shepherd and housemaid find him "in good humour and chanting verses inside the mound." Later, Njal's son, Skarp-Hedin, and Gunnar's son, Hogni, stand outside, to the south of Gunnar's burial mound. The moonlight is bright but fitful. Suddenly it seems to them that the mound is open; Gunnar turns round to face the moon. Four lights burn inside the mound, illuminating the whole chamber. They can see that Gunnar is exultant. He chants a verse.

> Hogni's generous father
> Rich in daring exploits
> Who so lavishly gave battle
> Distributing wounds gladly,
> Claims that in his helmet,
> Towering like an oak-tree

In the forest of battle,
He would rather die than yield,
Much rather die than yield.
(Magnusson and Palsson 1960, 174)

Gunnar, in this song of sublime egoism, brags of his heroic sacrifice. Skarp-Hedin takes his words as a green light to go out and kill. He refuses to acquiesce to Gunnar's 'unavenged' death and thereby stop the feuding. He and Hogni immediately set off to murder four of his father's enemies, and the terrible, ludicrous cycle of butchery and futile attempts at reconciliation at the althing continues.

Neil Corcoran contends that the poem "urgently desires an end to the terrible cycle, but it can imagine such a thing only in a mythologized visionary realm" (1986, 111). Heaney's fertility myths and elegiac visions are tendered with less credulity than his critics imply. They usually contain the seeds of their own annihilation. As soon as they emerge, they break down under the weight of historical facts. The poem that envisions the end of the revenge cycle with Gunnar's happy lunar gaze implies its bloody perpetuation. Heaney's beginnings are uncertain, his ends, and the apocalyptic ends they long for, undermined by historical certainties. His plots are modernist, antibiblical, fraught with epistemological and moral doubts about mythical promises, and sketch the agonized but regenerative flux of a mind at odds with itself.

Because history is the provenance of the dead, Heaney repeatedly invokes them to tell their story even though he concedes, like Eliot in "Little Gidding," that the language "of the dead is tongued with fire beyond the language of the living" (1969, 192). Digging down to disinter the truth about the past, he knows that histories of the dead are imagined ones—imagined by him or by others—and inevitably mediated by the devices of posthumous fictions. The further he searches beyond ideas about the thing for the thing itself the further enmeshed he becomes in refracting texts. His allusions to other books often include lighthearted indictments of their pretensions to historical accuracy. At the end of "Trial Pieces," for instance, he gently mocks Synge's Jimmy Farrell in *Playboy of the Western World*, who turns real cobbles into fictitious skulls and speculates, without appropriate archaeological evidence, that " 'an old Dane, / . . . drowned / in the Flood' " lies buried in Dublin. "The Digging Skeleton" again excavates Dublin's past with the hope of apocalyptically offering up actual deeds of the dead for judgment but ultimately plunges into a palimpsest of texts. The historical Danes Heaney would like to resurrect have been reduced to "anatomical plates" in decayed books. To complicate matters, Heaney approaches them through a poem by Baudelaire, which is not about Viking Dublin and which Heaney translates freely. The "mysterious candid studies" of the dead release a "gang of apparitions" whom Heaney questions, partly because they are so historically questionable. He wants to initiate a dialogue whereby the dead provide answers about the past. Unfortunately he is confined to a soliloquy in which he ventriloquizes for them. Ironically, he attacks not only traditional myths about the resurrected dead but also poets, like himself, who insist on digging them up and memorializing them in deceptive fictions. He asks, "Are you emblems of the truth?" and then imagines a posthumous response by one of the skeletons. "Even death / Lies. The void deceives. / . . . / Some traitor breath / / Revives our clay, sends us abroad." The traitor's breath is the inspiration of the poet (*spiritus* in Latin means breath), who betrays the dead by making them live again. Poets and historians alike misprize the dead by misreading them, as Harold Bloom would say.

Heaney's worries about bearing inaccurate witness to the dead are as poetic as they are political. He quotes Conor Cruise O'Brien's *States of Ireland* in "Whatever You Say Say Nothing," and no doubt knows O'Brien's vilification of the I.R.A. and Sinn Fein as fascist, aristocratic organizations so steeped in "the language of sacred soil and the cult of the dead" (1972, 319) that they are blind to both past and present, and therefore oblivious to saner policies for the future. Are Heaney's sacred sense of Irish soil and preoccupation with the dead mired in this kind of blindness, or does he knowingly rise above and redeem that blindness? For O'Brien the revolutionary nationalists wallow in political necrophilia. "Legitimate authority is derived only from the generations of the dead who died for Ireland, and is properly wielded in the present by the organization of men and women prepared to repeat the blood sacrifice" (318). Discussing O'Brien's views on the "unhealthy intersection" of art and politics with Seamus Deane, Heaney admits that

> the community to which I belong is Catholic and nationalist. I believe that the poet's force now, and hopefully in the future, is to maintain the efficacy of his own 'mythos,' his own cultural and political colourings, rather than to serve any particular momentary strategy that his leaders, his paramilitary organization or his own liberal self might want him to serve. I think that poetry and politics are, in different ways, an articulation, an ordering, a giving of form to inchoate pieties, prejudices, world-views. (Heaney 1977, 62)

Heaney's 'mystic' sense of the dead parallels the ideology of Sinn Fein. What saves it from becoming overtly political is its archaeological and analytic contemplativeness. Unlike the I.R.A., he is content to simply explain myths of blood sacrifice, worrying them into poems instead of reenacting them in the street.

The self-consciousness that haunts his poetry is perhaps the strongest antidote to his pious, mythic attachment to the dead and their 'heroic' deeds. He would agree with Richard Kearney who, in *The Crane Bag Book of Irish Studies* (for which Heaney wrote the introduction), asserts that writers must acknowledge the omnipresence and power of myth, "which always operates in a society regardless of whether this society reflectively acknowledges its existence." Otherwise it is uncontrollable. If "modern man has lost his awareness of the important role which myth plays in his life, it manifests itself in deviant ways" (1982, 262), such as in the fascist glorification of blood sacrifices and national saviors. Kearney takes up his argument again in *Ireland's Field Day*, a book to which Heaney contributed, and now applies it to the mythic assumptions of the I.R.A. "The IRA's ideology is *sacrificial* to the degree that it invokes, explicitly or otherwise, a 'sacred' tradition of death and renewal which provides justification for present acts of suffering by realigning them with recurring paradigms of the past and thus affording these acts a certain timeless and redemptive quality" (1986, 66).

The I.R.A.'s mythic acts hark back to Christian and earlier pagan "paradigms" of resurrection and revelation. When Kearney cites Rudolf Bultmann, who calls "for a radical 'demythologisation' of belief which will disengage the Judaeo-Christian Revelation from the magico-mystery rites and apocalyptic Saviour cults of pagan origin" (1986, 64), he asks for what Heaney has already delivered. By scrutinizing the epistemological gap between history and myth, absent event and present text, and by turning his apocalypse into a revelation of his own complex debate with fact and fiction, Heaney demythologizes the mysteries. Kearney's conclusion sums up Heaney's impulses and directives well. "We must never cease to keep our mythological images in dialogue with history; because once we do we fossilize. That is why we will go on telling stories, inventing and re-inventing myths, until we have brought history home to itself" (1986, 80). Heaney's revelations of the dead do exactly that; they expose the shadowy demarcations between story and history and tabulate the consequences of blind devotion to fossilized myths.

In speaking of unspeakable atrocities—whether perpetrated by I.R.A. myths or Iron Age fertility cults—Heaney walks a knife-edge between the desire to construct winning poems and the moral imperative to communicate ignominious defeats. Seamus Deane in a postscript to an Anglo-Irish literature issue of *The Crane Bag* alludes to Theodor Adorno's critiques of holocaust literature, but could be thinking of Heaney's bog poems when he despairs of "the way in which art falsifies atrocity (and perhaps all history) by rendering it in forms which afford it a meaning or a spiritual dimension which it does not have" (1982, 512). A poet like Geoffrey Hill, who addresses holocausts of history in the same breath as "the tongue's atrocities" that provoke and later distort them, strives for a curt, sardonic utterance that borders on silent memorial, as if linguistic restraint is both proper and preventative. "Silence is an alternative," George Steiner declared in his discussion of Adorno's injunction "No poetry after Auschwitz." "It is better for the poet to mutilate his own tongue than to dignify the inhuman either with his gift or his uncaring. . . . When the words in the city are full of savagery and lies, nothing speaks louder than the unwritten poem" (1967, 72, 73, 74). Within this debate Heaney chooses neither Steiner's silence nor Hill's extreme reticence, but a fascinated horror. He portrays the victims of atrocity with anatomical specificity, mulls over myths compelling those atrocities, and also guiltily recoils from the 'artful voyeurism' and mystery cults that, on one level, attract him.

Heaney's "mythical method," which has been so controversial, sets contemporary Irish history, especially the violent campaign of the I.R.A., against the background of the early Iron Age in Northern Europe. His critics complain that he emphasizes vague similarities and foregoes acute differences between present and past violence. What they ignore is his startling, didactic perspective in which Tacitus and a leader-writer for the *Daily Telegraph* can sit down at the same table to deliberate over persistent afflictions. He explains in *The Listener*,

> It turns out that the bogs in Northern Europe in the first and second centuries AD contained the shrines of the god or goddess of the time, and in order that the vegetation and the community would live again after the winter, human sacrifices were made: people were drowned in the bogs. Tacitus reports on this in his *Germania*. You have a society in the Iron Age where there was ritual blood-letting. You have a society where girls' heads were shaved for adultery, you have a religion centering on the territory, on a goddess of the ground and of the land, and associated with sacrifice. Now in many ways the fury of Irish Republicanism is associated with a religion like this, with a female goddess who has appeared in various guises. She appears as Cathleen ni Houlihan in Yeats's plays; she appears as Mother Ireland. I think that the Republican ethos is a feminine religion, in a way. It seems to me that there are satisfactory imaginative parallels between this religion and time and our own time. They are observed with amazement and a kind of civilised tut-tut by Tacitus in the first century AD and by leader-writers in the *Daily Telegraph* in the 20th century. (1972b, 790)

Although feminine deities of the politically sacrosanct land hover over Heaney's bog poems, the sacrificial victims receive his most intense scrutiny. Often Heaney treats deity and victim as one. Having 'died' into spiritual and sexual marriage with the goddess (Mother Ireland or Mother Earth), the devotee cannot be distinguished from the object of devotion. P. V. Glob, whose photographs and descriptions in *The Bog People* were the main impetus behind Heaney's bog poems, reminds us that the victims "through their sacrificial deaths . . . were themselves consecrated for all time to Nerthus, goddess of fertility—to Mother Earth, who in return so often gave their faces her blessing and preserved them through the millennia" (1969, 192). The sacrificial dead, whether Tollund Man or I.R.A. gunman, emerge as archetypes in Heaney's 'monomyth.' And on those tragic zealots who were sacrificed with the hope of reviving "romantic Ireland . . . dead and gone" ("September 1913," Yeats 1983, 108) or, more mundanely, crops in an Iron Age field, Heaney bestows his elegiac wreaths.

What makes Heaney's bog poems so ethically problematic are his personae who embrace the dead with erotic passion. In "Come to the Bower," the ritual communion with the girl is as titillating as any of the seduction poems by John Donne or Andrew Marvell, but the beloved in this case is a corpse. Heaney's persona feels his way, as if blinded by the feminine mystery, unpinning and unwrapping her until she is naked. If he wants to examine the bare bones of Ireland, he is hardly dispassionate in his quest. In fact, he resembles the typical conqueror, like Sir Walter Raleigh in "Ocean's Love to Ireland," who reaches for sex and gold with the same fist.

> I reach past
> The riverbed's washed
> Dream of gold to the bullion
> Of her Venus bone.

The dead girl's mons veneris is a mountain of gold bullion, flecks of which can be panned in her fertile streams. Heaney's "dark-bowered queen" may be Yeats's queenly Houlihan who, disguised as an old woman, stole the young Michael Gillane from his wife-to-be and states forebodingly, "Many a man has died for love of me" (Yeats 1965, 224). Yeats speaks for republican martyrs who sacrificed themselves to Ireland in the spirit of Wolfe Tone's United Irishmen. Heaney, on the other hand, speaks for and against the imperial colonizer, whose economic dreams are sexual as well as deadly. Femme fatale and homme fatal merge in a necrophiliac embrace. Heaney sees the differences in their political stances as differences in sexual preferences. One prefers sexual immolation; the other prefers economic and physical rape.

This strangely perverse elegy turns confessionally on Heaney as well as on his Catholic culture, of which he is a knowing product. His bog portraits have all the unseemly but prescient insight of Faulkner's tales of the American South, whose history of agrarian defeat in some ways resembles Ireland's. Like Faulkner's "A Rose for Emily," where the protagonist lies down with a corpse and dies in order to make permanent her marriage to the dead, antebellum South, Heaney's bog poems proclaim affection for the old dispensations of an agricultural Ireland. "Bog Queen," which speaks for the first documented body ever dug out of a bog (on the Moira estate in 1781), again expresses solidarity with the dead and delineates the kind of "terrible beauty" born from that fatal attraction. Heaney mythologizes the actual Danish Viking discovered by the turf cutter (and subsequently requisitioned by Lady Moira through bribery) into a symbol of Ireland's possession by Catholics and dispossession by Protestants. The bog queen subsumes legendary Houlihan and a contemporary Irishman fatally enmeshed in sectarian domains (as Heaney was at Mossbawn), "between turf-face and demesne wall," who would just as soon remain buried, but who in fact rises again with all the shabby and menacing gloom ("hacked bone, skull-ware, / frayed stitches") of Frankenstein's monster.

To let bygones be bygones is impossible in a culture wedded to the dead. A sacrificial victim, the bog woman is now resurrected by both religious denominations and transformed into a deity for whom further sacrifices are performed. She lies waiting for an apocalypse that will see her for what she is—a dead Dane, if the archaeologists are correct—knowing that she will be used and abused to justify conflicting causes. Her body is "braille / for the creeping influences," and "illiterate roots" ponder and die over her, because she is read, misread, or left unread by "blindmen battering blindmen." To the invading, sash-wearing Protestants she is their English queen, although her diadem has grown carious. To the Catholic turf cutter, she is the goddess of the sacred Irish soil as well as the Catholic girl punished for dating enemy soldiers. She says, "I was barbered / and stripped / by a turfcutter's spade." As the early Gauls shaved the heads of adulterous women, so the I.R.A. tars and feathers girls for 'traitorous' affairs with the British. The bog queen is covered with "soaked fledge," remurdered, and reburied. Like Jimmy Farrell's father 'killed' with a spade, or Finnegan after his mortal fall from his ladder, she rises again to continue the tragicomedy as mythic emblem of the Irish motherland who is consecrated and desecrated in turn.

The sad portrait of the weeping "Grauballe Man," named after the town in Jutland near where he was found in 1952, underscores the perseverance of blood sacrifice and blood feuds in modern Ireland. Glob explains that the man's neck was slashed from ear to ear and his naked body dumped in the bog around 310 B.C. during the midwinter celebrations. His grim death was intended to hasten the coming of spring. For Heaney the dead copulate with the dead only to reproduce noxious precedents for future conduct. The Grauballe man gives birth, strangely, to an image of himself ("bruised like a forceps baby"), whose death-in-life and life-in-death recall the mummified images in Yeats's "Byzantium." Heaney calls for an apocalypse that will judge beautiful icon against atrocious fact and highlight the reprehensible relations between the two. "Beauty is truth, truth beauty" only insofar as the "actual weight" of history's victims has been reembodied in tragic art. His Grauballe man, "perfected in . . . memory," is therefore

> hung in the scales
> with beauty and atrocity:
> with the Dying Gaul
> too strictly compassed
>
> on his shield,
> with the actual weight
> of each hooded victim,
> slashed and dumped.

In his essay "The Dying Gaul," David Jones reproduces a photograph of the statue "erected at Pergamon by an ally of Rome, King Attalos I, to celebrate his victory over groups of Celts operating in Asia Minor in the third century B.C." (around the same time the Grauballe Man was killed). He notes Virgil's description of Gauls raiding Rome. "They were assaulting the stronghold of a female earth-spirit, as well as the hill of Saturn and the mound of the buried head—and of course, also, a virtually impregnable military position" (1978, 50, 52). The naked Gaul is an emblem of the colonized provincial dying as he seeks revenge on an indomitable imperialist. For Heaney he is a timeless victim, whose contemporary incarnation is the Catholic victim in Northern Ireland. Tim Pat Coogan's encyclopedic study, The IRA, documents the kind of sectarian murder that Heaney places in an ancient context. He describes the Ulster Protestant paramilitary group, the U.D.A., and their methods of hooding Catholics to interrogate them before execution. "Scores of young Catholics [in 1972] were found with hoods over their heads and bullets through their brains. Others were found in a condition better imagined than described, with mutilations, throat cuttings and every form of atrocity" (1987, 554). For Heaney, Gaul and

Gael, Roman and Unionist, have simply traded places in a process that is all the more depressing for being archetypal.

Heaney's ambivalence toward the victimization of innocents and culprits alike reaches its most confessional pitch in "Punishment." The grim specifics of his autopsy again come from Glob, who recounts how an undernourished fourteen-year-old girl in the first century A.D. "was led naked out on to the bog with bandaged eyes and the collar round her neck, and drowned in the little peat pit" on the Windeby estate in Schleswig. Her head was partially shaved, and Glob cites Tacitus's remarks in *Germania* [referred to by Heaney in "Kinship"] that identify this as "a special punishment for adultery by women" (Glob 1969, 114, 153). Heaney's empathy for the girl culminates in a sensual, androgynous paean, but as he elegizes he also accuses. In step with the Schleswig police who first examined the girl's body, suspecting she was a recent murder victim, Heaney reconstructs the ritualistic crime by examining telltale clues. His verdict is triple-edged; he implicates victim, victimizer, and himself. He is the "artful voyeur" peeping across millennia at the Iron Age scene of adultery, a man more deeply culpable because he does nothing to stop similar types of punishment in the present. 'Punishment' killings and maimings have been longstanding practices of the I.R.A., and Heaney confesses to guilty bystanding in that arena too. During the 1940s, according to Coogan, "a favourite I.R.A. punishment of the time for serious dereliction of duty was wounding a man in the leg, or in both legs for more serious cases, with a revolver shot" (1987, 228). More recently, Catholic girls in Northern Ireland have been "cauled in tar" for repudiating I.R.A. totems and taboos.

The theme of self-inflicted punishment—of punishing one's own—is at the heart of Heaney's poem. Indeed, his poem is an act of self-punishment, in which he attacks himself for not standing up to and actively resisting the abhorrent reprisals of his Catholic tribe against those who, like himself, have abandoned its religious and revolutionary principles. His soul-scouring arises from the irreconcilable demands of civilized poet and tribal cohort, Christian superego and pagan id, as much as from divided Catholics punishing each other in Belfast. Confronted by atrocities, he admits he "would connive / in civilized outrage / yet understand the exact / and tribal, intimate revenge." In his exposition of the biblical allusions in the poem, Neil Corcoran points out, "The chilling irony of the allusions is that they both judge this act of tribal revenge by the more merciful ethic enshrined in the biblical religion, while they also implicate that religion in precisely those sacrificial rituals which join Jutland and Irish Republicanism. . . . if Heaney's dumbness is blameworthy, then neither 'connivance' nor 'understanding' can excuse it" (1986, 117). What exculpates Heaney and allays his guilt, at least partially, is the confessional, elegiac poem itself. His excuses may be 'dumb' in both senses of the word, but he seems more intent on explaining than justifying, on speaking for the contradictory, self-destructive forces in himself and his tribe than on formulating political policies to eradicate them. What exacerbates his critics, and Heaney as well, is the knowledge that speaking of troubles is no substitute for active reformation.

The poems in *North* call for revelations and judgments of Irish imbro-glios, just as Heaney's journalistic reporting in the late sixties and early seventies expatiates on the injustices in moods of anger and gloom. A *Listener* article covering the 1968 civil rights march in Derry reveals his tone turning from equanimity to rebelliousness. "Two years ago, in an article on Belfast, I tried to present both sides [Protestant and Catholic] as more or less blameworthy. But it seems now that the Catholic minority in Northern Ireland at large, if it is to retain any self-respect, will have to risk the charge of wrecking the new moderation and seek justice more vociferously" (1968, 522). He attacks the government for condoning the harrassment of pro-testors by police and Paisleyites, and for ignoring "the grievances of Catholic[s] . . . : unemployment, lack of housing, discrimination in jobs and gerrymandering in electoral affairs" (522). By invoking the dead rebels of Wolfe Tone's forces (just as Sinn Fein and the I.R.A. have done for de-cades), he envisions an uprising that seems more philosophical than militant. "This is probably the renaissance of an interest in the rights of man which began here (and was effectively ended, of course) with the United Irishmen in the latter part of the 18th century" (522). By December 1971 he is writing, in another *Listener* cover story, of "Belfast's Black Christmas," of personal humiliations at the hands of the British army, of victims "blown apart and those in cells apart," of bombs detonated in bars and stores. With a bow to Martin Luther King, he asserts, "I have a dream that one day this nation will rise up and live out the full meaning of its creed," but his dream for a successful Irish uprising, peaceful or otherwise, has been vanquished by the noise of explosions, police cars, and fire lorries. "There isn't much predictable now, except that the sirens will blare out the old and blare in nothing very new" (1971, 857, 858). By this time the infamous "Battle of the Bogside" had occurred, the British army had entered Northern Ireland (ostensibly to protect the Catholics), and the Provisional I.R.A. had split from the old I.R.A. to combat the British soldiers. Heaney's *Listener* article of 1971 articulates the despairing vision of cyclical violence that would achieve mythic proportions in *North*. Half a year later he would resign from his teaching post at Queen's University and leave Belfast for a cottage in Wicklow.

Insofar as it is a sustained revelation of Heaney's divided response to his home ground, "Kinship" is the central poem in *North*. What Heaney strives for in the poem is a candid explanation of a society mired in self-destructive instincts, conventions, and myths. The bog is his principal metaphor for the insidious, gravitational pull of myth and history. The bog resembles his poetry too, which breaks down and preserves the hierarchical icons that have led his society astray. His compositions are built from decompositions, just as the bog is "a windfall composing / the floor it rots into." Archaeologist and historian (in this case Glob and Tacitus) are his tutelary spirits, guiding him as he re-members the dismembered past and remythicizes the myths he shatters. To the end his apocalypse exhumes a past that exists only in mute relics and ambiguous signs. Glob's speculations on the fertility cults in which men and women were sacrificially disposed of are just that: speculations. Heaney relies heavily on Tacitus's accounts of Iron Age practices in the *Germania*. Yet Tacitus, according to one scholar, "gives no first-hand knowledge but relies on . . . other sources of information" (Warmington 1970, 120), namely Posidonius's *Histories*, Julius Caesar's *Gallic Wars*, Livy, Pliny the Elder, and evidence provided by Roman soldiers who had served in Germany. Archaeological evidence, Glob states, "agrees with what he tells us" (1969, 151). Still, mysteries persist. "The wet centre is bottomless," Heaney rightly says in "Bogland," despite his repeated efforts to plumb its depths.

When Heaney communes with Tacitus's ghost in the last section of "Kinship," imploring him to come back from the dead and "read the inhumed faces / of casualty and victim," he is really talking to the social historian in himself. He reads and rewrites Tacitus and simultaneously imagines Tacitus doing the same to him. Tacitus described the character, habits, institutions, folklore, religion, climate, and products of the Germanic tribes of his day; Heaney describes the cultural phenomena of his Gaelic tribe. He begins by 'misprizing' Tacitus's account of Nerthus, whose shrine and consecrated chariot reside "in an island of the ocean . . . a holy grove" so that it refers to Ireland and her cults. When Nerthus is carted around the mainland (presumably of Jutland and Schleswig-Holstein), battles cease; when she returns to the island, they recommence. Her slavish ministrants washing her in a lake, Tacitus records, are "straightaway swallowed." Hence "a mysterious terror and an ignorance full of piety" (Warmington 1970, 197) surround the goddess, whose effects are bafflingly murderous and regenerative. To show how closely he is connected to these myths, Heaney writes of his everyday experience as if it were part of a fertility rite. His 'raised' turf spade in section 3, which he sinks in the "tawny rut" of the ground, reenacts a sexual marriage with the goddess, Nerthus. Indeed, his spade becomes a votive gift to her, imitating the "cloven oak-branch nine feet in length" that Glob identifies as a symbol of "the goddess herself" (1969, 180). "They have twinned / that obelisk," Heaney comments, remembering that Nerthus's statue was sexually 'twinned' or hermaphrodite. Heaney 'twins' her in other ways too, so that the buried wagons once used to transport Nerthus during her spring journeys become a real turf cart that Heaney once rode in with his great-uncle, Hugh Scullion. Heaney allegorizes this incident so that patriarchal Protestant rides with matriarchal Catholic, Viking Njord (Nerthus's male avatar) joins with Celtic Nerthus, and his own 'manly pride' crosses with his 'feminine' penchant for sacrificial humility.

Crossing back and forth between past and present, Heaney keeps outlining a path of crucifying self-judgment upon which early affections are crossed out by a retrospective conscience. Running counter to his desire for Tacitus to join hands with a contemporary journalist and document "how we slaughter / for the common good / / and shave the heads / of the notorious, / how the goddess swallows / our love and terror," is his belief that modern and ancient 'reporters' adulterate the crucial tension between myth and history. His condemnation has scholarly precedents. E. H. Warmington, for example, blamed Tacitus's historical distortions on his "obedience to long-established ethnographic style and method, and to a traditional belief that all half-civilized nations had like qualities and customs" (1970, 121). Tacitus flaunted his historical presumptions with little concern for accuracy. In his own reporting, Heaney has attacked the "cliché-mongering movement" (1968, 522) of journalists from England for their similar devotion to "long-established" styles and stereotypes. The same accusation of mystification, of assimilating historical experience to long-established myths and narrative styles, ironically enough, has been hurled at Heaney.

Some ethnocentric distortion is unavoidable. With regard to mythic histories and mythopoetic historians, Conor Cruise O'Brien has observed, "Most history is *tribal* history: written . . . in terms generated by, and acceptable to, a given tribe or nation, or a group within such a tribe or nation" (1972, 16). Historiographic poets and scholars in Heaney's poems are usually affiliated with empire, English or Roman, and their accounts of conquered provinces tainted by condescension or disapproval. In "Ocean's Love to Ireland," Heaney's whipping boys are: Sir Walter Raleigh, who praised the imperial Queen Elizabeth in "The Ocean to Cynthia"; John Aubrey, who documented Raleigh's rape of a native maiden in his eccentric and biographically dubious *Brief Lives*; and Edmund Spenser, who spoke on behalf of Lord Grey concerning the massacre of Catholics at Smerwick. Other poems sarcastically invoke Tacitus, who spoke up for the Roman

Empire in his histories, and Diodorus Siculus, who also let myth and the mystique of empire take precedence over veracity. For Heaney these different figures exemplify the historian's dangerous and perhaps inevitable dependence on fictions. Diodorus's *Library of History*, for example, was intended to be a history from the creation of the universe to 59 B.C., the year of Julius Caesar's first consulship. Its didactic purpose was to snub democracy and applaud the strong man in history, as well as the 'good life' made possible by him. C. H. Oldfather points out that Diodorus's 'Universal History' assumed that "all mankind was coming to form a 'common' civilization, a 'common' society" and that "the whole Mediterranean world was now interested in the same things and what benefited one nation was of common value to all" (1933, xii). Although Heaney universalizes and mythologizes his particular historical moment, his notions of 'catholicity' and apocalypse have little of his mentors' presumptuous chauvinism.

Despite the efforts of journalists, historians, and poets to bear accurate witness to past and present atrocities, the atrocious events often dwarf these literary efforts with the sheer magnitude of their horror. The beheaded girl "outstaring axe / And beatification" in "Strange Fruit" becomes for Heaney an emblem of the martyr, who witnesses (*murtus* in Greek means witness) historical tragedy but remains independent of those who act as belated witnesses on her behalf. For Anne Ross, whose *Pagan Celtic Britain* Heaney quotes in "Feeling into Words," what "sums up the whole of Celtic pagan religion and is as representative of it as is, for example, the sign of the cross in Christian contexts . . . is the symbol of the severed head" (1980a, 59). For the Celts "the head was seemingly the centre of the life-force, capable of continued, independent life after the death of the body" (Ross 1967, 92). Sacks contends that the severed head as well as the other figures of martyrdom and dismemberment in Heaney's elegies could be symbolic of castration. In Greek fertility cults, which underpin the whole Western tradition of elegy, "castration was thought to defend the individual against mortality by conserving his *psyche*." The castrated head was also associated with the mutilated totem, the sacrificed god or goddess who rose from the dead, as well as the consoling tropes of elegies that guarantee the deceased's immortality. Sacks explains, "Just as the child performs a voluntary symbolic castration, and just as the vegetation deity suffers a particularly castrative martyrdom, so that the phallic principle of fertility may be renewed, so, too, the griever wounds his own sexuality, deflecting his desire, in order to erect a consoling figure for an ongoing, if displaced, generative power" (1983, 102). Heaney's erotic attachment to the dead and the fertility goddess (Ireland) also has to be severed in order for him to continue as a poet. The bog victims through a paradoxical apotheosis become the icons of his own

poetic power, and of the Irish psyche in general. They are abjured through a
sacrificial process that makes possible their longevity in the sublimated form
of art.

After all his psychomythic memorials, Heaney wonders why he labors
"through damp leaves, / Husks, the spent flukes of autumn" to expose the
dead and his moral quandaries in a culture bent on piling up more corpses.
He yearns to play the role of apocalyptic romantic hero sweeping away the
detritus of past and present so that, as Shelley wrote in "England in 1819,"
out of the "graves . . . a glorious Phantom may / Burst, to illumine our
tempestuous day" (Shelley 1945, 575). For both, revelation and revolution
are linked, but while Heaney exclaims prophetically, "If I could come on
meteorite!" his conditional clause acknowledges obvious uncertainty. He
admits that he has "missed / The once-in-a-lifetime portent, / The comet's
pulsing rose." The rose of salvation, which for Eliot reconciles history in a
timeless moment, for Heaney is always in the mythic past, illusory, unattainable. His apocalypse is Antaeuslike to the end, focused on dust and earth,
the "complexities of mire and blood," as Yeats put it in "Byzantium"
(1983, 248), and the relics of multitudinous defeats that also betoken the
demise of the old elegiac and apocalyptic tropes.

By ending *North* with a self-portrait of the artist as an outlaw on the
run, as the wood kerne or foot soldier pursued by Elizabethan troops,
"blowing up these sparks / For their meagre heat," Heaney offers a final
judgment of self and culture that is as unflattering as it is relentlessly judicious. If he is an escapist (he is writing from Wicklow after being accused by
Northern papers of betraying his roots), it is mad Northern Ireland that has
hurt him into that poetic role. Behind the madness is Hercules, symbol of
British and Irish Protestant power, "graiping him / out of his element,"
against which he fights with poems that seem to make little happen. "Hercules and Antaeus," which concludes the book's first section, expresses
solidarity with the dispossessed and damned: with Balor, the one-eyed rob-
ber god defeated by the legendary invaders of Ireland (the Tuath de Danaan);
with Byrthnoth, leader at the Battle of Maldon whose forces were massa-
cred by the Danes; with Sitting Bull, emblem of the American Indians
doomed by white colonizers; and ultimately with Catholic inhabitants of
Ireland deracinated by Protestant conquerors. The light he trains on these
victimized "mould-huggers" is stolen from Hercules' "spur of light," and
presumably with the knowledge that Hercules will taste defeat and die
too—by Antaean passion. The toxic love-shirt of the centaur, Nessus, which
his wife mistakenly gives Hercules to renew his passion for her, ultimately
kills him. Defeated Antaeus, paradoxically, will live on as an icon of martyrdom, providing "pap for the dispossessed." So will Hercules, as a reminder

that even the most invincible empires, rationalisms, and technologies are doomed.

The most precise image of Heaney's apocalypse of history and myth, and their symbiotic relations, is of Hercules and Antaeus locked in eternal combat. Victory and defeat, light and dark, reason and instinct, fact and fiction—all of which they represent—are merely transitional phases in a continuous dialectic. The recalcitrance of Irish troubles always rebuffs Heaney's dreams of utopian rapprochements. Nevertheless, he provides, as he said of Wordsworth's *Prelude*, "a working model for that evolution of a higher consciousness in response to an apparently intolerable conflict" (1984a, 1). To the end, his apocalypse seeks to reveal history for what it is. Abolishing or wholly transcending it, as in biblical and romantic eschatologies, will only perpetuate its nightmares. His apocalyptic method strives to exemplify the kind of vigilant conscience and consciousness desperately needed if a society like the one in Northern Ireland is to heal its wounds, which have festered partly because of history and partly because of myth for so many centuries. His apocalypse expresses hope, yet it is worldly-wise enough to know that justice may be ultimately unattainable.

6

CROSSING DIVISIONS AND DIFFERENCES

EVER SINCE CHARLES BAUDELAIRE IMAGINED "the miracle of a poetic prose" and Stephen Mallarmé challenged his contemporaries to refashion the metrical conventions promulgated by the "great general organs of past centuries," modern poets have tested their skills at the prose poem. For Mallarmé the urge to mix poetry and prose arose from a "crise de vers" (Fredman 1983, 2, 3), a disillusionment with the "artificial metronomes" of metrical orthodoxy, and a desire to explore "all possible combinations and interrelationships" (Mallarmé 1956, 36) that make up the music of language. Like the Modernists who followed him, Mallarmé managed to be revolutionary and reactionary at the same time. His aesthetic liberations promoted "democratic" prose to the status of "pure" poetry, but then refused to submit such "purities" to the masses. If prose was the common stuff of everyday speech, the aristocratic Frenchman would make it strut by giving it "un sens plus pur aux mots de la tribu" (Mallarmé 1977, 174). Mallarmé's poet, and Joyce's after him, was the artist-god, refining his creation into a symbolist mystery that only elite initiates were invited to appreciate.

With such hieratic origins, it is strange that the prose poem that became so popular in the 1960s and 1970s should be associated with the stridently democratic sentiments of the time. The prose poetry of Robert Bly, James Wright, and Gary Snyder, for example, and the later talk or performance poems of David Antin and other L-A-N-G-U-A-G-E poets level the old hierarchical assumptions of Mallarmé. Although Mallarmé declared that art "is a mystery accessible only to a very few" (1956, 11), his progeny in the post–World War II period employed prose as a tool to demystify the poetic and courted rather than condemned the common man. Seamus Heaney's uncollected sequence of prose poems, *Stations*, fits interestingly into this contradictory tradition. It was partly inspired by the tech-

99

nical examples and ideological concerns of Bly and Snyder, but it also drew on the technical accomplishments of the Symbolists and Modernists.

Like Mallarmé's prose poems, Heaney's *Stations* arose from a sense of crisis. The poems were composed at a critical juncture in his career, when he was allowing his formalist training to absorb the Whitmanesque spirit of the sixties. He completed several sections in California between 1970 and 1971, when he was teaching at Berkeley and reading William Carlos Williams, Robert Bly, Gary Snyder, and Robert Duncan. Shortly before, in 1968, he had translated a number of Baudelaire's *Petits poèmes en prose*. The cross-fertilization of American and French methods ended when he returned to the sectarian battles of Belfast in 1971. After departing from Northern Ireland to reside in the South that same year, he put the poems aside, only to take them up again and finish them quickly in May and June of 1974. In hindsight, it makes sense that Heaney's multiple psychological and geographical crossings would engender a "crise de vers" and find embodiment in a sequence whose title refers to the more traditional crises and crosses of his Christian heritage.

Heaney had written earlier sequences exploring the English/Irish, Protestant/Catholic bifurcations in his psyche and culture (such as "A Northern Hoard" in *Wintering Out*). *Stations* is unique in that it seeks to embody in poetic prose the candid, autobiographical style that in the sixties became known as Confessionalism. The thirteenth section, for instance, describes with characteristic intimacy and perplexity how the Troubles of the North have split him in half. He does not know which side to cheer for when German bombs fall on Protestant districts in Belfast. The traditional enemies of the Catholic nationalist faction have been punished, so the Germans appear to be heroes. The revelation has all the shock of Lowell's ambiguous identifications with Caligula, Mussolini, and Hitler, although Heaney's avowal is more guarded. Primed with megalomania, Lowell gesticulates grandly and carelessly; Heaney works stealthily toward negotiation and rapprochement. He asserts, "I moved like a double agent. . . . An adept at banter, I crossed the lines with carefully enunciated passwords, manned every speech with checkpoints and reported back to nobody." In line with the Jesuits of an earlier era, Heaney turns equivocation into a high art in order to fend off accusation and punishment. The judicious, measured style of *Stations* is above all the product of a culture besieged by enemies from without and within. The prose poem, which stalks the border between genres like a double agent, disguising the identities of both by blending them, depends on the sort of freedom Heaney must have felt in California and Wicklow. Removed from direct confrontation with the Troubles, he could experiment with a new form that, as he states in a letter, "the rather stricter, mocking and self-mocking atmosphere of Belfast would not have allowed" (letter to the author, 17 August 1988).

When Heaney contends in his lecture *Place and Displacement* that Wordsworth in *The Prelude* and Jung in his psychoanalytical writings agree "that the trauma of individual consciousness is likely to be an aspect of forces at work in the collective life" and that "a higher consciousness" is needed to assuage "an apparently intolerable conflict" (1984a, 3, 1), he could be thinking of the genesis of *Stations*. The book is his miniature *Prelude*. Following its epic forerunner, it investigates "the growth of a poet's mind" and the agonized devotion to a home ground torn by differences. Wordsworth, in fact, was on Heaney's mind when he began his sequence. His introduction recalls that the "first pieces had been attempts to touch what Wordsworth called 'spots of time,' moments at the very edge of consciousness which had lain for years in the unconscious as active lodes or nodes, yet on my return to Belfast a month after the introduction of internment my introspection was not confident enough to pursue its direction. The sirens in the air, perhaps quite rightly, jammed those other tentative if insistent signals" (1975, 3). Here the stations are broadcasting stations deep in Heaney's psyche, and vulnerable to the nearby uproar. Transcendence for Heaney is rarely embraced with the unambiguous rapture of an Emerson. So it is odd that he repeatedly finds himself, even against his better judgment, withdrawing from conflicts in order to envision them more clearly. If he poses as a soldier, as he does in "Kernes" and "England's difficulty," it is to fight for the artistic freedom to compose his poems. "Nesting-ground" suggests that he is a "sentry" devoted to the underground visionary world of poets and mystics rather than to the underworld of terrorists.

Boundary crossings mark the style and substance of *Stations*, and the most dramatic crossing for Heaney must have been the trip from Belfast to Berkeley. An article Heaney published in *The Listener* in late December 1971 records the glaring differences he experienced between Northern Ireland and California cultures, and how he felt deracinated but still intrigued by the latter. For the Irishman rooted in the harsh northern climate and its rigorous Catholic traditions, Californians seemed to float rootlessly from one blissful oasis to another. Rather than merge with the untethered folk around him, Heaney registered astonishment at their contentment. Writing shortly before Christmas, he attacked the commercialism that surrounded the holy day, and he mocked the countercultural groups that opposed commercialism as well. The hippies, in Heaney's view, were comical freeloaders depending on the capitalists for handouts and leisure. "The commune mores are occasionally an irritation to the Celt. It's the rip-off generation," he declared after being repeatedly pestered for money in the streets. And yet it was the "waifish hippy girl . . . [with] loose loops of hippy gear, piping 'Merry Christmas, Merry Christmas,' " who conjured up the seasonal rituals so familiar to Heaney's Catholic sensibility. He recounts, "We have lived in Berkeley for three months now and this is the first time I've heard an utterance on the street that has the shock of familiarity" (1970b, 903).

As usual, language provokes Heaney's most sensitive response. Assuming, as Hermine Riffaterre does, that prose poetry was and still is "revolutionary" (1983, 98) in its general aims, it is important to note Heaney's ambivalence toward the revolutionary language that was ubiquitous in Berkeley. While he mentions the Free Speech Movement of the sixties, the People's Park, and the protests that followed the American invasion of Cambodia, the rhetoric of the Black Panthers shocks him into making distinctions between the revolutionary language of America and Ireland— distinctions that reveal much about the style he chooses for *Stations*. So different from the "grotesquely violent" writings of the Panthers, those of the I.R.A. are rife with "romantic traditional invocations in the great line of Tone and Emmet and Pearse [and] even its furious anti-British propaganda has an old-world restraint about it." Bernadette Devlin, one of the most radical civil rights leaders in Northern Ireland in the late sixties, according to Heaney would never call a policeman a "fascist pig." He concludes, "In contrast to the revolutionary language of America, the revolutionary voice of Ireland still keeps a civil tongue in its head" (1970b, 903).

Throughout his vignette of American life, Heaney casts himself with conventional ritualists and reaffirms his Irish roots even though they seem as tangled and contradictory as those of his American compatriots. When he explains that "Northern Ireland has long been trapped in a ritualistic language that cannot, it seems, be unlearned" (1970b, 903), he celebrates the entrapment as he chafes against it. *Stations* opens to the revolutionary poetics and politics that he encountered daily in Berkeley but preserves the "ritualistic language" deployed with such brilliant effects in earlier volumes. As a result, when examined alongside the prose poems of Bly and Snyder, Heaney's assays into the form have a much more traditional feel. Rather than float free from Western culture, Heaney's poems continually burrow into it. His linguistic diggings expose Latin, Anglo-Saxon, Gaelic, and English roots so that, as in *Wintering Out* and *North*, etymology recapitulates history, especially its calamities and conflicts.

The section entitled "Patrick and Oisin," for instance, commemorates the historical period when Roman Catholicism sparred with Celtic paganism (his title is taken from Yeats's "Wanderings of Oisin" via Middle Irish dialogues between the Roman saint and the legendary Irish hero). Heaney recalls a similar dialogue in his own life, one in which the Celt dominates and the Christian retreats. He enshrines the Latinate sonorities of his early Catholicism even while elegizing its defeat by the resurgent Irish hero and all he represents. He relishes the "catechism with its woodcut mysteries and polysyllabic runs, its 'clandestine solemnizations,' its 'morose delectation and concupiscence' . . . [its] hard stones of 'calumny and detraction.' " As he grows up the old words and concepts give way to even older ones. Catholic orthodoxy wanes as indigenous Irish myths wax. Heaney concludes, "The phrases that had sapped my concentration atrophied, incised tablets, mossed and camouflaged by parasites and creeping greenery." The pagan Irish greening of his Christian sensibility is accompanied by a growing attentiveness to the hard-hitting energies of Anglo-Saxon and the flowing lyricism of Gaelic. The rich linguistic past is not purified or purged, as in the prose poems of Bly, James Wright, or Snyder. The dross remains in all its rich profusion, so that Anglo-Saxon 'moss' and 'sap' merge with Latinate 'concentration,' 'atrophy' and 'incise.' Through the dense roots the Irish past rises to color everything with its "creeping greenery."

The desire to give an Irish inflection to a complex linguistic inheritance owes much to the example of Joyce, as does the urge to write a prose as rich and artful as poetry. The individual episodes in *Stations* resemble Joyce's epiphanies, which were prose poems of a sort. Joyce's radiant moments, rather than reveal God as in the showing forth of Christ to the Magi in the orthodox epiphany, attempted to unveil the *quidditas* of objects and events. His *Portrait of the Artist* captured these evanescent moments of illumination and arranged them into a sequence that revealed, albeit ironically, his own evolution as an "artist-god." Just as Stephen Dedalus sees his mission as "a priest of eternal imagination, transmuting the daily bread of experience into the radiant body of everliving life" (1968, 221), Heaney presides over a eucharistic art whose Christ appears in artistic garb. The germinal idea for portraying the artist's early life as a succession of stations also may have come from Joyce. When Stephen plunges into his period of fervent Loyolan devotional exercises, Joyce comments, "Every part of his day, divided by what he regarded now as the duties of his station in life, circled about its own centre of spiritual energy" (148). Heaney's *Stations* focus on similar centers of energy, of tense crossings and crises, and with the same stylistic panache.

The influence of Joyce, emphatic though it is, was filtered through another more contemporary medium, which, in fact, stymied the poem for three years. Heaney told John Haffenden, "I did three or four . . . [sections of *Stations*] in California, and in that year Geoffrey Hill's *Mercian Hymns* arrived, and in some ways I hesitated" (Haffenden 1981, 67–68). His introduction admitted that Hill's sequence of prose poems, which conflated the poet's childhood with King Offa's ancient rule of Mercia, had a more debilitating effect. "What I regarded as stolen marches in a form new to me had been headed off by a work of complete authority" (1975, 3). The martial metaphors attest to a battle for originality Heaney felt he had lost. Heaney is partly mocking this poetic combat by playing the evasive Irish soldier (as he does in "Kernes") who historically is defeated by the authoritarian Englishman but somehow manages to escape. His respect for Hill and his imperious persona, however, is genuine.

The essay "Englands of the Mind" implies that his stolen marches— his prose poems—could continue only if he absorbed the technical apparatus that Hill paraded in front of him, such as his enchanting, polysemous patterns of entwined Latin and Anglo-Saxon roots. Heaney uses metaphors from architecture to describe this process. "The mannered rhetoric of these pieces is a kind of verbal architecture, a grave and sturdy English Romanesque. The native undergrowth, both vegetative and verbal, that barbaric scrollwork of fern and ivy, is set against the tympanum and chancel-arch, against the weighty elegance of imperial Latin" (1980a, 160). This "mannered rhetoric" is precisely what Heaney attempts to reconstruct in *Stations*, and most noticeably in "Patrick and Oisin." Aiming for an Irish rather than an English Romanesque, he uses the same images of vegetative undergrowth mantling Roman stonework to underscore his polyglot project. "In the stone-warmed kitchen, neighbours' names seeded and uncurled upon our tongues, a backbiting undergrowth mantling the hard stones of 'calumny and detraction.' " The spirited attacks of neighbors whose names no doubt derive from Irish and British roots give to the Latinate "calumny" and "detraction" a local vigor.

Hill's novel way of binding local tongues with ancient, foreign ones was also indebted to Joyce, as Heaney explains at some length.

There is in Hill something of Stephen Dedalus's hyperconsciousness of words as physical sensations, as sounds to be plumbed, as weights on the tongue. Words in his poetry fall slowly and singly, like molten solder, and accumulate to a dull glowing nub. I imagine Hill as indulging in a morose linguistic delectation, dwelling on the potential of each word with much the same slow relish as Leopold Bloom dwells on the thought of his kidney. And in *Mercian Hymns*, in fact, Hill's procedure resembles Joyce's not only in this linguistic deliberation and self-consciousness. For all his references to the 'precedent provided by the Latin prose-hymns or canticles of the early Christian Church,' what these hymns celebrate is the 'ineluctable modality of the audible,' as well as the visible, and the form that celebration takes reminds one of the Joycean epiphany, which is a prose poem in effect. But not only in the form of the individual pieces, but in the overall structuring of the pieces, he follows the Joycean precedent set in *Ulysses* of confounding modern autobiographical material with literary and historic matter drawn from the past. Offa's story makes contemporary landscape and experience live in the rich shadows of a tradition. (1980a, 160)

Heaney also combines autobiographical and legendary events, but there is no consistent figure—no Offa or Ulysses—underpinning his narrative except himself. His prose poems are epiphanies, bodying forth his evolving artistic spirit in a rhetoric often as linguistically rich as Joyce's and Hill's. They avoid, however, the additional complexity of 'the mythic method.'

Taking his cue from Joyce and Hill, Heaney strives with the help of Catholic rituals to recollect the cyclical rhythms of body and nature, blood and seasons, national and cultural history. His *Stations* pose a series of communions that set a divided mind and its divided world at one. The cross is Heaney's most poignant symbol for his crossed sympathies, not only between Catholic and Protestant factions warring in Northern Ireland, but also between the ideology of American free verse and the Anglo-Irish formalism of his background. Heaney's obsessive theme, which the prose poems stylistically underscore, is the anguish that a man feels when he persistently crosses between two camps. The impulse to borrow from diverse traditions and remain, for the most part, independent of each, characterized his dealings with the California poets who influenced his work. He commented to James Randall, "I didn't meet or become friends with the West Coast poets, but I became very conscious of the poetry of Gary Snyder. I saw Snyder, and Bly was living in Bolinas that year. . . . There was a strong sense of contemporary American poetry in the West with Robert Duncan and Bly and Gary Snyder rejecting the intellectual, ironical, sociological idiom of poetry and going for the mythological. I mean everyone wanted to be a Red Indian, basically" (1979a, 19–20). In *Earth House Hold*, published the year before Heaney arrived in California, Snyder interspersed prose poems between poems and prose accounts of working for the forest service in the western United States and traveling to Japan. Such chapters as "Buddhism and the Coming Revolution," "Poetry and the Primitive," and "Why Tribe" outlined his plan for a new society that would repudiate industrialism and "follow the timeless path of love and wisdom, in affectionate company with the sky, winds, clouds, trees, waters, animals and grasses" (Snyder 1969, 116). His essay "The Redskins" celebrated Native

American cultures for achieving this pantheistic program through the use of hallucinogens, remarking that "peyote and acid have a curious way of tuning some people in to the local soil" (107–8). Heaney would tune in, without the aid of hallucinogens, to the local soil as well. His *Stations*, however, broadcast a message persistently informed by the biblical narrative of fall and redemption, of paradise lost and redeemed, that Snyder in poems like "Milton by Firelight" mocked and renounced.

The passion behind the political poetry in California, despite his objections to its style and goals, still left an indelible mark on Heaney. "The most important influence I came under in Berkeley," he said, was the "awareness that poetry was a force, almost a mode of power, certainly a mode of resistance" (1979a, 20). The "mythological approach that Snyder and Bly were advancing" was one he turned to his own advantage in *Stations* and *North* (which he was composing at the same time). The skepticism bred out of close proximity to historical rebellions and calamities prevented him from embracing the American mythologists wholeheartedly. He could not accede so easily to their blueprints for utopia. "As far as I was concerned," he admitted, "their whole doctrine was too programmatic" (1979a, 20). He would maintain his freedom from his multiple sources, borrowing what he could use and rejecting the rest. Heaney's prose poems, in fact, never abandon the "intellectual, ironical, sociological idiom" that the West Coast poets attacked, although they merge it with the "mythological" idiom of the Americans. To see how different the result is, one could compare any poem in *Stations* with Robert Bly's "The Dead Seal near McClure's Beach," which Heaney probably heard or read in California, because it had been published in 1969. Bly mourns the effects of industrial wastes in a style expressive of the innocence of the victimized creature. His style flirts with sentimentality, his sentences are simple to the point of being simplistic, his diction reduced to the lowest common denominator, his rhythms attenuated. He begins unpretentiously, "Walking north toward the point, I come on a dead seal," and continues to describe how "his head is arched back, the small eyes closed, the whiskers sometimes rise and fall. He is dying. This is the oil. Here on its back is the oil that heats our houses so efficiently. Wind blows fine sand back toward the ocean. The flipper near me lies folded over the stomach, looking like an unfinished arm, lightly glazed with sand at the edges. The other flipper lies half underneath" (quoted in Fredman 1983, 52–53). Snyder's poetic prose surpasses Bly's in rhythmical vigor. Both join, however, in repudiating linguistic densities and the tortuous history of Western culture behind them, and in celebrating the kind of innocent consciousness that can live in solitary harmony with all natural beings.

Attracted to the "consciousness-raising that [was] . . . going on in the Bay area" (1979a, 20), Heaney would later state that an "evolution of a higher consciousness in response to an apparently intolerable conflict" was desirable as long as it shouldered rather than shirked the historical troubles that motivated it. Discussing "politics and transcendence" in his lecture *Place and Displacement*, he applauds Northern Irish poets who remained faithful to their formalist principles when the antiformalist poetics and anti-establishment politics of the sixties were all the rage.

> It is a superficial response to the work of Northern Irish poets to conceive of their lyric stances as evasions of the actual conditions. Their concern with poetry itself wears well when we place it beside the protest poetry of the sixties: the density of their verbal worlds has held up, the purely poetic force of the words is the guarantee of a commit-ment which need not apologise for not taking up the cudgels since it is raising a baton to attune discords which the cudgels are creating. (1984a, 7)

Encoded in this apology is a vote for the Symbolist program that advocates a pure poetry and aspires to the harmony of music. Heaney also backs the Modernist and Formalist tenets that aimed for a mimesis or at-one-ment between dense verbal constructs and the dense world's body, between po-etic paradox and historical and psychological divisiveness. Heaney remarked candidly of the poems in *Stations*, "I began them in California because the nature mysticism stuff was hot on the ground" (Haffenden 1981, 68). When he returned to Ireland he would cool this mystical heat with the ironic, scholarly intellect Bly and Snyder were trying to overhaul.

Almost every section of *Stations* contains a fertile crossing of opposi-tions that maps Heaney's progress from one mode of awareness to another. He begins as if umbilically attached to home and nature and then falls further and further into painful political, religious, and artistic quandaries. The first six sections describe rites of passage in which Heaney as a young boy discovers the pains and pleasures of bodily existence. He is consistently close to the elemental world of plant, animal, and mineral: sitting in a pea field, feeding a horse, gathering primroses by the hedge, listening to sand martins in a riverbank, gazing at golden sand at the bottom of a newly dug well, or sailing boats made from potatoes in a mud puddle called Botany Bay. His fascination with botanical and zoological splendors, harsh as they may be (Botany Bay refers to the place in Australia where Irish criminals were shipped), shifts as he begins to learn more about the sectarian roots of his Irish heritage. His recognition of religious and political differences inten-sifies from the seventh section, "Patrick and Oisin," to the fifteenth, "Trial

Runs," when he discovers what it means to be a Roman Catholic in Northern Ireland. As a schoolboy burrowing into history, he meditates on St. Patrick's legacy, the often disguised but nevertheless real brutalities instigated by William of Orange and the Protestant Ascendancy, the oddly distant terrors of World Wars I and II, and the difficulty of detecting genuine enemies and deciding how to deal with them once they are detected.

The first section covers Heaney's preschool days, the second his days at Anahorish, and the third his journey away from home to St. Columb's in Londonderry. His departure amounts to a retreat, both religious and scholastic, and resembles Stephen Dedalus's period under the tutelary influence of the Jesuits at Belvedere. Here his training as a genuine writer begins. The poem ends with a new faring forth. Now a student at Queen's University, Belfast, he affixes the pseudonym Incertus to his poems and tentatively tests his wings in artistic flight. He encounters the reality of experience in different arenas and from different perspectives. He begins in sensuous contact with the bodily world (like the fetal Stephen) and (like Stephen at Christmas dinner) learns of sectarian politics in Ireland. Again the narrative he traces is essentially oedipal, and can be illuminated by both Freudian and Lacanian perspectives. His development, as charted in his other poems, is a struggle away from captivating mother figures whose sexual allure promises stagnation or death. He also struggles with the Law of the Father, the patriarchal codes ingrained in Northern Irish politics and language. Traversing between his various Symplegades, he strives to incorporate their differences productively rather than to repress them destructively, as his culture has managed to do for so many centuries. Art in the end is his therapeutic mirror in which he will try to envision himself and his culture as they really are.

To get a better view of the maze of mirrors that is his culture, Heaney as usual flies above it. The structure of *Stations* can be explained vegetatively as well as aeronautically and psychoanalytically. Rooted in his home ground, Heaney extends his tendrils into language, politics, and religion (he says in "Patrick and Oisin," "My hand was a tendril reaching with the others"). These exploratory forays are rebuffed by the shock of contemporary affairs. In "Cloistered," he enters a wintry retreat, withering toward his Catholic roots, and then struggles toward a vernal resurrection. He is born again as a writer by the end. The original caul covering the head of the fetal poet has been transformed into a literary cloak and mask, though it "lies there like a mouldering tegument." Still a neophyte ("I crept before I walked," he asserts), at last he has discovered his vocation. A sensitive poetic plant (a tegument is the outer covering of a plant), he is ritualistically at one with the pulsating rhythm of all organisms, whether natural or man-made. Following Joyce's Icarus/Dedalus, he is ready to soar toward the sun. Heaney's preoccupation with 'organicism' took some of its impetus from Coleridge, Keats, and Wordsworth. It found additional support in Theodore Roethke. Although he does not mention Roethke in his discussions of *Stations*, it was Roethke who provided him with the imagery for his first section, "Cauled," and with the larger model of a sequence tracing the imagination's passage from a vegetative Eden through psychological perplexities toward artistic redemptions. His review of Roethke's *Collected Poems*, "Canticles to the Earth" (published in *The Listener* in 1968, two years before he began his prose poems), stresses the American poet's "apocalyptic straining after unity" in which the poet's progress is articulated in terms of snails, bugs, geraniums, rivers, pine trees, and every other natural thing. "Growth, minute and multifarious life, became Roethke's theme," he observes, and with regard to *The Lost Son*, which contains the greenhouse poems, "Now the free, nervous notation of natural process issues in a sense of unity with cosmic energies and in quiet intimations of order and delight" (1980a, 191–92). While Heaney's notations may not be as freewheeling as Roethke's, he aims for the same documentation of the mind's battle for organic unity.

For Heaney and Roethke sex is the most constant reminder of the biological root of human existence. As with the ancient fertility rituals that intrigue both poets, and perhaps because of their interest in Freud, sex is seen as the original and originating force behind all life, an analogue of the prime mover's power to create the cosmos and the poet's to produce poems. Heaney gives priority to sexual impulses and to the sense of the creative life as a vegetative ritual by making his original station a recapitulation of a child's sexual experience in a pea field. The plants are unmistakably phallic, the child's gestures toward them masturbatory.

> Green air trawled over his arms and legs, the pods and stalks wore a fuzz of light. He caught a rod in each hand and jerked the whole tangle into life. Little tendrils unsprung, new veins lit in the shifting leaves, a caul of shadows stretched and netted round his head again.
> He sat listening, grateful as the calls encroached.
> They found him at the first onset of sobbing.

A childhood reminiscence in *Preoccupations* describes how Heaney "got lost in the pea-drills in a field behind the house" at Mossbawn, and how, after imagining the event for so long, he transformed it into his private mythology. The pea field became a "secret nest," the "*omphalos*. . . . the navel . . . the center of another world" (1980a, 17), an Eden from which the child would inevitably fall.

Roethke's *The Lost Son*, which guided Heaney's tale of himself as a lost child in the pea-drills ("They thought he was lost" is the first line of *Stations*), obsessively charts sexual returns to omphallic and womblike origins. The pleasures of solitary stimulation are matched by contrary feelings of guilt, doubt, fear, and contrition. Having lost his father at the age of fifteen, and having been lost once as a child in a similar field behind his father's greenhouses, Roethke searches frantically for a paternal guide and a path toward salvation. Sex unifies him ecstatically, or at least reassuringly, with primordial, vegetative life; anxiety convinces him of his separateness and his need for the redemptive "light within light" ("The Lost Son," 1975, 55) he mentions at the end. Another poem, "Cuttings (later)," however, was Heaney's richest source for images combining vegetative growth with human sexuality. The spermatic sprouts, throbbing veins, and watery sucking in "Cuttings" all have their corollaries in "Cauled." Roethke writes;

> I can hear, underground, that sucking and sobbing,
> In my veins, in my bones I feel it,—
> The small waters seeping forward,
> The tight grains parting at last.
> Slippery as fish,
> I quail, lean to beginnings, sheath-wet. (1975, 35)

This commemoration of erotic beginnings appeared at the beginning of Roethke's greenhouse sequence. It is one of the few passages Heaney quotes in his review. Another is from "The Meadow Mouse," which perhaps encouraged Heaney to depict himself in "Cauled" as "a big fieldmouse in the middle of the rig."

The enjoyment of a phallic or womblike Eden was as shortlived for Roethke as it was for Heaney. Heaney could be speaking of his own troubled progress sketched in *Stations* when he observes of the "Cuttings" passage, "Such celebration . . . was prelude to disturbance and desperation. Out of Eden man takes his way, and beyond the garden life is riotous; chaos replaces correspondence, consciousness thwarts communion, the light of the world fades in the shadow of death. Until the final serenity and acceptance of all things in a dance of flux, which comes in the posthumous *The Far Field*, Roethke's work is driven in two opposite directions by his fall into manhood" (1980a, 192). Roethke's final sequences, Heaney suggests, combine the formal New Critical side of his oeuvre with "the long Whitmanesque cataloguing" (1980a, 193) side. *Stations* seeks similar unities for its crossed and crucifying antinomies in a sequence whose music and dance is weighted with historical awareness.

To recognize the real world's brutalities, the romantic poet usually has to be kicked out of Eden with a jolt. In the second section, "Branded," the idealized naturalist in Heaney suffers just such a jolt when he is literally kicked by a horse. As in *Death of a Naturalist*, he discovers that the pastures surrounding his farm are not Arcadian groves but a sectarian community bristling with violence. Plucking "straws from the stack that stands in the haggard like a gold apple bitten," he resembles Adam picking his apple of bitter knowledge. His fall is essentially a journey from a prereflective, childhood at-one-ment with nature through division and pain toward imaginative transcendence. His body falls but his spirit ascends. "His small head hits the ground like a pod splitting open to the faraway acreage of the sky." His vegetal life as a pea pod—an obvious constriction—has been broken open to the dispensations of imaginative vision. The moon, that Yeatsean symbol of metamorphoses in the imaginative life, heralds the boons of Heaney's fall. As he weeps in bed, "slowly motes compose the opening of a hairy canopy [the horse's] as the pastern unclouds its moon and again the shod hoof strikes and brands him." Horse-struck and moonstruck, he is the branded victim as well as the branding artist, discomposed but also composing himself, like the blacksmith hammering horseshoes in "The Forge." The redemptive power of the imagination allows him to strike back at what struck him.

Thesis and antithesis flourish throughout *Stations* from a single seed. Like a plant bending toward the sun, Heaney's germinal imagination synthesizes fractious materials as it grows. The third section, "Hedge-school," again sketches the child's divided sensibility, his irrepressible tendency to abandon undifferentiated, vegetal Edens where "the white thorn was green as the blackthorn" and confront disturbing differences. Picking primroses by the hedge for the May altar turns out to be a frighteningly sexual experience which, like the hedge itself, enforces a sense of dividedness. He has all the ambivalence of Stephen Dedalus toward sex, although his description of flowers as sex organs with cosmic dimensions smacks more of D. H. Lawrence and Ted Hughes.

> Primroses grew in a damp single bunch out of the bank, imploding pallors, star plasm, nebula of May. He stared himself into an absence. "Pull them for the May altar and hurry up." He knelt and reached the stems. Pod ridges. Legs of nestlings.

The flowers have less religious than anatomical significance for this young poetic botanist. His familiar stems, pods, and nestlings, because they draw him away from prereflective bliss and remind him of such things as cosmic voids and the mysteries of sex, in the end worry him to tears.

These childhood recollections continually map out privileged pastoral spots as centers to which Heaney has become increasingly tangential. Phallocentric and gynocentric images proliferate as he discovers his links to the creative power of an omphalos that is ultimately androgynous—phallus and womb in one. Heaney responds with fear and bewilderment, as boys often do, but situates himself on the perimeter as a spectator whose curiosity matches his trepidation. His examination of the sand martins' dark holes in the poem "Nesting-ground" is typical. Peering in, he is overcome by gruesome fantasies of sex and death. He recalls "a rat's nest in the butt of a stack where chaff and powdered cornstalks adhered to the moist pink necks" and "the cold prick of a dead robin's claw." New life seems just as grotesque as old. Frightened by generation's ominous cycle, "he only gazed. . . . he only listened," even though "he could imagine his arm going in to the armpit" to touch the living source. In "Sinking the Shaft," with its obviously phallic overtones, the plunge into a new consciousness of occluded things again beckons and repulses the growing boy. The workers digging the well for Heaney's proverbial pump ask, "Are you not for coming down, young Heaney?" The child, predictably, keeps his distance. The short essay "Mossbawn" describes the same pump as Heaney's "omphalos . . . , marking the centre of another world" (1980a, 17). Fears of sex and death intermingle, a cross vexing Heaney's youthful Catholic imagination. To him, "it was a big wound," a vaginal opening resembling Christ's wounds. Unlike doubting Thomas, however, believing Heaney refuses to plunge in. He is already the "inner émigré," bearing witness to turbulent centers but upholding his right to stand apart.

Heaney's "baptism in the gutter," as Yeats would say, comes later. Just as Yeats weighed contrary impulses in "Dialogue of Self and Soul," surveying the "fecund ditch" where they were combative as well as procreative, so Heaney in "Water-babies" indicates a greater willingness to encounter fundamental facts. World War II bombers "warbled far beyond" and the boys played heedlessly in their "Botany Bay" by the pump. Heaney describes his altered or "baptised" vision metaphorically. "Perversely I once fouled a gift there and sank my new kaleidoscope in the puddle. Its bright prisms that offered incomprehensible satisfactions were messed and silted: instead of a marvelous lightship, I salvaged a dirty hulk." The soiled kaleidoscope salvages Heaney too; his later art depends on his stubborn adherence to the transformational powers of water and earth, and a renunciation of the child's prismatic vision.

After *Death of a Naturalist*, Heaney's naturalism made a surprising comeback. As the innocent pastoralist retreated, the Darwinian naturalist sanctioned by Ted Hughes and D. H. Lawrence advanced. According to *Stations*, the transition occurred when Heaney began to learn that the crossed oppositions in nature and self were also intrinsic to his literary, religious, political, and linguistic heritage. Artistic culture, he implies, is also composed of species struggling to survive. Plumbing his Irish past, he can hardly ignore factions clashing and evolving. His naturalistic vision sharpens to scrutinize all cultural activity against a background of riotous vegetation, as if a jungle rather than a church or museum were its proper arena. He focuses on bloody games and confusing wars with the conviction that these are the norms rather than the exceptions. Again and again he identifies with the "enemy," the victim, the indigenous Irishman whose ancestors are Catholic rather than Protestant. "Silence, exile, and cunning" are his weapons for survival. The battle depicted in "Patrick and Oisin," for example, is fought between Heaney's different cultural allies; stones and vegetation represent the two sides. As the pagan warrior-poet of ancient Ireland gives way to the Christian soldier, foreboding cathedral stones overshadow the native Irish green. Maturing, Heaney reverses the historical process, allowing the naturalism of the pagan to triumph and the supernaturalism of the church to deteriorate. He elevates the Irish language and the legends it embodies, relegating imperial Latin and Catholic dogma to a secondary position.

Heaney applies his organic model of vegetative struggle to political, linguistic, and religious history too. The eighth section, "Sweet William," depicts a garden of burgeoning Sweet William flowers, which remind him of his childhood view of the world as Eden. His idealism was perhaps reinforced by his experience at Anahorish, the school where Protestant and Catholic students mingled peacefully. Now, as one of the "less-deceived," he knows beauty is a mask for prejudice and atrocity. Like Ted Hughes, he begins to see bloody conflict beneath every leaf. Once perceived as idyllic, now the flowery "blooms infused themselves into the eye like blood on snow, as if the clumped growth had been spattered with grapeshot and bled from underneath." Sweet William conjures up bloody images of the Battle of the Boyne along with the victorious William of Orange who made Protestant domination of Northern Ireland certain for centuries to come. Confronting Sweet William in all its botanical, artistic, and political manifestations, Heaney concludes, "And the many men so beautiful called after him, and the very flowers, their aura could be and would be resisted." For

Heaney, the Battle of the Boyne rears out of history's compost every July during the Orange Day celebrations, a perennial *fleur du mal* that should be repudiated rather than plucked and cherished.

The wars and competitive games in the middle sections of *Stations* are all overshadowed by the battle between William III and James II in 1690. Oppositions take on an unmistakably sectarian inflection. "The discharged soldier" in section 9 is a shell-shocked casualty of Flanders during World War I. He is also a casualty of the older battle fought on Irish turf. "Drunk again, full as the Boyne, staggering home on the old club foot." We are never really sure which side he is on, partly because Heaney's allegiances are confused. Oscillating between factions—Roman and Celtic, English and Irish, Catholic and Protestant, German and British—Heaney and the soldier seem to objectify the divisions and confusions that tear apart Northern Ireland.

The same confusion over opponents surfaces in "The Sabbath-breakers." The Gaelic football game described is between two Catholic teams whose oppositions are ambiguous. They oppose each other, they oppose the dictates of the Sabbath, and they oppose the Protestant bigots who try to break up the Sabbath game by cutting down the goal posts the night before. "Call it a pattern. We called it a tournament," Heaney recounts at the start. The chivalric combat of the game quickly mutates into the traditional pattern of religious vengeance in Northern Ireland. The "roundhead elders," those descendants of Cromwell's Parliamentary party who butchered thousands in Ireland in the 1600s, are Heaney's true opponents. In the next section, "Kernes," he and his Catholic mates find a representative target in the arrogant Anglophile, Dixon. Reenacting medieval guerrilla battles between Irish foot soldiers (kernes) and their English rivals, they pelt Dixon with sod. Again Heaney wears a disguise, "a glib he hadn't even ruffled," imitating the Irish highwaymen who wore their hair long over their faces to escape recognition.

The two following sections, "England's difficulty" and "Visitant," return to more contemporary battles. Still, friends and foes blend confusingly. "The word 'enemy' had the toothed efficiency of a mowing machine," Heaney reflects, mocking the convenient stereotype that reduces opponents to straw figures. For the Catholic child growing up in Ireland during World War II, England and Germany both appear to be enemies, and Germany is even perceived as an ally for bombing "the bitter Orange" parts of Belfast. So Heaney confesses he is the "double agent" who "crossed the lines with carefully enunciated passwords, [and] named every speech with checkpoints and reported back to nobody." How could he report back to somebody if he did not know which side he was fighting for? "He's an artist," his compatriots proclaim, as if confirming his freedom to scout and judge all positions. So when he meets the German bomber pilot who parachutes to safety near his home, he suspends judgment in order to see the man as he really is. As a result, the German POW "walked back into the refining lick of the grass, behind the particular judgements of captor and harbourer . . . treading the air of the image he achieved." Heaney's artistic eye has refined and transformed him from a stock image of war propaganda into a more complete image of flesh and blood.

If "all wars are boyish," as Robert Lowell claimed (repeating Melville) in "Christmas Eve under Hooker's Statue," child Heaney learns to prevent local skirmishes by striving for adult diplomacy. In "Trial Runs," the soldiers return to Northern Ireland after fighting the Axis on the continent only to witness their unity divided by archaic sectarian pressures. Heaney's parents defuse the explosive situation by bantering about religious differences with their neighbors. Their friendly, two-faced masks are donned for the sake of peace. Heaney recognizes that beneath the disguises they are "big nervous birds dipping and lifting, making trial runs over a territory." Ultimately their masks and high-flying intentions crash. As Heaney investigates language, politics, and religion in Northern Ireland, he does not evade his double-edged responses to them but inspects them unflinchingly. By linking private dilemmas with public ones, and by mapping his own evolution in terms of the evolution of his culture, he offers a ritual design that is archetypal rather than idiosyncratic, a trial run over a fractured territory that maps old wounds as if for the first time.

Heaney's journey to St. Columb's College from Anahorish (in 1951) heralds a new development in his quest for artistry and is therefore dramatized as a vegetative bursting out (as well as another station, another crossing). "The sun . . . incubating milktops and warming the side of the jam-jar where the bean had split its stitches" is an emblem for Heaney's second birth. Another Dedalus, Heaney has been incubating for a long time without accomplishing very much. He is a fetal bean laboring to sprout. To sanctify this birth, this new crossing, the master who announces the scholarship "crossed [Heaney's] . . . palm with silver." The rite of passage is characteristically expressed in biological and Christian terms. Heaney also goes to Anglo-Saxon tradition to stress the primitive and heroic attributes needed to succeed. The famous Anglo-Saxon poem, "The Wanderer," presents Heaney with an exemplary aesthetic and ethical model because it too crosses poetry with prose (it first appeared in *The Exeter Book* as continuous prose) and crosses pagan with Christian virtues as it memorializes the ascetic, penitential hero in exile. The Anglo-Saxon wanderer's fate or *wierd* is to ply the seas in search of a master, a ring-giver or "gold-friend." With his losses lying about him, he stoically declares,

In the earth-realm all is crossed;
Wierd's will changeth the world.
Wealth is lent us, friends are lent us,
man is lent, kin is lent;
all this earth's frame shall stand empty.
                                    (*Earliest English Poems* 1966, 73)

Heaney's ocean crossings and peregrinations in Ireland are similarly fraught
with adversities. He ends his version of "The Wanderer," "I have wandered
far from that ring-giver and would not renegue on this migrant solitude. I
have seen halls in flames, hearts in cinders, the benches filled and emptied,
the circles of companions called and broken. That day I was a rich young
man, who would tell you now of flittings, night-vigils, let-downs, women's
cried-out eyes." Emptiness prevails. The Anglo-Saxon meadhalls destroyed
by monsters, as in *Beowulf,* have their contemporary analogues in Irish bars
blown up by the I.R.A.

The last poems in Heaney's sequence outline the artist's withdrawal
from society's turbulence into the 'cave of making,' where aesthetic ideals
are pursued with religious devotion. The monastic "Cloistered" implies that
at St. Columb's the ascetic disciplines of the priest dovetail with those of the
writer. As was true for Joyce, it is Heaney's Catholic schooling that impels
him, ironically, to become a priest of the imagination rather than of the
church. "Cloistered" fondly recalls the ritualistic pattern of his teenage
years, which prepared him for the artistic success that came shortly after. "I
could make a book of hours of those six years, a Flemish calendar of rite and
pastime." Sprouting vegetatively before, now Heaney retreats, a dormant
bulb quietly contemplating his spiritual origins. He travels back in time,
comparing himself to a medieval scribe, an "assiduous illuminator," repress-
ing all sensual distractions to ply his subliminal craft.

The intensity of this budding artist's withdrawal engenders a last
flurry of contrary movements. Heaney paints a psychoanalytic portrait of
the artist as a young man, who as both martyr and narcissist takes pleasure
in self-inflicted wounds. Repression, the order of the day, has reduced the
monastic youth to a condition of "exhilarated self-regard," of sublime egotism in which sexuality is not so much purged as displaced momentarily.
Heaney admits, "I was champion of the examination halls, scalding with lust
inside my daunting visor." Poetry and repression are intimately linked for
this artist, whose passion threatens to break down the walls containing it.

Acknowledging the benefits of his Christian education, he also attests
to its liabilities. Icons of crucifixion and their power to abet rather than
alleviate sacrificial bloodshed fade into the background as Heaney's imagi-

nation pursues a more natural course. "The stations of the west" records his growing separation from his Irish Catholic heritage and its penchant for sanctimonious martyrdom. Here, on his retreat in the Gaeltacht in western Ireland where only Irish is spoken, he tries to act as an oracle for Gaelic and Pentecostal tongues but fails. Like Synge on the Aran Islands, he listens "through the wall to fluent Irish," but he is homesick for English. He is encouraged to speak in tongues; still the Holy Spirit balks. This moment of failure is crucial, because it intimates that he will be spokesman and apostle for neither Holy Ghost nor holy Ireland, neither Catholic right nor Catholic left, neither unionist nor nationalist. Instead, he will be a poet who witnesses their fission and fusion. He concedes at the end, "Neither did any gift of tongues descend in my days in that upper room when all around me seemed to prophesy. But still I would recall the stations of the west, white sand, hard rock, light ascending like its definition over Rannafast and Errigal, Annaghry and Kincasslagh: names portable as altar stones, unleavened elements." Rather than adopt the role of prophet, advocating destructive revenge and apocalyptic recreation, Heaney chooses the less stentorian, more down-to-earth role of "inner émigré." Although his separate peace may be escapist, his respect for the place names and hard, objective facts has the same moral weight as Hemingway's injunction against "abstract words such as glory, honor, courage . . . and sacrifice" in *A Farewell to Arms* (1929, 184–85). For both writers a stubborn empiricism countervails the emotionally charged ideals that have propelled them, along with their countries, toward suicidal ends.

An attentiveness to geography and biology is one cure for romantic excess; a principled ambivalence is another. "Inquisition," the penultimate poem, again reveals Heaney crossing sectarian lines as a double agent under fire. Refusing to throw his lot in with the Catholics, he also refuses the peaceful invitations of the Protestants. He is Janus-faced to the end. Even his title demonstrates ambiguity. The Inquisition, the Catholic tribunal established in the thirteenth century to discover and punish Catholic heretics, according to Heaney's sardonic version is a Protestant group in a pub's men's room that indiscriminately treats all Catholics as heretics. The rowdy, drunken Protestants, it turns out, are ecumenical rather than suppressive. One blurts out, "Ah, live and let live, that's my motto, brother. What does it matter where we go on Sundays as long as we can still enjoy ourselves." Heaney's response is two-faced: "The door was unexpectedly open and I showed them the face in the back of my head." The face he shows is no doubt conciliatory. What it conceals is his fear, uncertainty, and anger.

His last section, "Incertus," shows how a mask of uncertainty—the one he wore as a neophyte poet at Queen's University—can be a defense against the dangers of too much certainty. Where unambiguous assertions of faith issue from one militarized camp or another, a judicious "faults-on-both sides tact" can be a politic alternative. Heaney takes an ethical stand against the self-righteous arrogance that destroys writers as well as nations. His ideal of organic unity provides a model for a democratic state in which different factions work in creative proximity, just as contrary sympathies do in his mind and poems. As the sequence of prose poems crosses back and forth between these differences, Heaney repeatedly returns on himself, bringing his highest hopes for peaceful coexistence down to earth for candid analysis and raising his deepest fears and biases up for lofty moral scrutiny. Doggedly self-reflexive, Heaney in *Stations* offers a spiritual autobiography that amounts to a self-crucifixion. By stressing natural and supernatural analogues of his artistic development, he makes his story both biological and biblical and contributes an intriguing self-portrait to the many-roomed house of autobiographical fiction.

7

THE ANXIETY OF TRUST

H EANEY'S CAREER HAS ADVANCED IN WAVES disturbed by a central event, each new pulse collapsing only after the tensions impelling it have been exhausted. His image of the family's drinking water shaken by the train in "Glanmore Sonnets IV" (the "small ripples . . . vanished into where they seemed to start") brilliantly captures this contrapuntal progress. Following Blake's assertion that "without Contraries is no progression," Heaney has made sure that his surges are always complemented by equally powerful countersurges. His early pastoralism in *Death of a Naturalist* relied on an opposing antipastoralism for credibility and contemporaneity, just as in *North* the apocalyptic desire to raise the dead for judgment and to invoke history as a guide to a saner future achieved pathos from the counterrevelation of Irish history as a dark, tragic mire of bloody feuds and mindless sacrifices.

In this series of oscillating movements, *Field Work* marks a new departure and is crucial to an understanding of the books that come after it. Seismic Ireland is still the central event resonating through the poems, but from his new position in the South Heaney registers the quakes in a different way. The narrow, constricted poems like "Punishment," in which Heaney excoriated his failure to become more actively engaged in the political events of Northern Ireland, modulate now into a more relaxed, melodic verse. When asked by Frank Kinahan whether substance determined style, Heaney remarked, "The line and the life are intimately related, and that narrow line, the tight line [in *North*] came out of a time when I was very tight myself." Lengthening his lines in *Field Work*, "the constriction went, the tension went." Stunned by the severed heads and strangled victims of Iron Age fertility rites and their modern-day equivalents in Northern Ireland, Heaney in *North* took on a grim Anglo-Saxon abruptness and ornamental density. He believed that the musical grace of the English iambic line was "some kind of affront, that it needed to be wrecked." In the pastoral

119

landscape of Glanmore, surrounded by a Catholic majority, he felt that he had reached "a kind of appeasement" (Heaney 1982a, 411–12). To the playwright Brien Friel, he confessed he wanted to open "a door into the light" and to close his "door into the dark" (1979a, 20).

In one of the most perceptive reviews of *Field Work*, Christopher Ricks pointed out that "the word which matters most is 'trust'. . . . Heaney's poems matter because their uncomplacent wisdom of trust is felt upon the pulses, his and ours, and they effect this because they themselves constitute a living relationship of trust between him and us." In an "Ireland torn by reasonable and unreasonable distrust and mistrust" the "resilient strength of these poems is in the equanimity even of their surprise at some blessed moment of everyday trust" (Ricks 1979, 4). At first glance, it would seem that Heaney's new trust arose from his new sense of a 'trusting' audience, of the assumed covenant between himself and his new community of predominantly Catholic and Republican citizens in the South. While his new trust was more artistic than political (it depended more on private impulses than public compulsions), and while he wanted "to bring elements of . . . [his] social self, elements of . . . [his] usual nature" (1982a, 411) toward center stage in *Field Work*, there are few signs that he trusted his audience any more than he had in the past, and little to prove he trusted his newfound door into the convivial light any more than his old door into the primal dark. Although the diction and rhythms of *Field Work* resemble the kind of relaxed, accessible style Robert Lowell popularized in *Life Studies* and later volumes, and although he strives for the colloquial luminosity of Dante's verse, like these two precursors Heaney gives equal time to the unenlightened darknesses he finds in himself and in those around him.

Just as "the light of Tuscany" wavers through the clear pool in "The Otter," Heaney wavers in *Field Work* between trusting and distrusting 'transparent' communication with his new, receptive community. His anxiety over trust is nothing new. Early on, Heaney admits, he "had absolutely no confidence as a writer qua writer" (1982a, 407); he affixed the pen name, Incertus, to his first poems. From Hughes and Kavanagh he learned the "thrill . . . of trusting . . . [his] own background," which was the dark hinterland of bogs, beasts, and rural laborers in Northern Ireland; he claims, "Philip Hobsbaum . . . gave me the trust in what I was doing" (1979a, 14). Writing *North*, his most successful book up to that time, his confidence swayed. If he trusted his predilections, he distrusted those of his audience. "I was expecting *North* to be hammered, actually. I thought it was a very unapproachable book. But I was ready for the reaction, because I trusted those poems" (1982a, 412). *Field Work*'s "wisdom of trust" is similarly counterpointed. To Frank Kinahan he conjectured, "I suppose, then, that the shift from *North* to *Field Work* is a shift in trust: a learning to trust melody, to trust art as reality, to trust artfulness as an affirmation and not to go into the self-punishment so much. I distrust that attitude too, of course" (1982a, 412). Antaeus, proponent of dark, instinctual beliefs, and Hercules, skeptical light-bringer and demolisher of irrational credences, continue to wrestle in Heaney's mind, just as they did in *North*.

Moving to the Republic of Ireland for Heaney was both a flight to freedom—away from the burdensome "position of . . . a representative of the Catholic community" (1979b, 28) in the North—and a return to old responsibilities and anxieties. His freedom from agonizing over "the political colouring" of his utterances, he told Robert Druce, was illusory. His dreams of political freedom were rebuked by the atrocious situation he could not leave behind. Moments of transcendence, as in "Oysters," decline into disturbing meditations on old acts of imperialist aggression and privilege. He recalls Rome but is thinking of England too (as it gluts itself on Ireland).

> Over the Alps, packed deep in snow,
> the Romans hauled their oysters south to Rome:
> I saw damp panniers disgorge
> the frond-lipped, brine stung
> Glut of privilege.

Heaney wants to celebrate uncluttered sensuality and the transcendental light beyond politics, much as Robert Lowell wanted to free himself from Roman religion and politics in "Crossing the Alps," but history's gravity continues to tug. His anger is kindled by the fact that his "trust could not repose / In the clear light, like poetry or freedom / Leaning in from the sea." Part of the reason, he explains, stems from the "Irish Catholic . . . distrust of the world" and "distrust of happiness" stamped on his childhood psyche. Among the Irish, as among the Spanish and Russians, he claims, "There's a more elegiac and tragic view of life; they're less humanist; they're less trusting in perfectibility" (1982a, 408–09). This mistrust of humanist ideals stimulates Heaney's preoccupation in *Field Work* with bestiality. Guided by Ted Hughes, Heaney examines a zoological array of otters, skunks, oysters, dogs, pismires, badgers, cuckoos, corncrakes, and other species. Ascents to humane, civilized orders are everywhere undercut by "saurian relapses." If Heaney consecrated his idea of poetic and political freedom by leaving Belfast, his poems return obsessively to witness its bestial ways, and to explain how his former environment was the breeding ground of his distrust.

In his essay "Responsibilities of the Poet," Robert Pinsky (who had reviewed *Field Work* in 1979) could be thinking of Heaney when he links 'responsibility' to 'sponsor' and 'spouse,' and explains the poet's contradictory need "to feel utterly free, yet answerable" (1987, 423) to the community around him. Pinsky declares that the poet does not need an audience so much as the compulsion within himself to respond to one. He is responsible to the living, to spouse, and to readerly sponsors. Opposing this is his responsibility to the dead and unborn. "One of our responsibilities is to mediate between the dead and the unborn: we must feel ready to answer, as if asked by the dead if we have handed on what they gave us or asked by the unborn what we have for them" (424). The poet is responsible for his culture, for witnessing its exemplary and unexemplary acts, and for reinvigorating its language. This plunges the poet into quandaries. Pinsky explains, "The poet's first social responsibility, to continue the art, can be filled only through the second, opposed responsibility to change the terms of the art as given—and it is given socially, which is to say politically" (426). These contrary forces form the fundamental tension in *Field Work*, where marriage poems speak of tearing responsibilities toward spouse and art, and political poems speak of similar tearing responsibilities toward poetic freedom and tribal demands. A poem like "Casualty" elegizes a member of the Catholic community but also rebukes that community's terms and ethics by celebrating the dead man for renouncing tribal expectations. Commemorative poems to artistic sponsors, whether to Lowell or Ledgwidge, uphold their freedom from the august dead in order to mock them as well as to praise them. "Ugolino" and other Dantesque poems again demonstrate a responsible willingness to be the beneficiary of a "trust," to accept the riches of tradition and pass them on. Heaney also wants freedom from tradition and insists on altering the past to fit his needs and beliefs.

Neil Corcoran has argued that "the major poetic presence in *Field Work* . . . is not Lowell . . . but Dante" and cites Heaney's serial encounters with the dead and his "awareness of the intimate relationship between the personal and the political or historical" (1986, 129–30) as the two most obtrusive resemblances. Heaney himself has written in "Dante and the Modern Poet" that it was the way the exiled and embittered Florentine poet "could place himself in an historical world yet submit that world to scrutiny from a perspective beyond history, the way he could accommodate the political and transcendent" (1985, 18) that stimulated his attempts to emulate him. Dante's exploration of political and psychological divisions makes him seem Heaney's contemporary ally rather than his ancient master. "The main tension" felt by poets in Ireland, and felt by Dante in a Florence ripped apart by Guelph and Ghibelline, Heaney claims, "is between two often contradictory commands: to be faithful to the collective historical experience and to be true to the recognition of the emerging self" (1985, 19). In this case, however, Heaney is referring to Dante's influence on *Station Island*, not on *Field Work*. Although Dante certainly reinforced Heaney's thematic concerns in the earlier volume, its texture of diction and imagery is always closer to the poetry of Robert Lowell.

The echoes of Lowell are so unmistakable that several critics accused Heaney of playing magpie to the American poet's magisterial song. Lowell's powerful, burnished rhetoric and his penchant for long chains of adjectives reverberate throughout *Field Work*. Lowell's example was liberating as well as constraining. His furiously candid self-scrutiny, his guilty dramas of the poet's conflicting responsibilities to marriage, society, and art, and his sad confessions of failure to spouses and sponsors encouraged Heaney to mine a rich new vein.

Heaney's relation to Lowell is perhaps best characterized not by Harold Bloom's 'anxiety of influence' but by a perplexed 'anxiety of trust.' When asked about his friendship with Lowell, Heaney remarked, "There was a certain trust and intimacy. He had a great gift for making you feel close, and he had tremendous grace and insight" (1979a, 22). His review of *Day by Day* praised Lowell as one of the exemplary masters, "obstinate and conservative in his belief in the creative spirit, yet contrary and disruptive in his fidelity to his personal intuitions and experiences" (1980a, 221). And in the memorial address delivered after Lowell's death, he specifies what he trusts most in Lowell's art, and what he feels obligated to entrust to others. Of his demanding sponsor he attests, "He was and will remain a pattern for poets in his amphibious ability to plunge into the downward reptilian welter of the self and yet raise himself with whatever knowledge he gained there out on to the hard ledges of the historical present, which he then apprehended with refreshed insight and intensity, as in his majestic poem 'For the Union Dead,' and many others, especially in the collection *Near the Ocean*" (1978b, 37). It is interesting to note that Heaney originally distrusted the majesty of "For the Union Dead." In a review published in 1966, he tells of "reading and wondering about the title poem," of wanting "to feel that it is an achievement as solemn and overwhelming as it seems to be." He concludes, "Although I find it once public and personal, dignified and indignant, I miss the impregnable quality that comes when a poem is perfectly achieved. The transitions, if not arbitrary, are not inevitable and the rhythm in the middle stanzas does not body forth the ominous tone" (1966, 23). Heaney's personal and literary bonds with Lowell obviously grew closer over the years, yet uncertainty and doubt remained. "Heaney's trust in other poets is itself part of his art," Christopher Ricks claims (1979, 5). It may be more correct to say that his art is a force field in which trust and distrust exist in tense proximity.

A profile in *The Observer*, "Poet Wearing the Mantle of Yeats," divulged some of the reasons for Heaney's wariness of Lowell. According to the anonymous author, Heaney "has found it hard to live down a reputation for obligingness," some of "which goes back to the trick that a mad Robert Lowell played, crankily testing him out, when Heaney visited him in hospital in 1976. (The previous night Lowell had broken out of hospital to award Heaney the Duff Cooper Memorial Prize.) 'Would you like some of this Benedictine?', Lowell invited him. Heaney eyed the bottle suspiciously, was reassured that it did indeed contain Benedictine, and took a swig of what turned out to be after-shave" (1987, 7). Heaney's elegy to Lowell in *Field Work* is certainly no gullible obeisance to the American poet; it is a knowing testimonial that also testifies against Lowell for his notorious shenanigans. Heaney delivers a responsible avowal of indebtedness, flattering the sponsor by imitating him. He also writes a declaration of independence that slyly mocks the great artist's great faults. Lowell made Heaney drink after-shave. Heaney imagines Lowell drinking a bitter potion too.

> You drank America
> like the heart's
> iron vodka,
>
> promulgating art's
> deliberate, peremptory
> love and arrogance.

The metaphorical American "spirits" Lowell drinks are the sublime spirits of the dead (Jonathan Edwards, Cotton Mather, Captain Ahab), whose violent spiritual devotions reflect his own. Lowell, the literary master, also wields some of the peremptory arrogance of a political taskmaster. After all his nickname, Cal, referred to Caligula, and in "Beyond the Alps" he identified with the later imperialistic tyrant, Mussolini, stipulating that "the skirt-mad Mussolini unfurled / the eagle of Caesar. He was one of us / only, pure prose." For Heaney, whose poetry from the start has registered the most minute tremors of imperialistic aggrandizement (even in the very consonants and vowels of his words), the Latinate "deliberate" and "peremptory" suggest Lowell's de-liberating, emperorlike ways.

"Elegy," in fact, is as much an allegory of invasion and conquest as Heaney's etymological poems in *Wintering Out* and historical narratives in

North. Enthralled by Lowell, he identifies with other Irishmen "enthralled" by imperial conquerors and distrusts his reverence. Lowell and his art appear as a figurative ship mastering the "ungovernable" Irish sea, a sea that Heaney has historical reasons to fear.

> As you swayed the talk
> and rode on the swaying tiller
> of yourself, ribbing me
> about my fear of water,
>
> what was not within your empory?

The master here is dictating how the conversation flows. He is also swaying with inebriated enthusiasm as his ego cuts ahead like the ship's prow. The empory, the territory of the emperor, is that ground possessed by Lowell that Heaney wants to repossess, just as he so often talks of reclaiming Catholic Ireland once possessed by Protestant England. Heaney settles his differences with Lowell by inscribing them into his tribute. Lowell, after all, was tracing the same route as past empire builders (the Raleighs and Spensers), sailing from England with his aristocratic wife, Lady Caroline Blackwood, to property owned in Ireland.

As Heaney fills out his life study of Lowell, the older poet emerges as linguistic imperialist "Englishing Russian," a curmudgeonly artist "bullying out" sonnets to Harriet and Lizzie, and Roman gladiator (*retiarius*) throwing a net over his victim to hold him down (the sort of event Caligula would applaud with great glee, although Heaney is no doubt referring to Lowell's artistic "fishnet of tarred rope" in "Fishnet" [Lowell 1973, 15]). He is also that uproarious sailing carnival, the "night ferry," that crosses regularly between England and Ireland. Ultimately, the portrait of Lowell turns out to be an ambivalent response to a heroic artist's tragic flaws. Heaney's line, "Your eyes saw what your hand did," a borrowing of Lowell's confession in "Dolphin," reveals Lowell as the self-interrogatory, self-accusing, and self-punishing poet that he was. An emperor, he is also a humbled slave, rendered timorous and pedestrian by his severe conscience. A shielding and shielded patriarch, he is also the shieldless victim. He is the majestic clipper ship and ordinary ferry, conquering seaman and conquered islander, ungovernable plunderer and governed native. Like the other artists memorialized in *Field Work*, he becomes Heaney's double, an ambiguous persona dramatizing his own confusions. Heaney too can be "imperially male," as he confesses in "Act of Union" (*North*), and explore a psyche and heritage divided by masterful and servile impulses. Encountering Lowell, he strives for empathy. At the same time he submits the other poet's masterful images and authoritarian ways to a vigilant distrust, attacking himself in the process.

Heaney's other elegies fasten on artists for similar reasons of identification, self-diagnosis, and judgment and test the risks that trusting others involves. Trusting Lowell was made more difficult because of the different traditions the two poets represented. At the end of "Elegy" it is "the fish-dart" of Lowell's eyes "risking, 'I'll pray for you,' " that reminds Heaney of the Anglo-Protestant (turned Catholic and then agnostic) dangerously risking intimacy with the Catholic Irishman (although lapsed), and the long history of sectarian distrust that such a gesture implies. In his elegy to Sean O'Riada, the famous Irish composer who died in 1971, Heaney borrows Lowell's style ("a black stiletto trembling in its mark" is classic Lowell), but his bond with the other artist is more intimate from the start. O'Riada resembles Heaney's actual father rather than his artistic father, Lowell. He "herds" the orchestra with his baton, as Patrick Heaney once herded cattle in County Derry.

> He conducted the Ulster Orchestra
> like a drover with an ashplant
> herding them south.
> I watched them from behind,
>
> springy, formally suited,
> a black stiletto trembling in its mark,
> a quill flourishing itself,
> a quickened, whitened head.

The political and religious implications of this gesture are born out at the end. "He was our jacobite, / he was our young pretender." That is, he resembled the defeated Catholic James II and his son rather than William of Orange and his Protestant followers. As in the Lowell elegy Heaney tends to obscure O'Riada with a plethora of metaphors. He, like Lowell, is a boat and fish, but also a drover, knife, quill, head, fisherman—but "more falconer than fisherman"—king, king's son, gannet, minnow, and wader. He invokes this multitudinous bestiary for a definite purpose: to underscore the artist's necessary but problematic trust in feral instinct and his related bestial distrust of too much cerebration. "He had the *sprezzatura*," Heaney declares, the nonchalance and natural skill of an animal, "trusting the gift, / risking gift's undertow." As Lowell certainly knew, the muses are often Sirens, dragging the artist down into oceanic depths. Heaney celebrates O'Riada's courage in courting the muse through risky submission rather than controlled exertion (he works by lying down "like ballast in the bottom of the boat / listening to the cuckoo"). Heaney, too, will take his chances. He will risk getting pulled under as he learns to trust the Lowellish melodies of *Field Work*.

Some of the political and religious tergiversation that appeared in the Lowell elegy reappears in the elegy to Francis Ledgwidge, which in some ways is a rewriting of Lowell's "For the Union Dead." Here, rather than the bronze statue of Colonel Shaw and his Negro infantry, "the bronze soldier hitches a bronze cape / That crumples stiffly in imagined wind." The historical monuments for both poets inspire meditations on the vestiges of old divisions in their personalities and nations. For Lowell the American Civil War still trembles through television news of racial strife in contemporary Boston. His mind is similarly split between despair and a violent, primitive desire to follow Colonel Shaw, plunge into battle, and die in the struggle for moral reformation. Lowell suffers a further division because of his affiliation with Southern culture (the agrarian Fugitives, Allen Tate and John Crowe Ransom, were his early mentors) and his native New England culture of transcendentalists and abolitionists. For Heaney, Ledgwidge is another Lowell, an emblem of loyalties split between North and South, Protestant and Catholic, British unionist and Irish nationalist. Heaney explains in a review of Alice Curtayne's biography that Ledgwidge was a Catholic from Southern Ireland and a Sinn Fein sympathizer who supported the Easter Rising of 1916. Paradoxically, he also accepted patronage from an Anglo-Irish lord and allowed his first book to be "introduced to the world by a Unionist peer" (1972a, 408) and finally joined the British army to die fighting alongside his traditional foes in 1918. As Lowell captures the native haunt of Colonel Shaw on his retrospective walk around Boston, so Heaney walks with his Aunt Mary around Drogheda where Ledgwidge engaged in "genteel trysts with rich farmers' daughters" (1972a, 408). The abrupt transitions between Heaney's personal memories, his speculations on his aunt's life during the Great War, quotations from Ledgwidge, and his vision of him in a Tommy's uniform in the Dardanelles at Ypres, however, lack Lowell's uncanny ability to make disparate elements cohere. Nevertheless, Heaney resurrects Ledgwidge as spokesman for his Catholic and republican pieties and through him delivers a moving address.

> In you, our dead enigma, all the strains
> Criss-cross in useless equilibrium
> And as the wind tunes through this vigilant bronze
> I hear again the sure confusing drum

You followed from Boyne water to the Balkans
But miss the twilit note your flute should sound.
You were not keyed or pitched like these true-blue ones
Though all of you consort now underground.

Having betrayed his community's trust by following the English army on a massive Orange Day march into World War I, Ledgwidge now consorts with dubious allies and obvious enemies—uselessly, since as a corpse he can do nothing to redress the many divisions he was prey to.

Heaney tries to redress his nation's wounds by simply addressing them, although as he witnesses exemplary figures of the past he also announces his own sectarian proclivities. He expresses solidarity with the dead, tracing his vacillations in terms of theirs, and, like the dead in Revelation, he awaits a last judgment that will pitch him toward heaven or hell. His eschatological anxiety, as he once said of Lowell, "arises from one felt responsibility clashing against another." His essay "Current Unstated Assumptions about Poetry" speaks of Lowell's covenants with different factions, again in terms of trust and judgment. Lowell's *Life Studies* "trusts that it has an audience" (1981, 648) that will empathize with the poet's divisive responsibilities to family, literature, society, and history and understand his inevitable failings. Heaney could be referring to his own ideals when he says of Lowell's, "We respond to Lowell's implicit trust in poetic art as a vocation. We register and are fortified by the commitment that has made possible the note of command. . . . we feel that this writer is forging his covenant with the past and the future" (1981, 649). When Heaney accepted the Bennet Award from *The Hudson Review* in 1982, he seized the occasion to remind himself and his audience "of the responsibilities of the creative life," and then spoke of his own sense of a trusting covenant. "I thank and congratulate the sponsors of this prize for ratifying in such an open-handed way that covenant we all hope for between artist and audience" (1982–83, 519). With so many commitments, it is no wonder the poet often found himself rattling moral chains of his own devising.

Domestic covenants between father and son, which were collapsing in "Elegy," are mended in "The Harvest Bow." Here Heaney's father is a shield for his son, an icon the poet yearns to trust and revere, but the son's image reflected in the shield is the "lockjawed, mantrapped" one that Heaney delineated in "An Afterwards." For both father and son the shield represents the hard, silent, repressed mask that conceals and reveals the violence of their instinctual energies. Heaney's father is overtly brutal and appealingly mellow. He laps "the spurs on a lifetime of gamecocks" and whacks "the tips off weeds and bushes," yet in "mellowed silence" he weaves the beautiful harvest bows. The poem owes some of its pastoral quiet to Keats's "Ode on a Grecian Urn" and "To Autumn" (Keats was Heaney's original poetic father). Heaney, however, is hardly as sanguine about art's ability to reconcile opposites as his early sponsor. Truth and beauty, like Heaney's contradictory need for both contemplative quiet and a bullhorn to speak against political atrocities, are at violent odds. The poem is as much a confession as an aesthetic treatise, as much a guilty, distrustful exploration of the tangled genealogical roots of Heaney's social quietism as an apology for them.

    For Neil Corcoran, "Harvest Bow" can "be considered a revision of 'Digging' " (1986, 151). In addition, it harks back to "Boy Driving His Father to Confession," an uncollected poem written at about the same time (1965), in which a tender filial relationship is disturbed by the son's growing sense of disillusionment. Heaney recounts, "Four times [I] found chinks in the paternal mail / To find you lost like me, quite vulnerable." The chinks, in this case, reveal little of the man beneath the armor. So Heaney wonders, "What confession / Are you preparing? Do you tell sins as I would? / Does the same hectic rage in our one blood?" By the time he wrote "The Harvest Bow," father and son had been reconciled, paradoxically, by their mutual feelings of otherness. The bow twisted out of what Keats once called "the alien corn" is an emblem of their alien status, of their social unease and political disenchantment, their indifference to vocal protest against and active participation in current events. Both affirm the silent, peaceful art of making. But for both the silencing that necessitates art seems unduly repressive. Heaney groped "awkwardly to know his father" as a young man in "Confession." Now he offers "a knowable corona" that knots them together. To the question "Do you tell sins as I would?" he answers, "I tell and finger . . . [the bow] like braille, / Gleaning the unsaid off the palpable." His familiarity with his father's silences allows him to forge an understanding that approaches complete trust. His father no longer has to tell his son "what is going on / Under that thick grey skull," as Heaney rather indecorously put it in the earlier poem. Identifying with his otherness, his patriarchal silences, Heaney can now "read" his father's mind with all the assurance of a blind man reading braille.

    Like Stephen Dedalus searching for real, artistic, and mythical fathers in *Ulysses*, what Heaney keeps finding at the end of his quests is himself. His father appears as his artistic shadow, not a cattle dealer worrying about the price of grain and farm equipment so much as a cultural totem, an exemplary artistic patriarch, an O'Riada or Lowell, who trusts the "gift and worked with fine intent" until his masterful "fingers moved somnambulant." From the talismanic harvest bow Heaney conjures up an image that implies that the child is father to the man. Trusting his paternal sponsors as he would himself, Heaney also submits both self and other to wary scrutiny. The submerged oedipal quarrel with his father in "The Harvest Bow" is fundamentally a quarrel with himself. Knowing that poetry is born from this inner battle, Heaney also yearns for a peaceful reconciliation. The poem's motto, "The end of art is peace," which is taken from Yeats's "Samhain: 1905" in *Explorations* and which Heaney places on the first page of *Preoccupations*, is ironic, because both poets distrust peace as anything but a momentary pause in art's continuing, potentially tragic, yet ultimately fruitful dialectic. After the father's shaping "intent" is found culpably apolitical and his gift judged a seductive snare, Heaney implies that neither his spirit nor the corn's spirit have been put to peaceful rest. If peace were permanent, art would end permanently too. To rest in peace is a temptation that Heaney, like "the spirit of the corn," has slipped from at the end.

Poetic quarrels with real and artistic fathers have obvious corollaries in Heaney's political and marital poems. They too recognize the ineluctable conflict in the central arena of creation. They hoist the white flag for peace and then, in more sober mood, cannot swear allegiance to it. Heaney's marriage poems have been praised for their "unromanticizing exactitude," and yet they seem natural offshoots of what Geoffrey Hill (borrowing a line that Keith Sagar applied to Ted Hughes) has called the "major Romanticism of our time": the struggle to negotiate a productive alliance between the individual mind and everything that is beyond it. Or, as Sagar puts it, to find "a way for reconciling human vision with the energies, powers, presences, of the non-human cosmos" (Hill 1984, 15). Hill points out that the urge to distrust all peaceful reconciliations is also part of the inner dynamic of Romanticism. "Romantic art is thoroughly familiar with the reproaches of life. Accusation, self-accusation, are the very life-blood of its most assured rhetoric" (1984, 3). Heaney's marriage poems, which trace separations and reunions, domestic squabbles and partial mendings, fit neatly into this Romantic loop. What is startling and disturbing about them is their tendency to envision women as part of the "non-human cosmos," as animals, trees, or, even more unflatteringly, as mud or water. Heaney, though, is not as insouciant as he first appears. Rather than relegate women to a demeaning niche on the phylogenetic scale, he proposes to break down stuffy views of marriage and squeamish attitudes toward sexual and artistic creation. His vision is androgynous and pantheistic, not misogynist. His metaphor of marriage on its most primal level involves a trusting at-one-ment between self and other, individual vision and actual fact, and he depicts this bond ecologically, in terms of human interaction with animals, vegetation, and minerals.

The tension that shudders through these poems again arises from the two charged poles of trust and distrust. Christopher Ricks remarks of Heaney's

Lowellish "The Skunk," a poem about the separation from his wife when he taught in California, that it "is an exquisitely comic love-poem, and you have to love your wife most trustingly, and trust in the reciprocity, before you would trust yourself to a comparison of her to a skunk" (1979, 4). It is the skunk and not the wife, however, that dominates the poem, although wife and skunk ultimately merge into a figure of otherness, of what Heaney has called in his discussion of another animal poem, "The Badgers," "the night-self, the night part in everybody, the scuttling secret parts of life" (1979a, 21). "Night," in fact, is repeated five times in "The Skunk." It has some of the religious connotations of St. John of the Cross's dark night, just as it does in Lowell's "Skunk Hour," where the otherworld in which he searches for love, divine or profane, is hellishly unfulfilling. Heaney is more contented, and more enthusiastic than Lowell about the religious alliance of sacred and profane, Christian and pagan. His totemic skunk is first compared to a celebrant wearing ecclesiastical vestments ("the chasuble") at a funeral mass. The skunk is a kind of medium, whose purpose is to deliver the poet into the spirit world. The word *wife* has a similarly magic power. It transubstantiates what is absent (Heaney's real wife) so that the word's "slender vowel" takes on her bodily form and his wife's presence permeates "the night earth and air / of California." In "The Skunk," the process by which the otherness of Heaney's wife is sacramentalized in the California night is complex but lyrically provocative.

> The beautiful, useless
> Tang of eucalyptus spelt your absence.
> The aftermath of a mouthful of wine
> Was like inhaling you off a cold pillow.

Heaney deftly turns his uxorious skunk and his letter writing to his wife into a miniature fable of what David Jones (in a book Heaney had read by this time) described as man's "extra-utilist, or sacramentalist" (1978, 178) vision. "The Incarnation and the Eucharist cannot be separated; the one thing being analogous to the other. If one binds us to the animalic the other binds us to artefacture and both bind us to *signa*, for both are a showing forth of the invisible under visible signs" (1978, 171). For Heaney sacred and profane love intermingle as ordinary words and even ordinary objects become signs bodying forth the invisible presence of his wife.

The poem ends with a candid "bodying forth" of sacramentalized wife and skunk, "damasked like the chasuble" at mass. The ornamental garment is stripped off, the "ordinary" body unveiled. Voyant and voyeur comically merge as Heaney watches his wife disrobe before bed. During her ultimate re-veiling, "the black plunge-line nightdress" she puts on recalls the black chasuble in the first stanza, although this ceremony is erotic as opposed to funereal.

Heaney's journeys into the fecund night often resemble prayers and Catholic meditations, although with a deliberately sexual slant. "Homecoming," where "love is a nesting trust," as Ricks observes (1979, 5), also articulates a prayer for the self's deliverance. Here a male sand martin "veering / breast to breast with himself" is Heaney's symbol for the self-preoccupied artist. His flight is a meditative one, a transport from the diurnal ego toward the desired other. The meditation requires "a glottal stillness," an attentive tuning in to an autochthonous demiurge. His wife once again becomes the dark lady, both earth mother and muse, sand martin and sandy bank in which she nests. Heaney prays for the kind of self-occlusion that will lead to a luminous revelation.

> Mould my shoulders inward to you.
> Occlude me.
> Be damp clay pouting.
> Let me listen under your eaves.

Again the wife is rather unflatteringly anatomized, and again she becomes a projection of the poet's oracular night self, his creative unconscious, his m/other. Despite his promise to open a door into the light in *Field Work*, he keeps opting for a door into the dark.

The mythic equation between women, nature, and imagination implicit in Heaney's poetry from the start receives a pared-down elucidation in these later poems. Few early poems, for example, have the passionate brevity of "Polder," where the wife is cast as a stormy sea dyked and transformed by her husband into a fertile land (*polder* is the Dutch word for reclaimed land).

> I have reclaimed my polder,
> all its salty grass and mud-slick banks;
>
> under fathoms of air, like an old willow
> I stir a little on my creel of roots.

As usual, Heaney seems hesitant to explore the sexual politics and gender stereotypes that these poems suggest and as a result is vulnerable to feminist attack. In "The Otter," an amphibious Heaney (reminiscent of Ted Hughes in "An Otter" and "The Thought-Fox") enters the animistic otherworld to write his poem, and characteristically the otter *is* the other, his wife and muse. She delivers the poem like a gift after the poet's sexual plunge into what he partially fears (the symbolic waters). Risk and trust, for Heaney, is as important to lovemaking as to poetry writing. After his wife 'swims' on her back, she 'gives birth,' "printing the stones," close cousin to Hughes's 'Thought-fox' printing the page after "it enters the dark hole of the head" (Hughes 1982, 1).

As for Stephen Dedalus, who quests for a father and in the end finds a mother (the mythic female, Molly Bloom, after all is the *telos* of the novel), Heaney's ultimate symbol of the unified self he yearns for is a woman. Not to be outdone by Joyce, who mythicized his wife into an archetype of all wives, mothers, and daughters, whether Virgin Mary or pagan fertility goddess, Molly Bloom or Anna Livia Plurabelle, Heaney transforms his own Marie into an emblem of a universal élan vital, then launches forth to make her example his own. This is the gist of the title poem, "Field Work," where loosened meters and relaxed diction underscore the journey toward spontaneous fecundity and the trust in his wife that mirrors his trust in himself. The poem commences in separation and concludes, after national and personal boundaries have been crossed and old suppositions negated, with the poet at one with his anointed image. Although Heaney dramatizes his process of 'individuation' in terms of multiple crossings, he chooses bodily symbols rather than the Cross to carry his meaning. Still, Christ the wounded, healing God is behind them all.

Trust and faith are obviously more pressing issues when wife and husband are on different sides of the world. In "Field Work," Heaney faithfully travels back across the Atlantic to wife and home and, unlike Ahab, persistently seeks an emblem of concord rather than of adversity, of contraries crossed in a regenerative unity rather than crucified into oblivion. Ring symbols of moon and coin highlight this 'marriage-in-separation.'

> Our moon was small and far,
> was a coin long gazed at
>
> brilliant on the *Pequod*'s mast
> across Atlantic and Pacific waters.

As the poem progresses, it counters images of destruction, disease, and death with those of burgeoning fertility. It traverses a *via negativa* from imaginary, nocturnal unions in California to actual, sexual unions in Ireland. Even though he proposes that his mythic image of woman, his mandala of a unified self, is "not the mud slick . . . and pock-marked leaves," "not the cow parsley in winter / with its old whitened shins," "not even the tart green shade of summer thick with . . . fungus," but the radiant "sunflower, dreaming umber," his intention is to subsume these negatives rather than pit them against each other.

The ritualistic finale reenacts a strange, touching scene of marital rapprochement. To Yeats's observation that "love has pitched his mansion in / The place of excrement" (1983, 259–60), Heaney adds Lawrentian details: "Catspiss smell, / the pink bloom open." He presses the flowering currant to his wife's skin for her "veins to be crossed / criss-cross with leaf-veins," and "anoint[s] the annointed / leaf-shape" with his thumbprint. Comparable to a stigmata of the cross, the new mark testifies to crucifying trials and exemplary faithfulness. The divisions in the poem between husband and wife, imagination and reality, 'perfect' animal existence and 'imperfect' human travail, vegetation goddess and actual woman, are fused in the final mark made by the leaf and mould. "You are stained, stained / to perfection," Heaney declares at the end, thinking of the redemptive ordeals through which both wife and poem have passed.

Freedom and responsibility, trust and doubt, rend the political poems in *Field Work* as well as those dramatizing marital and literary relations. A witness to sectarian killings, Heaney invokes the dead to corroborate his dilemmas. Almost without exception his victims are innocent bystanders (like himself), who for one reason or another refused to get embroiled in political battles but also refused to get out of their way. Those innocents who avoid the Troubles, going about their business as if nothing unusual is happening, usually end up dead. "Too near the ancient troughs of blood / Innocence is no earthly weapon" (Hill 1985, 61), Heaney might say with Geoffrey Hill ("Ovid in the Third Reich"). With Hill he feels obvious empathy for the unearthly innocents, yet he distrusts their freedom from worldly exigencies. His elegy for Sean Armstrong, for example, tells how his Queen's University friend who "dropped-out" to pursue the pot-smoking, communal life-style of the sixties, only to return to work at childrens' playgrounds in Belfast, was "changed utterly" by an assassin's bullet.

> Drop-out on a come-back
> Prince of no-man's land
> With your head in clouds or sand,
> You were the clown
> Social worker of the town
> Until your candid forehead stopped
> A pointblank teatime bullet.

In this Lowellish life study, when Heaney observes, "Yet something in your voice / Stayed nearly shut / . . . It was independent, rattling, non-transcendent / Ulster," he is also observing his own reluctance to speak out. His portrait of iconoclastic independence is a confessional self-portrait that delineates his distrust of political absentmindedness, especially when it leads to martyrdom.

Louis O'Neil, Heaney's drinking friend who was blown up by the I.R.A. in his father-in-law's pub (the bombing was a reprisal for the Bloody Sunday murders by British paratroopers), is another authorial double—the illiterate, nearly silent, slyly independent self Heaney would like to trust but ultimately distrusts. The poem describes a series of turnings in which his friend, having turned his paradoxically "observant back" on political imposi-tions like curfews, in death turns back toward Heaney, reminding him that his "tentative art," which also turns its "observant back" on straightforward engagements with the Troubles, is partly to blame for their continuing cycle. When Heaney asks, "How culpable was he / That last night when he broke / Our tribe's complicity?" he turns the question on himself, because he too seeks to break free from tribal complicity. The futile turning away from sins of commission only perpetrates sins of omission. Like the figures bound to Yeats's gyres and Eliot's stairways, Heaney seems entrapped in purgatorial anxiety. If Heaney's purpose in "Casualty" is to bury the dead, he fails. O'Neil's ghost is "revenant" at the end, haunting him with accusa-tions of guilt.

Heaney's attitude toward the I.R.A. is deeply ambivalent and perhaps the fundamental wound behind his many festering political anxieties. In "Triptych," he elegizes Christopher Ewart-Briggs, a British ambassador mur-dered by the I.R.A. in 1976, and again plunges into the familiar dialectic, yearning for freedom and fertility—"a stone house by a pier. / Elbow room. Broad window light" with a down-to-earth vegetation goddess "car-rying a basket full of new potatoes, / Three tight green cabbages, and carrots"—while painfully aware that his quest for poetic freedom and cre-ativity only makes his sectarian affiliations more agonizing. His psyche is as riven as Ireland itself. His nation's "saurian relapses" and negative sea changes (its "comfortless noises" allude to those in *The Tempest*) are his own. He hopes "forgiveness finds its nerve and voice." When he examines his native ground, he finds only a "flayed or calloused" corpse whose voice has been strangled in blood. His emblems of religious transcendence recall Lowell's statue of the Lady of Walsingham in "The Quaker Graveyard in Nan-tucket," whose face, "expressionless, expresses God" (Lowell 1944, 19), and which again rebukes his dream of trust, freedom, and deliverance. "On

Boa the god-eyed, sex-mouthed stone" is "two-faced, trepanned," a mirror image of Heaney's own ambiguous stance, echoing the poet's "silence with silence."

Among the Christian ruins on the islands in Lough Beg, and the ruins Christian factions have littered across Ireland for centuries, Heaney finally acknowledges his own vestigial Catholicism, since it provides a way to confess to collusion and work toward therapeutic redemption.

> Everything in me
> Wanted to bow down, to offer up,
> To go barefoot, foetal and penitential,
>
> And pray at the water's edge.

He feels impelled "to bow down" partly because "the helicopter shadowing" the march at Newry forces him to, and partly because of his urge for a womblike withdrawal from all political activities. As Stephen Dedalus was shocked by the word *foetus* carved in the desk at his father's old school (because it suggested his failure to be artistically born), Heaney is shocked by his similar failure to be politically born and to establish a credo he can trust and act on. He wants to return home, as in "The Toome Road," to that "untoppled omphalos" of Mossbawn where political and religious turmoil was eclipsed by pastoral calm and where beliefs were more certain, more stable. He distrusts that nostalgia too, just as he distrusts the peaceful 'snare' of the harvest bow. As "Triptych" attests, engaging in the protest march fails to remove his conviction that he has not done enough.

Field Work often depicts Heaney walking through a mine field of his own design. He knows where the mines are, locates them, defuses them, but as he keeps versing and reversing over the field almost against his will he plants new ones. The things he is most devoted to—his Irish heritage, poetic craft, marriage—exercise his rigorous sense of responsibility to the breaking point. He wants to 'respond' to 'sponsors' and 'spouses,' actual and imaginary, literary and familial. Nevertheless, their diverse claims fill him with moral anguish. Freedom from those claims is a transcendence hoped for and renounced. Working against *Field Work*'s partial relaxation of the constrictions scored into the tight stanzas of *North* is the worry spurred by that relaxation. To slip through the harvest bows that promise deceptive peace and to escape the paramilitary groups assuring prolonged violence requires persistent vigilance. Those who relax in *Field Work* often get shot or blown up.

Heaney insists that his art, marriage, and politics depend on trust. Freely availing himself of that constellation of otherness—audience, wife, spirit, animal, vegetation, the earth itself—he also recoils in uncertainty and distrust, always fearing bedevilment by the forces that originally succored him. The 'others,' as the poems show, comprise a 'compound ghost,' which is really Heaney's multifaceted mask or shadow. If they are all representations of the original Mother, his attitude is ambivalent but ultimately conciliatory. In his own psyche he will wed symbolic Mother and Father, discursive spontaneity and silent, repressive intellect, and from their differences produce poems that underscore their difficult alliances. Although many of the poems in *Field Work* resemble trial pieces (perhaps not as accomplished as the "Trial-Pieces" in *North*), they are courageous in their willingness to explore new territory, to trust hunches and take risks. Some careers would wilt under the intense self-scrutiny Heaney applies to himself and his art. His career seems to gain force and immediacy because of it. As Heaney said of Lowell, whose influence is noticeable in almost every poem in *Field Work*, he "dared to perceive himself historically, as a representative figure" (1981, 648). Heaney also dares to test his poetic accomplishments with unprecedented self-questionings and self-accusations. The result of his psychological and political investigations is an art representative of the adversities and tensions that have made Ireland what it is.

8

HEANEY'S SWEENEY

THE DEBATE over imitation and originality in poetry has a prestigious history, and nearly every critic and poet from Aristotle to Emerson, T. S. Eliot to Harold Bloom, has rattled a saber for one side or the other. Yeats claimed to be obsessed by imitation. In *Per Amica Silentia Lunae* he declares, "I was always thinking of the element of imitation in style and in life, and of the life beyond imitation" (1959, 334). He then quotes an old diary of his. "All happiness depends on the energy to assume the mask of some other life, on a rebirth as something not one's self, something created in a moment and perpetually renewed; in playing a game like that of a child where one loses the infinite pain of self-realisation in a grotesque or solemn painted face put on that one may hide from the terror of judgment" (334). The poet plays at reincarnation, Yeats suggests, like an actor playing different roles in order to escape the punishment of self-consciousness and conscience. For Yeats, originality and creativity are paradoxically bound to repetition and imitation.

Yeats's "Anima Hominis," which praises Christian saints and heroes of the Middle Ages for striving to "resemble the antithetical self" through "imitation of Christ or of some classic hero" (1959, 333), predicts the direction Seamus Heaney takes in *Sweeney Astray* (1983) and *Station Island* (1984). Both books return to medieval legends for much of their material. In the long title poem, "Station Island," Heaney dons the masks of Dante and St. Patrick and, *in imitatione Christi*, makes the mythic journey into the underworld, confronting the shades of tutelary friends and artists as he goes. The "Sweeney Redivivus" section of *Station Island* orchestrates another ghostly drama where the seventh-century Irish hero rises from the dead to speak for the living. What emerges is a portrait of the divided, irascible Sweeney that is fundamentally a self-portrait of Heaney: the artist adored by an audience he mistrusts, who studies and documents the mili-

138

tary maneuvers in his Northern homeland from the safe distance of a Southern wood, who mocks the pretensions of politicians and identifies with those creatures (like the birds) who can fly above such things, and who relishes the solitude of the hermit-artist and his ability to scrutinize everything, including his life and art, with 'scrupulous meanness.' Sweeney is the poet who bears witness to cultural affairs while declaring his independence from them. He resembles Heaney who asserts in an essay on art and politics in Northern Ireland that "the artistic endeavour . . . is not obliged to have any intention beyond its own proper completion" (1984a, 8). The distrustful, hermetic Sweeney is the modern self-reflexive artist, devoted to art for its own sake, but bent on deconstructing all claims for art's preeminent status and exposing the sociopolitical institutions, values, and events that determine art in the first place. Part aesthete, Sweeney fashions an art that unravels ethical and aesthetic presuppositions as it posits them, like "the twine [that] unwinds and loosely widens / backward through areas that forwarded" it, as Heaney says in "Unwinding." Flying above nets of church and state like Dedalus, his bird's-eye view informs everything he writes.

Yeats once stated that "the poet finds and makes his mask in disappointment, the hero in defeat" (1959, 337). If this is true, what disappointments inspired Heaney to adopt Sweeney as his mask, and who really is Sweeney? Is he simply Heaney's alter ego, a foil for self-conscious parries and ripostes, as some, including Heaney, would lead us to believe? Does he exemplify heroic triumph and artistic fertility born out of despair, as Yeats would contend, or is he closer to the doomed victim, the modern anti-hero: alienated, impotent, and incapable of success? Is he, as Heaney declares at the beginning of *Sweeney Astray*, primarily "a figure of the artist, displaced, guilty, assuaging himself by his utterance" (1983, viii), continually torn asunder by conflicting aesthetic aspirations and social duties? Or is he more ancient: the wild man or saint whose figures were so popular in the literature and legends of the Middle Ages? What, finally, is Heaney's attitude toward Sweeney? Does he pity him for his excruciating trials and abhor his transgressions, or does he identify with him and doggedly translate his poetry out of artistic envy?

The introduction to *Sweeney Astray* stresses similarities as opposed to differences between Heaney and Sweeney. Suibhne, the legendary and perhaps historical king in the original Middle-Irish poem, *Buile Suibhne*, which began to take shape in the ninth century but referred to events in the seventh, reigned in an area of Northern Ireland that Heaney knew intimately. "My fundamental relation with Sweeney," he says, "is topographical. His kingdom lay in what is now south County Antrim and north County

Down, and for over thirty years I lived on the verges of that territory. . . . When I began work on the version, I had just moved to Wicklow, not all that far from Sweeney's final resting ground at St. Mullins" (1983, ix). Sweeney's sociopolitical problems are comparable to Heaney's; they begin in the North and are partially resolved in the South. A pagan Celt, Sweeney resents the evangelical and imperialist intrusions of Christians and focuses his rage on St. Ronan Finn, chasing him off his land when he tries to mark out the foundations for a new church. To exacerbate the insult, he tosses Ronan's psalter into a nearby lake, and when one of his psalmists sprinkles holy water on Sweeney at the battle of Moira (A.D. 637), Sweeney kills him with a spear. For this and other blasphemies Ronan utters a curse that ultimately transforms the king, who is already partially deranged from the horrors of battle, into a neurasthenic bird that will flit from tree to tree for the rest of his life. Exposed to Ireland's rough weather, isolated from companions, home, and wife, and maddened by his uprooting, Sweeney is for Heaney the prototype of the Irish exile or "inner émigré" (as he refers to himself in "Exposure") who never quite escapes the forces that set him in motion. Although another priest, Moling, restores his sanity and reconciles him to Christianity in the end, the original prophesy that Sweeney will "die at spear-point" still pertains. The jealous husband of a cook who has been feeding Sweeney milk kills him. All is not lost, since "his spirit fled to heaven and his body was given an honourable burial by Moling" (1983, 77).

Topographical affinities aside, Heaney must have felt a profound psychological bond with the Celtic king who fled from battles in Ulster to take up the more solitary ardors of contemplation and poetry in the South. Some critics, however, were quick to distinguish Heaney's sojourn in Wicklow from Sweeney's frenzied tree hopping. Barbara Hardy in her essay "Meeting the Myth" recalls how Heaney "made the disarming admission that he chooses Sweeney for his rhyme with Heaney, explaining [on the BBC 'Kaleidoscope' program] that he was not driven mad, though he did move to exile among the trees of Wicklow." As "Yeats used the mask or the image to summon opposition," she declares, Heaney in the "Sweeney Redivivus" poems employs his persona to "assert and reassert the securities of personal experience." If he distorts Sweeney by making him seem complacent, it is because Sweeney's "punishment for sacrilege and aggression imagined as a state of acute unease, nakedness, exile and madness" (Hardy 1982, 157, 159, 158) in *Buile Suibhne* is simply too foreign to Heaney's characteristic equanimity and élan. According to Hardy, by comparing himself to Suibhne Geilt Heaney makes his situation seem more melodramatic than it actually is or was.

Although Heaney may pretend to be Sweeney (even to the extent of climbing a tree to be photographed for a *Harvard Magazine* article [November/December 1985, 88] appearing after *Sweeney Astray* was published) he is surely aware of his problematic relationship with his mask. Critics, who downplay Heaney's emotional unease, his painful sense of exposure, political failure, and exile, have simply succumbed to another disguise that Heaney is adept at projecting: that of the jovial, free-spirited, Irish bard. Neil Corcoran is right when he avers, "Sweeney is, above all, the name for a restless dissatisfaction with the work already done, a fear of repetition, an anxiety about too casual an assimilation and acclaim, a deep suspicion of one's own reputation and excellence." He identifies Sweeney as the "mask antithetical to much that the name 'Seamus Heaney' has meant in previous books" (1986, 180, 174). These turbulent emotions have always festered under the hard, orderly surfaces of Heaney's poems just as "the flax-dam festered in the heart / of the townland" in "Death of a Naturalist." The Sweeney mask allows Heaney to reenact the fate of the poet *in extremis,* take the measure of his own fate, and distance himself from gothic excesses. Donning the tattered costume of the madman, Heaney externalizes the *hysterica passio* pent up in the politically beleaguered, exiled poet he identifies with and moves toward catharsis. If his confessionalism is histrionic it is also therapeutic, and perhaps more successively so than those brands practiced by Lowell, John Berryman, Plath, Anne Sexton, and Roethke, whose demons were not so easily exorcised. Through self-dramatization as a ludicrous, mythical bird, Heaney flies over the cuckoo's nest that trapped many of his precursors.

Hardy diminishes the anguish of exile in the Heaney/Sweeney persona when she recounts, "In the 'Kaleidoscope' interview . . . Heaney said he thought of himself as belonging to the North, but felt at ease everywhere in Ireland" (1982, 158). In the 1987 interview with *The Boston Phoenix,* Heaney contradicts this avowal of comfortable, omnipresent at-homeness. He feels exiled wherever he goes, he says, whether it is Belfast, Wicklow, or Boston. His second-class status as a Catholic in Ulster only intensified his awareness of exile on friendlier turf later on. "I never had a feeling of comfortable consonance between myself and a place. The travel reinforces a condition that would be there anyway," he told the *Phoenix* reporter (RD 1987, sec. 3.3). Heaney's friend and fellow poet, Brendan Kennelly, illuminates Heaney's complex relationship with his mask more incisively when he describes Sweeney as a "mad Adam driven alone through a lunatic Eden" and points out that "the language of the poem reflects this gulf—between the 'civilized' and the outcast, the accepted and the accursed, agonized aimlessness and calm resoluteness, the man of pain and the men of purpose." In the end, Kennelly convincingly observes, Heaney seeks a balance between both factions, just as he has done in all his poems. The pain, however, is not minimized. *Sweeney Astray*, Kennelly believes, "will come to be seen as a compelling poem of human pain—the vague yet vivid pain of the waking imagination, an almost unutterable loneliness." For Heaney, pain and praise are often two sides of the same coin, which leads Kennelly to conclude, "One feels that this balance, urbanely sustained, is the product of a long, imaginative bond between Mr. Heaney and Sweeney" (1984, 14).

The pain of the famous nomadic poet who pursues his penitential art with "silence, exile and cunning" finds similar expression in Heaney's "The Wanderer," the prose poem in *Stations* that he wrote not long after beginning his version of *Buile Suibhne*. Here he juxtaposed personal trials against their ancient Anglo-Saxon correlatives: "halls in flames, hearts in cinders, the benches filled and emptied, the circles of companions called and broken" (1975, 19). The Anglo-Saxon scop's penchant for clear, rugged diction, which he emulated in "The Wanderer," was obviously on Heaney's mind while translating *Buile Suibhne*. His introduction compares the "bareness and durability" and "the hard weather of the Anglo-Saxon 'Seafarer' " (1983, viii) to his Gaelic model. And his essay, "The God in the Tree," discusses P. H. Henry's *The Early English and Celtic Lyric*, a study that links "The Seafarer" and "The Wanderer" with *Buile Suibhne*. The medieval preoccupation with the penitential journey that vacillates between complaint and paean, melancholic acknowledgment of wierd and commemoration of heroic deeds, is their common denominator. Heaney explains, "Both spring from a way of life at once simple and ascetic, the tensions of asceticism finding voice in the penitential verse, and the cheerier nature lyrics springing from the solitary's direct experience of the changing seasons" (1980a, 183). It was this tension between personal pain and praise for nature that sustained Heaney's interest in *Buile Suibhne*. He recalls in his introduction, "It was . . . its double note of relish and penitence, that first tempted me to try my hand at it and gave me the encouragement to persist" (1983, viii).

Both P. H. Henry and Nora Chadwick, Celtic scholars whom Heaney commends in "The God in the Tree," tell how early Anglo-Saxon and Irish Christians practiced "a very interesting and characteristic form of ascetic discipline known as *peregrinatio*, 'peregrination,' 'wandering,' literally 'pilgrimage' " (Chadwick 1961, 80). Chadwick distinguishes this from missionary work, and stipulates that it was a kind of exile, sometimes voluntarily taken to seek out God, at other times involuntarily accepted as a punishment for sins or crimes. As a prelude to her analysis of *Buile Suibhne*, Chadwick asserts that "peregrination and penance . . . are among the most important developments of eremitism in the Early Celtic Church" (102).

Sweeney's sin is a blatant one: he attacks St. Ronan and murders his acolyte. His humiliating metamorphosis from king into bird and his enforced *peregrinatio* among the trees comprise his ascetic penance, the poems he composes along the way his consolation.

Heaney shares with a difference his persona's obsession with sin, guilt, penance, and poetry. Although Sweeney suffers enforced exile for his sins, Heaney's sin is that he *chooses* exile. Sweeney runs from Ulster's atrocities because he has committed heinous crimes. Heaney's crime, at least in his eyes, is that he renounces direct political engagement with Northern Ireland's Troubles in order to devote his energy to poetry. In *North*, which Heaney composed while translating *Buile Suibhne*, he confesses to a guilty evasion of the Troubles in poems like "Punishment" and "Exposure" and punishes himself for witnessing but not preventing those who punish others unjustly. In "Exposure," what is being exposed is Heaney's propensity for political quietism and escapism. Is he a coward and deserter or a saintly man severing his attachments to the sinful world? Perhaps he is both.

> An inner émigré, grown long-haired
> And thoughtful; a wood-kerne
>
> Escaped from the massacre,
> Taking protective colouring
> From bole and bark, feeling
> Every wind that blows.

A deserting foot soldier (kerne), he is also Sweeney the bird-man camou-flaging himself in the trees and vigilantly avoiding the nefarious feuds of Ulster. As in Celtic times, when "voluntary exposure becomes an important penitential discipline and literary motif" (Henry 1966, 192), Heaney sub-mits to exposure as a form of self-chastisement. But again his chosen exile in the Wicklow woods is as much penance as sin.

To consider writing and translating an exemplary 'punishment' or confessional 'exposure' may strike some as masochism or martyrdom. Nev-ertheless, this is how Heaney sees it. "Station Island," which Heaney pre-pared for by translating the first two cantos of the *Inferno* as well as the Ugolino cantos he included in *Field Work*, was "a kind of penance," he told the *Phoenix* reporter, "like a big wheel I felt I had to turn myself on for a while" (RD 1987, sec. 3.3). The actual pilgrimage to Station Island, with its barefoot circuits on sharp rocks, its painful fasts and sleepless nights, was also a kind of penitential torture (at least William Carleton, one of Heaney's "familiar ghosts," viewed it that way). Along his *via dolorosa* a monkish voice admonishes him, "For your penance / translate me something by Juan de la Cruz," and Heaney plunges into the Catholic mystic's "dark night" to begin his work. St. John of the Cross, Dante, and Sweeney merge for Heaney into a single persona (this is particularly evident in his essay on Dante and the *Divine Comedy* playfully entitled "Treely and Rurally"). Voluntary or involuntary exiles, they join Heaney as he journeys through his dark wood of Irish troubles. Through translation Heaney appropriates their masks, manipulating their medieval voices and texts so that they speak for his and his country's contemporary need for atonement.

For Robert Graves, who retells Sweeney's story in *The White Goddess*, the anguish of the poetic life is a given; it is as medieval as it is modern, as pagan as it is Christian. Graves regards Sweeney as part Christian saint (his leaping among the trees is what "medieval Latin philosophers described . . . as *spiritualizatio, agilitas* and *subtilitas*, and applied . . . to cases of levitation by ecstatic saints" [1948, 451]), part pagan wild man "feeding on sloes, hollyberries, watercress, brooklime, acorns," part lover who threatens and is threatened by his beloved, but most importantly the poet who suffers horrible afflictions in his inspired devotion to the muse, the White Goddess. He concludes, "The tale seems to be devised as an illustration of the *Triad* that it is 'death to mock a poet, death to love a poet, death to be a poet. . . . This must be the most ruthless and bitter description in all European literature of an obsessed poet's predicament." Yet Graves also points out that the poetic life has its redemptive moments. Sweeney's sufferings were by no means absolute; he "enjoyed life to the full in better weather" (456).

Graves describes Sweeney's trouble as a conflict of interests between "service to the White Goddess, on the one hand, and respectable citizenship, on the other" (456). Heaney's dilemma is uncannily similar, and as a result Sweeney becomes his "useful mask—or a very useful objective correlative" (1979b, 34). His introduction to *Sweeney Astray* underscores the poem's "quarrel between free creative imagination and the constraints of religious, political and domestic obligation" (viii). We can assume that Heaney is referring to all his commitments and flights (aeronautical as well as political) in the seventies and early eighties. For a man deeply rooted in the pastoral soil of County Derry, the frequent trips to America and other countries must have made the bird (Suibhne makes international flights too, between Scotland and Ireland) rather than the peat or potato digger a more credible emblem. Shortly before beginning his translation in 1970, Heaney made the trip to Berkeley, California, for a year's teaching; upon returning to Belfast he resigned from Queen's University, moved to Wicklow, and afterward to Dublin in 1975. In 1979 he returned to America to teach, this time at Harvard, and after receiving the Boylston Chair of Rhetoric and Oratory, he began commuting monthly, from January to May, between Dublin and Cambridge. The first version of *Sweeney Astray*, which was completed quickly and intended as a children's story and radio program, was abandoned only months after Heaney arrived in Glanmore. Seven years later, another uprooting and flight renewed his inspiration; after his first semester at Harvard he "just jumped on it" (quoted by Corcoran 1986, 33), this time in a friend's house on Long Island. House hopping, college hopping, and continent hopping, alone and with his family, must have been exhausting and disorienting, making Suibhne's frenzied flights all the more appropriate a correlative for his own.

Some critics badgered Heaney for emphasizing his hero's picaresque 'straying' over his madness, his geography over his psychology. Denis Donoghue in *The New Republic*, for instance, complained that the modifier 'astray' in Heaney's title failed to do justice to *buile* in the Gaelic original. " 'Astray' doesn't, even in the north of Ireland, have the force of '*ar buile*,' which means frenzied. In the north, I remember, we said that someone was 'astray in the head,' meaning daft or simpleminded: not the same ailment" (1984, 28). If Heaney's title downplays Sweeney's madness his story unleashes it. The rhetoric is often reminiscent of Ted Hughes. When "the herded armies clashed and roared out their war cries" at the Battle of Moira, "a dark rending energy" assaults Sweeney. Hughes's Crow, another demonic bird-man all too familiar with the cacophony and carnage of battlefields, would empathize with Sweeney's spasmodic response.

> His brain convulsed,
> his mind split open.
> Vertigo, hysteria, lurchings
> and launchings came over him,
> he staggered and flapped desperately,
> he was revolted by the thought of known places
> and dreamed strange migrations. (sec. 11)

Sweeney's paradoxical attitudes toward violence—he kills mercilessly before realizing suddenly that he is horrified by violence—to a certain extent mesh with Heaney's. Confronted with Irish hostilities and their repercussions, both "would connive / in civilized outrage / yet understand the exact / and tribal, intimate revenge," as Heaney exclaims in "Punishment." Sweeney is "a kind of figure like Poor Tom in *King Lear*," Heaney told Druce, "a civilised man in disguise, tasting the primitive facts" (1979b, 35). Like

Hughes's Crow and Wodwo, the mythical savage and estranged nature spirit, Sweeney both embodies and reflects on the primordial world to which he is mysteriously but emphatically attached.

Heaney's guilt arises from his tribal feelings of revenge butting up against his rigorously civilized conscience. He 'connives' with liberal do-gooders and well-wishers by paying lip service to plans for social reformation, pretending that only barbarians entertain murderous thoughts. When naturalistic attitudes reassert themselves, he confesses that all 'civilized' people share a primitive 'blood consciousness.' His guilt is compounded by the suspicion that the moral shock of the 'innocent' saint and the high-minded ideals of the 'liberal' poet may have the same root in political cowardice, in the inability to confront barbarism face to face and fight against it. This is what the *geilt* in Suibhne's name implies, and why Heaney feels such an affinity for his Celtic ancestor. P. H. Henry shows in his study of early Celtic and English lyrics, which Heaney praised as "learned and thrilling" (1980a, 183), that the Gaelic word *geilt* jibes with the old English word *gylt* and can signify guilt, fear, exile, cowardly flight, and exclusion. Similarly, the Gaelic term can refer to "terror, fear, dread, cowardice, timidity," and, further-more, "one who goes mad from terror; a panic-stricken fugitive from battle; a crazy person living in the woods and supposed to be endowed with the power of levitation; a lunatic" (Henry 1966, 199). Henry links *geilt* etymo-logically to Gaelic words for flying and singing and a Greek word for a bird and then provides a long gloss on *geilt* taken from a Norse source that derived its information from Ireland. Individual words can contain whole poems encoded in their etymologies, as Heaney so convincingly proved in *Wintering Out*. *Geilt* encapsulates most of *Buile Suibhne* in one syllable, and most of the compulsions and deeds that Heaney found so relevant to his own experience. Henry explains.

> There is also one thing, which will seem very wonderful, about men who are called *gelt*. It happens that when two hosts meet and are arranged in battle-array, and when the battle-cry is raised loudly on both sides, that cowardly men run wild, and lose their wits from the dread and fear which seize them. And then they run into a wood away from other men, and live there like beasts, and shun the meeting of men like wild beasts. And it is said of these men that when they have lived in the woods in that condition for twenty years, then feathers grow on their bodies as on birds, whereby their bodies are protected against frost or cold; but the feathers are not so large that they may fly like birds. Yet their swiftness is said to be so great that other men cannot approach them. . . . For these people run along the trees as swiftly as monkeys or squirrels. (200)

Although Heaney has yet to sprout feathers, his perch halfway up a tree in the Harvard photograph suggests he might like to. If he has to become a wild man or levitating saint to achieve artistic freedom, he seems almost prepared to put on a bird's plumage or an ascetic's robes to do so.

According to some Celtic scholars, the original Suibhne practiced the poverty, chastity, and solitude of eremitical saints and indeed may have been one. Nora Chadwick connects Suibhne to the desert saints. "A close analogy to these *gealta* of the Irish Christian church, who shun the society of men and live alone with wild nature under the open heavens or even in the trees, is found in the recluses of the Syrian desert" (1961, 109). Greek writers referred to them as "tree-dwellers" and "gazers" because, like Suibhne, they often lived in trees and foraged local vegetation. Stories of the Syrian ascetics could have reached Ireland by word of mouth or by manuscript and then acted as powerful models in the anchorite tradition that, during the sixth and seventh centuries, was the most distinguishing feature of the Irish Celtic church.

The Roman church disapproved of recluses like Sweeney. St. Patrick's arrival in Ireland around A.D. 432, St. Augustine's in Kent in A.D. 597, and the Synod of Whitby in A.D. 663 (the group which imposed on Celts the Roman method of dating Easter) were all attempts to crush the eremitical tradition by bringing Christianity in the British Isles into closer conformity with the church of Rome. That church's central, urban form of ecclesiastical governance finally predominated after much resistance. For a country like Ireland where central towns were rare and scattered pastoral communities abundant, a centralized church seemed unsuitable. Chadwick believes that Suibhne's nature poetry, praising the anchorite's close contact with the beauty of the birds and trees, is a deliberate defense of the Celtic church as it faced obliteration by the authoritarian depredations of Rome. The pagan superstitions associated with Suibhne and recorded by the monks could have been "a protest against the levelling intellectual influence of the Roman Church" (1961, 158), a kind of rearguard assay by the retreating monasteries designed to prolong 'the Age of Saints' which, Chadwick believes, was effectively finished by the eighth century. With respect to Sweeney's poetry of penitence and praise, she says,

> There can be little doubt that the lyrical poetry, with its passionate
> defence of the Anchorite life, its emphasis on writing, and above all its
> devotion to simplicity and austerity, and its ever-recurring reference to
> nature and the wild things of the country, is conditioned and immedi-
> ately stimulated, despite its sweetness and spontaneity, by the impulse
> to defend the free life of the Celtic monks among these things against

the encroachment of a Church governed by law and order and a
centralized foreign official authority. (1961, 159)

Heaney also decenters and deconstructs the powerful institutions associated
with the insurgent Roman Church, siding with the marginal Celts, their
monastic independence and their preoccupation with writing. A poem written during the period he translated *Sweeney*, "Remembering Malibu," reaffirms his allegiance to the "cold ascetic," "monk-fished, snowed-into Atlantic"
with its "beehive hut" above "steps cut in the rock." Against the smother-
ing demands of empires, whether American or Roman, Heaney asserts the
artist's right to withdraw to a secluded outpost for contemplation and
writing.

As *Sweeney Astray* develops, however, its protagonist seems more wild
man than saint, more fanciful lunatic than orderly, contemplative anchorite.
The original writer who composed the text "at any time between the years
1200 and 1500," according to O'Keeffe (1913, xvi), was drawing on other
texts (whose poems may have been composed by Suibhne and his friend, St.
Moling, in the seventh century) as well as oral tradition, which had embroi-
dered Suibhne's antics into their final form. Chadwick believes that the
hilarious distortions of Suibhne's saintly ardors were caused by the storyteller's
ignorance of as well as contempt for Celtic Christianity. A product of
Romanization, "the *fili* [the bard] has given full rein to his humour and the
elaborate story of Sweeney is virtually a satire on the early religious communities whom the medieval writer did not understand and with whom he has
little sympathy, though he has remembered the tradition and reproduced it
faithfully enough" (Chadwick 1971, 276). Elsewhere she maintains, "Extreme asceticism, such as that of Suibhne and the 'many *gealta*' in Ireland in
his day, soon become transformed by the laughing Irish shanachie" (1961,
109) into rollicking comedy. One of the attractions of this hybrid text for
Heaney lay in its iconoclastic humor. For a poet determined to defuse and
break apart the dangerously seductive icons of his culture, *Buile Suibhne*
provided an irresistible opportunity for extended scrutiny and mockery, just
as it did for Flann O'Brien in his uproarious rendition of Sweeney in *At
Swim-Two-Birds*. Reconstructing Suibhne into a saintly eremite, Heaney
simultaneously deconstructs his hallowed image by exposing him as a ludicrous wild man.

The many inconsistencies and paradoxes in *Buile Suibhne*—between
paganism and Christianity, Celtic and Roman Churches, military heroes and
pacifist saints—arose from the various biases of the bards and scribes who
passed the tale along and from the history of conflicting allegiances in
Ireland that determined them. O'Keeffe, in fact, believes that the Christian

characters, St. Ronan and St. Moling, and the narrative of Suibhne's infractions against the former that are redeemed by the latter originally formed a separate tale. "I venture to suggest that the original story attributed the madness to the horrors which he witnessed in the battle of Magh Rath, and that the introduction of St. Ronan and St. Moling may be a later interpolation" (1913, xxxiv). This would divide Sweeney into two characters: the belligerent pagan king who hates the church but finally accepts it and the sensitive convert whose nerves are so shattered by the savagery of battle that he opts for the hermit's ascetic devotions. Rather than detract from the story's credibility and coherence, the confusion actually enriches it. It makes Heaney's mask polymorphous and ambiguous, which is what he wants. It allows him to play engaged king and otherworldly saint, and to play the opposed roles against one another for ironic and moral effect.

The Irish king who hurls his spear at St. Ronan and the one who flees the spears at the battle of Moira may be different characters. What apparently unifies them is their enchantment with wildness. O'Keeffe has pointed out, "The account of Suibhne's madness seems to bear some resemblance to the widely dispersed story of the Wild Man of the Woods of which the Merlin legend is perhaps the most conspicuous offshoot" (1913, xxxv). Kenneth Jackson corroborates this view in his revealing essay, "The Motive of the Threefold Death in the Story of Suibhne Geilt," adding, "The particular sub-type of the wood-dwelling Wild Man who has gone mad in a battle, becomes a prophet or makes friends with a prophet . . . seems peculiar to the Celtic lands" (1940, 544). Heaney follows Sweeney into the wilderness for poetic rather than prophetic reasons; still, his art amounts to a kind of *vox clamanto in deserto*. His enchantment with ascetic rigors in the wilderness is longstanding. "Remembering Malibu" celebrates an earlier exile on the Pacific coast because the ocean "was wilder and colder / than my notion of the Pacific / / and that was perfect, for I would have rotted / beside the luke-warm ocean I imagined." To Druce he described his exile to Wicklow as taking his "family into the wilderness" (1979b, 26). Barbara Hardy in her essay "Meeting the Myth," while distinguishing Heaney from Sweeney, claims that the latter is "closely related to the wodwo or savage man of myth, legend, and many literatures. The classic text on the subject, as interesting to a study of these Sweeney poems as Jessie Weston's *From Ritual to Romance* is for 'The Waste Land' is Richard Bernheimer's *Wild Men in the Middle Ages*" (1982, 163). Is Heaney, then, a modern equivalent of the medieval "savage man"?

The portrait of the wild man that Bernheimer pieces together from numerous medieval artifacts resembles Heaney/Suibhne only in a tangential way. For Bernheimer the wild man is an archetypal creature who glories in the primordial desires of the id. That is, he is irrepressibly violent, sexual, or a combination of the two. "The wild man's strength is the mainspring of his actions, driving him in a continuous effort to release the explosive force which is in him by trying it out in combat," he says, and adds, "in the Middle Ages the wild man's inability to control his sexual passions was regarded as an essential part of his primitive personality" (Bernheimer 1970, 34). Although Suibhne throws a few spears at the beginning of his adventures, for the most part he is nonviolent and abstemious, even at the end of the story when he is accused (falsely) of philandering with the swineherd's wife. Indeed, he lives more like a real wild animal than a mythologized one. Bernheimer reveals that in medieval iconography the wild man usually sported an intimidating club, shaggy hair, or a loin ornament and came to represent the nexus of creative and destructive forces in nature. He was a vegetation god, dying so the earth would grow fertile and flourish, "a personified obstacle to the return of spring, a winter demon who had to be killed so that his icy breath would not impede the sprouting of greenery" (56). Heaney allows him some of these vegetal attributes (he is "the green spirit of the hedges" [1983, ix], according to his introduction). He is hardly the hirsute thug that Bernheimer describes trampling through the underbrush in pursuit of women and enemies. He is more penitent poet than violent hedonist, more flitting bird than thrashing ape. He rises above society's lurid treasures while the wild man typically absconds with them; he renounces what his double trounces.

It makes more sense to view Suibhne as an ambiguously Christian wild man and not a boorishly pagan or barbaric one. At first he appears godless, later his penitential quest turns toward God, and at last, abetted by St. Moling, his faith in God is confirmed. He is buried in consecrated ground and his soul ascends to heaven. Bernheimer is more to the point when he says, "One can realize the seriousness of his [the wild man's] plight by considering that, according to the widely accepted Augustinian doctrine, knowledge of God, however dim, was the prerequisite and basis for any further mental activity. So long as his spiritual blindness prevailed, the wild man had to be portrayed as either out of his mind or without one" (1970, 12). Exiled from society and God, Sweeney suffers periodic bouts of madness, but at the end when he prays to god and decides, after years of mistrust and faithlessness, to return to both community and communion, in Heaney's version, "then a glimmer of reason came back to him and he set out for his own country, ready to settle there and entrust himself to the people" (sec. 63). Bernheimer mentions that medieval writers could find a handy biblical precedent for the godless *wyld* man, whose brutality was "synonymous with what we call mad or frenzied" (12) in the figure of Nebuchadnezzar. For defaming and repudiating God, this king also had to survive as a bird-man in exile, scrounging sustenance from the fields. As Daniel recounts, he "was driven from men and did eat grass as oxen, and his body was wet with the dew of heaven, till his hairs were grown like eagles' feathers, and his nails like birds' claws" (Dan. 4:33). Sweeney's fate is no different.

What emerges from Bernheimer's study is the conviction that the wild man was one of civilization's discontents who revelled in a life of "bestial self-fulfillment, directed by instinct rather than volition, and devoid of all those acquired tastes and patterns of behavior which are part of our adjustment to civilization" (1970, 4). For the romantic imagination his archaic charm "lies in the fact that his manner of life, in its stark simplicity, is regarded as a paragon of virtue lost in the unfolding of civilization" (102). In this romanticized form, he is the noble savage, an ancestor of Adam roaming his pristine paradise and freely plucking its fruit. Suibhne's green world, by contrast, is more purgatorial than edenic, and while appreciating nature's indubitable splendors he misses civilization's amenities and camaraderie. Unlike Bernheimer's wild man, he is neither rapacious brute nor Wordsworthian pastoralist. He possesses a remarkably realistic eye for nature's cycles of affliction and appeasement, rugged bestiality and uplifting beauty. At one point he cries out,

> I am the madman of Glen Bolcain,
>
> wind-scourged, stripped
> like a winter tree
> clad in black frost
> and frozen snow.
>
> Hard grey branches
> have torn my hands,
> the skin of my feet
> is in strips from briars
> and the pain of frostbite
> has put me astray. (sec. 21)

As inevitably as winter turns to spring, his view of nature turns from bitterness to celebration.

> Sweetest of the leafy stalks,
> the vetches strew the pathway;

the oyster-grass is my delight,
and the wild strawberry.
. . . .
I love the ancient ivy tree,
the pale-leafed sallow,
the birch's whispered melody,
the solemn yew.
. . . .
I would live happy
in an ivy bush
high in some twisted tree
and never come out. (sec. 40)

This paean to nature gains intensity from the opposite recognition of nature's cruelty.

Sweeney is both saintly and scientific naturalist journeying penitentially away from personal and public sins in order to atone for them, his tale a vacillation between contradictory moods which approximate Heaney's. To what extent, then, does Heaney actually identify with him? A partial answer is that in order to translate *Suibhne Geilt* into credible, dramatic English Heaney *had* to identify with him. Discussing the exigencies of translation with Robert Druce, Heaney said of Sweeney, "I began to think of him as being like myself. You have to do that . . . when you're working" (1979b, 34). The first version of *Sweeney Astray*, completed in April 1973, made the correspondences between himself and his alter ego explicit, and the original clash between Sweeney and Ronan was allegorized into an altercation between Catholic nationalist and Protestant unionist in Northern Ireland. Later chagrined by "a strong sense of bending the text" to his sociopolitical context, and by creating a bastardized version "infected with the idiom of the moment" (1979b, 32, 33), Heaney decided to aim for a more faithful transcription. The dialectical relation with his mask did not subside; it simply became more subtle.

Three essays published in the 1980s, "Treely and Rurally" (1980), "Envies and Identifications: Dante and the Modern Poet" (1985), and "The Impact of Translation" (1987), all reveal, in their oblique ways, the complexity of Heaney's identification with Sweeney. The essays are all related (the second even lifts a whole section from the first), and all focus on ways in which modern poets translate and transform foreign texts, how they remake them in their own images. T. S. Eliot is Heaney's whipping boy because he imposes his urbane, melancholic personality to such an extent on models such as Dante that only a simulacrum of the original remains. Accusing Eliot's 'translations' of blind manipulation, Heaney is staking his own claims for Dante and Sweeney and asserting that his political afflictions and rugged, vernacular poems are closer to those of his medieval masters. This assertivenss surely derives some of its vehemence from envy—not so much of Eliot as of Dante and Sweeney. "The impact of translation upon poets and poetry in English," Heaney claims, "has involved two main lines of reaction which might be characterized as 'envy' and 'identification.' " Modern poets tend to identify with the martyrs and victims of totalitarian oppression, past and present, and envy not "the plight of the artist but . . . the act of faith in art which becomes manifest as the artist copes with the tyrannical conditions" (1987, 6). Although he admits that the translating poet has to at least *pretend* to be the author he translates, he expresses "resentment that such poetic identification has issued in a kind of unwarranted annexation" whereby "what was once wrung valiantly from history . . . become[s] available at such greatly reduced emotional prices" (12). According to Heaney, the new martyrologists from Eliot to present-day American surrealists have not paid sufficiently for what they have purchased.

It is surprising that Heaney should be so vindictive toward Eliot when his Sweeney and Dante masks are also serviceable fictions rather than believable realities. Contemplating Yeats's use of a Dantean mask in "Ego Dominus Tuus," he reveals a good deal about his own translation-as-self-dramatization when he comments, "Energy is discharged, reality is revealed and enforced when the artist strains to attain the mask of his opposite; in the act of summoning and achieving that image, he does his proper work and leaves us with the art itself, which is a kind of trace element of the inner struggle of opposites, a graph of the effort of transcendence" (1985, 5). When Yeats wears the mantle of Dante he is doing his "proper work" rather than indulging (like Eliot) in an improper masquerade that disfigures or sentimentalizes the original.

Yet Heaney must know he is walking the same tightrope between mask and masquerade in his translations of Suibhne and Dante. "When poets turn to the great masters of the past, they turn to an image of their own creation, one which is likely to be a reflection of their own imaginative needs, their own artistic inclinations and procedures," he writes in "Envies and Identifications" (1985, 5). Heaney is hardly Dante, whose exile was enforced under penalty of death and whose narrative structure in the *Divine Comedy* was inherited from Aquinas and medieval Catholicism. And he is hardly Suibhne, who kills out of religious intolerance and chatters in the trees. On the other hand, both provide him with convex mirrors, as in John Ashbery's poem about Parmigianino, and in these glasses they are able to glimpse their self-portraits, however exaggerated.

Heaney's method of versifying original texts (he calls *Sweeney Astray* a version rather than a translation) derives its confidence to alter and cut from precedents set by Ezra Pound and Robert Lowell (especially his *Imitations*), even though he chides both poets for their classical and elitist assumptions. Both, he argues, converted "the great tradition" into "a kind of cultural air-raid shelter" (1987, 10) to which they retreated in order to escape the warring democratic 'mobs.' Heaney also withdraws from warring 'mobs' and approaches the traditional *Buile Suibhne* as Pound approached "The Seafarer." Pound's dictum for translators, "Don't bother about the WORDS, translate the MEANING" (quoted by Kenner 1972, 150), is Heaney's. Confronting the fragmentary "Seafarer," which had probably been Christianized and "improved" by a monk with literary ambitions, Pound set to chiseling away all the encrustations with the hope of delivering a vigorously modern approximation. Heaney chisels with similar brio, acknowledging the deletion of twenty-one stanzas and a prose passage. As Mary Kinzie points out, "Above all, Heaney restores to the lines before us what anyone reading the O'Keeffe version realizes is a promise of electrifying keenness. . . . Heaney elevates the poems from archaeological curiosity into a text with enormous urgency" (1988, 40). One could compare almost any passages to illustrate Heaney's method of condensation. Kinzie chooses section 40 (1988, 49–50).

O'KEEFFE:

I flee before the skylarks—
'tis a stern, great race—
I leap over the stumps
on the tops of the mountains.
When the proud turtle-dove
rises for us,
quickly do I overtake it
since my feathers have grown.
The silly, foolish woodcock
hen it rises for me
methinks 'tis a bitter foe,
the blackbird (too) that gives a cry of alarm.

HEANEY

The skylarks rising
to their high space
send me pitching and tripping
over stumps on the moor

and my hurry flushes
the turtle-dove.
I overtake it,
my plumage rushing,

am startled
by the startled woodcock
or a blackbird's sudden
volubility. (sec. 40)

Heaney's pared-down, depoeticized version gains energy from the slimming. The literalists still chastise Heaney (just as they chastised Pound) for recasting the complex patterns of meter, rhyme, assonance, and alliteration of the Gaelic original into a simulacrum of his trademark style.

Evidently Heaney vacillated between the different options *Buile Suibhne* presented. Finally he chose to act on all of them. After discovering in Sweeney a convenient persona, he confessed in an interview that "the question is, in a sense, whether one is content to take Sweeney as he appears in the manuscript, and to invest that version of the manuscript with things from within myself. Or whether to take Sweeney out of the old fable, and make him *Sweeney Redivivus*, and make him bear other experiences" (1979b, 37). He did both, and in both cases modernist experiments with imitation, free translation, dramatic personae, and mythopoesis directed his enterprise.

Heaney's "envies and identifications" are often submerged, just as the examples of Pound and Eliot are often suppressed. One of the most important influences on *Sweeney Astray* and "Sweeney Redivivus" came from a poet whose work Heaney acknowledged as both challenging and defeating. It was shortly before tackling *Buile Suibhne* that Heaney abandoned his sequence of prose poems, *Stations*, because of Geoffrey Hill's *Mercian Hymns*. He postponed work on *Stations* until moving to Wicklow, where he completed it shortly after finishing the first draft of *Sweeney Astray*. Resembling *Mercian Hymns* in many ways, *Sweeney Astray* was so different stylistically that it must have seemed a viable alternative to the English poet's work of "complete authority." Hill's exploration of cultural roots and reenactment of significant moments in his development as a poet were also achieved through a mask (through Offa, the legendary eighth-century Anglo-Saxon king). Hill is overtly modernist in his procedures, creating a dense, disjointed narrative with all the verbal panache of a *Ulysses* or *Waste Land*. Heaney's foray into his tangled past is not so ambitious (although it would be in "Station Island"). Both blocking agent and catalyst for Heaney, *Mercian Hymns* eventually dispersed his "stolen march" in four different directions: he translated *Buile Suibhne* (Hill's *Mercian Hymns* were also derived in part from translations—found in *Sweet's Anglo-Saxon Reader*); he rendered his own narrative of trials and triumphs in a sequence of prose poems; he conflated Sweeney with his modern-day self in "Sweeney Redivivus"; and he incorporated his mythopoetic techniques on a grand, modernist scale in "Station Island." Hill, on the other hand, managed to accomplish all four feats in one sequence.

Heaney's strategy may have been designed to avoid a head-on collision with Hill's *Hymns* by confronting them on several flanks at different times. Similarities certainly abound between Hill's conception of Offa and Heaney's of Sweeney, even though Offa tends to be the authoritarian victimizer and Sweeney the authoritarian's victim, Offa the social and political animal and Sweeney the antisocial and apolitical animal. Still, the two suffer the tragic flaws, guilt, and madness to which kings are often heir. They represent the genius or *zeitgeist* of their respective cultures and psyches. Offa, Hill declares, is "the presiding genius of the West Midlands" (1985, 201), a kind of local vegetation god. Sweeney is similarly "the green spirit of the hedges" (Heaney 1983, ix) in Heaney's Ireland. Both figures are artificers whose sins are entangled in and partly responsible for their accomplishments. They struggle tortuously toward God like shadowy plants twisting toward the sun. Their comic and tragic guises allow their authors to laugh and cry out at their own reflections.

For Hill, Offa is "a creature of legend" (1985, 201) as well as "an objective correlative for the inevitable feelings of love and hate which any man or woman must feel for the *patria* . . . [and] an objective correlative for the ambiguities of English history in general" (Haffenden 1981, 94). For Heaney, Sweeney is "a literary creation," "an historically situated character, although the question of whether he is based upon an historical king called Sweeney has to remain an open one" (1983, vii), and an objective correlative for his ambivalence toward the *matria*. While mad England hurts Offa into poetry, sardonic as it is, mad Ireland stimulates Sweeney's more caustic lyrics. Both poems chart a cycle from derangement to sanity, sin to redemption, life to death to afterlife. Both kings commit murders and embrace penitential journeys (Offa killed his political foe, Ethelbert, and took a pilgrimage to Rome to atone). Both are naturalists (Offa "had a care for natural minutiae" [Hill 1985, 118]) and see in the wilderness their own wildness reflected. Discontented with civilization, Offa deprecates institutions like the church, state, school, workplace, and family, but remains irascibly committed to them. Sweeney's break and reunion with civilization is more extreme, but similarly ambivalent. Both are doomed by fate (Offa by his wierd, Sweeney by Ronan's curse) and fulfill their natural and supernatural destinies, oscillating between excruciating trials and godly triumphs.

Through madness and defeat Sweeney wins his paradoxical victory of sanity, grace, and resurrection. A deracinated modern artist, he is less the impotent lost soul haplessly wandering through the waste land than the explorer or saint enduring ascetic ordeals in the wilderness, and discovering in its pristine splendors a redemptive vision. Recalling Coleridge's ancient mariner, who is afflicted with similar penitential woes and for similar reasons, his whole quest leads to a final act of reconciling love. The mariner learns:

> He prayeth best, who loveth best
> All things both great and small;

For the dear God who loveth us,
He made and loveth all.

Sweeney's deathbed confession arises from a similar affirmation of nature, society, and God. Sweeney even speaks in the balladlike quatrains of the mariner.

> There was a time when I preferred
> the turtle-dove's soft jubilation
> as it flitted round a pool
> to the murmur of conversation.
>
> There was a time when I preferred
> the blackbird singing on the hill
> and the stag loud against the storm
> to the clinking tongue of this bell.
> . . . .
> To You, Christ, I give thanks
> for Your Body in communion.
> Whatever evil I have done
> in this world, I repent. (sec. 83)

That Sweeney pays a mortal price for his renewed faith in humanity and God reveals that, finally, he is more saintly penitent than raving fool.

Like Flann O'Brien in his hilarious lampoon of Celtic myths, *At Swim-Two-Birds*, Heaney laughs at Sweeney too. He is drawn to the tale like Shanahan and Furriskey when Finn, with bardic aplomb, exclaims, "The first matter that I will occupy with honey-words and melodious recital . . . is the reason and the first cause for Sweeney's frenzy" (O'Brien 1951, 90). Heaney vows to avoid the mellifluous chords and roseate pallors of the Celtic idiom that O'Brien satirizes. He no doubt sympathizes with Shanahan who interrupts the Yeatsian Mr. Storybook to push for a more Joycean vernacular, the kind that is (laughably) represented by the proletarian "Jem Casey, Poet of the Pick." Shanahan says, "Now take that stuff . . . about the green hills and the bloody swords and the bird [Sweeney] giving out the pay from the top of the tree. Now that's good stuff, it's bloody nice. . . . It's the stuff that put our country where she stands to-day. . . . But the man in the street, where does he come in? By God he doesn't come in at all as far as I can see" (105–6). Ironically, the poem he recites by Jem Casey, "The Workman's Friend," is as sentimental and hackneyed as the Celtic Twilight mode he mocks. It is a jingle that returns in every quatrain to the refrain, "A PINT OF PLAIN IS YOUR ONLY MAN." It puts the scholarly and fastidious Finn to sleep. Heaney's *Sweeney Astray* aims to weld the vernacular idiom favored by Shanahan with the 'sublime' Celtic idiom trumpeted by Finn. "I wanted it to have an Irish tang," Heaney once said (1979b, 36). His *Sweeney Astray* and "Sweeney Redivivus" are not only invigorated with an authentic sense of Irish legend and landscape; they provide Heaney with new ways of exploring artistic dilemmas as old as Sweeney. His multilayered mask allows him to shift between comedy, tragedy, and farce and to make contemporary Irish history resonate with the impact of myth. Through translation and impersonation, Heaney reveals the differences as well as the correspondences between his situation and Sweeney's. The persona he fashions out of archaic Celtic materials is an entertaining disguise that reflects some of Sweeney, some of Heaney, and some of us.

9

GHOSTLY COLLOQUIES

Poets, like nomads, cultivate a patch of ground until it is exhausted, then push on to greener lands. Seamus Heaney's first ground is his home ground, Northern Ireland, and the books from *Death of a Naturalist* to *North* map its "terrible beauty" in a verse as compressed as it is resplendent. *Field Work* documents new territory and, as the title implies, a willingness to try out new tools and new techniques. "I'm certain that up to *North*, that was one book," Heaney says in an interview; "in a way it grows and goes together" (in Haffenden 1981, 64). The sonnet sequence at the center of *Field Work* entitled "Glanmore Sonnets," with its numerous purgatorial journeys, acts as a bridge between the Northern emphasis of his earlier work and the lighter Southern music he orchestrates so brilliantly in *Sweeney Astray* and *Station Island*. The "Sonnets" begin with a complex conceit that compares a farmer's "turned-up acres" with a woodworker's lathe-turned artifacts and a poet's turnings (his tropings and agonized self-questionings). As was the case for Eliot and Yeats, who depicted bewildering dilemmas in terms of spiraling staircases and spinning gyres, Heaney's object is to encounter and transcend demons of his past. The first sonnet ends, "Breasting the mist, in sowers' aprons, / My ghosts come striding into their spring stations. / The dream grain whirls like freakish Easter snow." Having turned away from the North, he now turns back to face its inescapable ghosts. The conjunction of vegetative dream-ritual and Christian resurrection is typical of Heaney and reminiscent of Eliot at the beginning of *The Waste Land* where he compares the resurgence of painful memories to Christ's Passion and to menacing vegetation breeding out of the dead land of snow. Both poets echo Dante, whose descent into hell and encounters with old ghosts also commence in April *in imitatione Christi*.

Dante and Eliot resurface as tutelary presences in "Station Island," Heaney's longest and most ambitious poem to date. As with "Glanmore

Sonnets," Heaney's miniepic conjures up figures from his past. Before, he watched them "striding in" to repeat Christ's Stations; now he strides out, a pilgrim communing with them as he turns on the sharp, circular rocks of Station Island in Lough Derg. In contradistinction to Eliot who bears witness to the general destruction of World War II in his Dantean section of "Little Gidding," Heaney recalls specific victims of political atrocities in Northern Ireland. "Station Island," Heaney asserts (recalling a phrase from Eliot's poem), "is a sequence of dream encounters with familiar ghosts" (1984b, 122), in which the ghosts are always more particularized and more mundane than Eliot's. Uncomfortable with abstract philosophizing upon "the gifts reserved for age / To set a crown upon your lifetime's effort" (Eliot 1969, 194), they tend to discourse on such matters as "wind and rain in trees" and "tinkers camped / under a heeled-up cart." Simon Sweeney, an actual person Heaney knew of as a child, initiates his series of dialogues with the dead.

Most of Heaney's dramatis personae, in fact, oppose the sort of lofty enterprises like pilgrimages and theological disquisitions that Eliot sanctioned (in "Mr. Eliot's Sunday Service" the poet ridicules a common man by the name of Sweeney; Heaney tends to hang on his every word). William Carleton's ghost, for instance, is enraged by Heaney's intention to go to Lough Derg, and offers the grotesque, down-to-earth explanation of all rites of purification as rites of putrefaction. We are worms, he says, eating through the earth to renew its body and our own, and when we die only maggots will purify our flesh. Timeless moments, for Carleton, are will-o'-the-wisps. His scientific ruthlessness is reminiscent of the surgeon, Bobby, in Sean O'Faolain's story "Lovers of the Lake," whose animosity toward his girlfriend's plan to take the Lough Derg pilgrimage dwindles only after great resistance. Other dream characters accuse Heaney of otherworldliness, and with similar didactic intent. A young priest disillusioned with his early, naïve spirituality, berates the poet as a tourist simply "going through the . . . motions" of the pilgrimage without actually believing in their efficacy. Patrick Kavanagh rises from the grave to exclaim, "Forty-two years on / and you've got no farther." He assumes Heaney, like himself forty-two years before, mechanically repeats age-old rites that now mean nothing. Colum McCartney, Heaney's second cousin who appeared in "The Strand at Lough Beg" in *Field Work* (with an epigraph from Dante's *Purgatorio*), castigates the poet in "Station Island" for whitewashing ugliness and proffering saccharine accounts of death. James Joyce approaches him at the end in a brilliant valedictory passage of *terza rima* that also scorns Heaney's penchant for otherworldly exercises. Adopting "a voice like a prosecutor's," he warns Heaney away from all rituals, including those at Station Island that distract him from his art. "Hard and sharp as a blackthorn bush," Joyce remains rooted in the ground and advises Heaney to do the same.

The comical conjoining of seemingly devout pilgrims with overtly sacrilegious ones may have been inspired by Chaucer, a poet for whom Heaney had an early affection. In his article "Discovering a Tradition," he mentions Chaucer as an author in his undergraduate course whose work gave "real onsets of pleasure and epiphany" (in Broadbridge 1977, 22). "Station Island" like *The Canterbury Tales* employs a pilgrimage more as a "frame narrative" than as a central dramatic event. It provides the occasion for the characters to speak out, so that the poem in the end is more a collage than a flowing, synchronized story. If the "frame" had been a journey to Sligo, the narrative might remain essentially the same, just as Chaucer's tales would change little if the pilgrims were traveling to Oxford or Cambridge rather than to Canterbury. The religious pilgrimage in both cases creates a significant context. It remains in the background to create an ironic contrast with the unholy acts and tales of the pilgrims. Heaney's ambivalence toward his characters, coupled with his genuine respect for rituals that instill humility and assuage guilt, is also reminiscent of the medieval poet who retracted his *Canterbury Tales* as "translacions and enditings of worldly vanitees" but indulged wholeheartedly in their worldly topics when he was telling them.

In an interview in 1979, several years before "Station Island" was published, Heaney described the new style he was aiming for in his sequence. He chose "The Wild Swans at Coole" as an example, because "the voice of the . . . lyric isn't a self-entranced voice. It's clear, bare. . . . I use the word public because it's not inwardly turned, it's set *out*. I think that the first voice I have is an inward musing, entranced at its best, but I would love to master a voice that could *talk out* as well as go into a trance" (Haffenden 1981, 70). A year later Dante's *Divine Comedy*, with its protagonists turning inward and downward as well as outward and upward and its trancelike vision of the mysteries expressed in the vernacular, would serve as an even more potent example.

His long review of C. H. Sisson's translation of *The Divine Comedy* and George Holmes's *Dante* indicates some of the fruits of Heaney's apprenticeship to Dante. He begins by debunking Eliot, whose famous essay on Dante stressed linguistic and religious matters over political ones. When Eliot is the target, Heaney's tone is usually barbed. Here Eliot is "the Yankee *raznochinet* . . . mutating into the English vestryman" (1980b, 14). Dante is his oracle of the Catholic mind of Europe and an apotheosis of its central tradition, who speaks the universal language that all poets should echo. Incensed by Eliot's claims for a central hegemony, Heaney speaks for

162	SEAMUS HEANEY

marginal traditions "cut off by historical disintegration and sealed in the dialects of their tribes" (1980b, 14) and marshals Eliot's diction against him. Heaney seeks to redress Eliot's hierarchical view. "It is curious that this born-again Anglican and monarchist did not make more of the political Dante, the dreamer of a world obedient to the spiritual authority of a cleansed papacy and under the sway of a just emperor, where, without bitterness or corruption, Christ and Caesar would be hand in glove" (1980b, 14). The essay, "Envies and Identifications: Dante and the Modern Poet," published after *Station Island*, repeats this passage in an expanded attack on Eliot and his way of recreating Dante. When Eliot "makes Dante's confident and classically ratified language bear an almost allegorical force" and when he invests it with "the illusion of absolute authority, of a purity beyond dialect and tribe," he "does less than justice to the untamed and thoroughly parochial elements it possesses" (1985, 12, 9, 12). Heaney offers Osip Mandelstam's view of Dante as a corrective example. For the Russian poet, instinct is the *Commedia*'s engendering force. Dante is less the scholarly expounder of Aquinas than the natural genius who, like a bee, is "endowed with the brilliant stereometric instinct" to fabricate a "thirteen-thousand-faceted form" (1985, 15).

Heaney praises Mandelstam for bringing Dante back "from the pantheon," where he had been installed by Eliot and Pound, "to the palate," where "he makes our mouth water to read him" (1980b, 16). Mandelstam's celebration of Dante, Heaney intriguingly suggests, was partly a result of his exile. Having renounced the poetry of social realism dictated by the state (and having suffered Stalin's wrath as a consequence), he now indulged in Dante's music rather than in his ideology. Exile offers Heaney a similar freedom from political and religious bonds. His identification with his two models is qualified by Dante's having been driven from a city torn by feuds—by ruling Guelf and rival Ghibelline, and by Guelf factions of Black and White (which Heaney might be alluding to at the beginning of section 8, "Black water. White waves")—and Mandelstam's having been driven toward mental and physical breakdown during his interrogations and two exiles. He is not sentenced to death if he returns to Belfast, as Dante was if he returned to Florence, or sentenced to years of hard labor, as Mandelstam was. He is an "inner émigré" but a self-determined one. The distance afforded by this 'exile,' however, allows him to scrutinize literary personalities and political enemies engaged in history "from a perspective beyond history" (1980b, 18), and this, according to his essay, is what he finds most exemplary in the *Commedia*.

Numerous reviewers pointed out that Joyce, another self-imposed exile, acts the role of Virgil to Heaney's Dante. By the end of "Station

Island" Heaney is not sure who is guiding whom, or whether he wants to take the rather cold, skeletal hand of Joyce in the first place.

> I stepped on ground
>
>> to find the helping hand still gripping mine,
>> fish-cold and bony, but whether to guide
>> or to be guided I could not be certain
>
>> for the tall man in step at my side
>> seemed blind, though he walked straight as a rush
>> upon his ash plant.

Joyce's literary direction was always toward greater verbal intricacy, greater abstraction from the vernacular. Heaney's is the reverse. His religious journey, like Eliot's, has simplified rather than complicated his diction. Although "Station Island" resembles the dream-collage of *Finnegans Wake*, it has none of the other book's deliberate complexity. Joyce was cool to the artist's social, religious, and political commitments; Heaney is warm. He threatens to guide Joyce to a more sensible position while, at the same time, Joyce tries to guide him away from the senseless, archaic rituals performed at Lough Derg. "Silence, exile and cunning" for Heaney are tactics to be confessed rather than ecstatically embraced. The appeal of Heaney's 'confessional' poems comes from the willingness to bow down over old haunts and speak with humility and candor for the troubled conscience. Joyce celebrates his willful detachment from church and country; Heaney makes the artist's ambivalent attachment to them the crux of his work.

Heaney is ambivalent toward his precursors, and also toward the very idea of pilgrimage. In a sense he goes on pilgrimage to purge the guilt aroused by participating in such ceremonies as pilgrimages. His poetry, he decides, is a ritual similar to the one commemorating St. Patrick's original penitential vigil of fasting and praying on Loch Derg because it recollects sacrificial passions in a symbolic way. Heaney worries, as he does in "Punishment," that his circumspect involvement with 'sacrificial acts' is an evasion, a cop-out, that in transforming political and religious 'sacrifices' into artifice he drains them of their original blood. How to speak of unspeakable suffering and how to bear witness to atrocious facts in fictions designed to appeal is a problem he has addressed before. Seamus Deane, in the concluding chapter of *Celtic Revivals*, goes so far as to say that Heaney, along with Thomas Kinsella, John Montague, and Derek Mahon, are "changing our conceptions of what writing can be" by emphasizing its "confrontation with the ineffable, the unspeakable thing for which 'violence' is our helplessly inadequate word" (1985a, 186). In "Station Island" Heaney speaks through the mouths of antagonists. His method is excruciatingly self-reflexive. He uses words to scrutinize the duplicity of words and like Plato accuses poetry of mendacity. Poetry pretends to re-member a dismembered past, re-presenting what is absent, and Heaney reminds us that its pretence can be deceptive and callous. As he turns on himself, he also turns his failings into a partial success. His metaphor of the poet circling on the sharp rocks of St. Patrick's Purgatory aptly embodies his agonizing conundrums.

How to dramatize the artist's painful self-consciousness has preoccupied Heaney from the start. His earliest poems depict falls into poetic consciousness as departures from an edenic farm that precipitated frightening descents into supernatural realms of nearby bogeys and bog spirits. His essay "Mossbawn" describes the outer limits of his childhood farm as a zone of menace but also a place where the poetic imagination, having abandoned its natural constraints, could wander. "We'd heard about a mystery man who haunted the fringes of the bog here, we talked about mankeepers and moss-cheepers, creatures uncatalogued by any naturalist, but none the less real for that" (1980a, 18). These spirits were figments of an early 'supernatural' imagination haunted by fear and guilt. In the first section of "Station Island," the mystery man reappears as Simon Sweeney, who rhymes with Heaney in more ways than sound. He is an image of abandonment, like the bogeys of the bog, who instills fear in the growing boy. He declares, "I was your mystery man / and am again this morning." Remembering how the man frightened him (like the slime kings invading the flax dam or the rats behind the hen coop), Heaney is once again provoked into redemptive flight, a pilgrim "light-headed, leaving home / to face into my station."

Heaney's dream encounters are highly personal, yet he strives to make them archetypal. His protagonists and antagonists attain more general status when Heaney aligns them with mythical figures of the past. Simon Sweeney, for instance, is a Sabbath-breaking tinker who recalls the iconoclastic hero of *Sweeney Astray.* At the start of "Station Island," he is the actual man Heaney used to meet on his way to school as a child. His command, "Stay clear of all processions," fails to keep Heaney from the "quick bell-notes" of the church. Ironically, it frightens him and sends him more quickly on his way.

For the poet, Sweeney is a guardian of the dark wood, an accuser who threatens to trap the potential pilgrim and prevent his journey toward redemption. He resembles Eliot's "Sweeney Among the Nightingales" as he "guards the horned gate" (Eliot 1969, 56), although he has little of the other's sexual boorishness. He is what Joseph Campbell, in his discussion of the heroic journey, calls the "threshold guardian" (1949, 77), and for

Heaney he personifies the sort of doubts and fears that Dante scored into the opening scene of *The Divine Comedy.* He quotes the famous beginning, as translated by C. H. Sisson, in his review "Treely and Rurally."

> Half way along the road we have to go,
> I found myself obscured in a great forest,
> Bewildered, and I knew I had lost my way.
>
> It is hard to say just what the forest was like,
> How wild and rough it was, how overpowering;
> Even to remember it makes me afraid. (1980b, 14)

Heaney aims for a quicker pace in lines that transpose Dante's dark wood to his own backyard.

> It left you half afraid.
>
> When they bade you listen
> in the bedroom dark
> to wind and rain in the trees
> and think of tinkers camped
> under a heeled-up cart
>
> you shut your eyes.

Dante passes through the dark wood and, like Campbell's archetypal hero, "ventures forth from the world of common day into a region of supernatural wonder: fabulous forces are there encountered and a decisive victory is won: [so that] the hero comes back from this mysterious adventure with the power to bestow boons on his fellow man" (Campbell 1949, 30). This is the "nuclear unit of the monomyth," Campbell asserts, borrowing his last term from James Joyce. Writing about Dante, Heaney echoes Campbell's words in his description of *The Divine Comedy.* "However the drama is deepened by individual encounters, its greatness has to do with an overall sense of having come through. Allegorical, theological, political, personal, encyclopedic, all these it is, but its big shape is the archetypal one—of faring forth into the ordeal, going to a nadir and returning to a world that is renewed by the boon won in that other place" (1980b, 14). "Station Island" situates this mythical design of separation, initiation, and return firmly on Irish ground.

Summoning Dante as his model, Heaney dramatizes his own sense of 'coming through' as a poet. Of his departure from Belfast for Wicklow, where he put "the notion of being a writer at the centre of the lived, day-to-day life," he reveals, "That was coming through some sort of barrier for me. I think that I consecrated myself at that point" (Haffenden 1981, 65). The first section of "Station Island" refers obliquely to myths of the golden bough to enshrine Heaney's personal sense of breaking away from the past. Virgil's Aeneas must break the golden bough in the oak grove before descending into the underworld to encounter familiar ghosts; Heaney's alter ego, Sweeney, breaks boughs with his saw in order to initiate a similar journey. A distant relative of the old King of the Wood at Nemi—the focus of James Frazer's encyclopedic study, *The Golden Bough*—Sweeney must be surpassed before the new king can be consecrated. Despite the fact that Heaney's boughs are yellow rather than gold, and his consecration poetic rather than priestly or political, they possess some of the aura of their mythic forbears.

> When cut or broken limbs
> of trees went yellow, when
>
> woodsmoke sharpened air
> or ditches rustled
> you sensed my trail there
> as if it had been sprayed.
> It left you half afraid.

Frazer explains, "Within the sanctuary of Nemi grew a certain tree of which no branch might be broken. Only a runaway slave was allowed to break off, if he could, one of its boughs. Success in the attempt entitled him to fight the priest in single combat, and if he slew him he reigned in his stead with the title of King of the Wood. . . . According to the public opinion of the ancients the fateful branch was the Golden Bough which, at the Sibyl's bidding, Aeneas plucked before he essayed the perilous journey to the world of the dead" (1922, 36). Although Sweeney does not brandish a sword against intruders, the trail to the grove is sprayed, as if by a skunk, and the odor seems just as potent and off-putting.

Sweeney *is* Heaney, or at least one of his patriarchal personae. He embodies his iconoclastic, nonliterary heritage that attacks poetic pilgrimages as superfluous. The "pursuit of the verbal icon" and the act of writing in general has always aroused suspicion in Heaney. Seamus Deane put it succinctly in his *Irish Literary Supplement* review of *Station Island*, "Seamus Heaney gets better and better as time goes on and guiltier and guiltier about being so." For Heaney, he explains, writing is embroiled in multiple betrayals: of "experience by becoming a substitute for it," of "privacy by bringing it out into language," and of "political commitment by using up its passion without pursuing its goals" (1985b, 1). Committing words to paper is also a betrayal or violation of familial ghosts, of ancestors who could not do the same. Heaney confesses, "There is indeed some part of me that is entirely unimpressed by the activity [of poetry], that doesn't dislike it, but it's the generations, I suppose, of rural ancestors—not illiterate, but not literary. They, in me, or I, through them, don't give a damn" (Haffenden 1981, 63). Sweeney is the apotheosis of Heaney's rural ancestors who oppose the pursuit of icons, verbal or religious. He poses a threat, but his instinctual power when properly tapped promises an advantage. As he does with so many of the laborers in his poems, Heaney seeks to establish common ground. He yearns for rapprochement with his ancestors and finds it in their mutual commitment to *poesis*, to skilled artisanship, whether in farming or rhyming. In fact Sweeney's "bowsaw, held / stiffly up like a lyre," is a lyrical instrument, like the many penlike spades and versing and reversing ploughs that Heaney so frequently extols. A religious and literary iconoclast, Sweeney cuts down the old icons, the old gods inhabiting the wood, just like Heaney—to let new shoots burgeon from the old stalk.

Having overcome his fear of the dark wood and his agonizing doubts about his vocation as a writer, Heaney plunges forward, a little like Piers Plowman at the beginning of his visionary pilgrimage when he espies a "fair field full of folk." He seems partly drawn by friendly corn spirits ("a crowd of shawled women / .... wading the young corn") into a field "full / of half-remembered faces, / a loosed congregation / that struggled past and on." Vestiges of vegetation rituals ceremonialize his inspired beginning. Robert Graves, whose *White Goddess* informs many of Heaney's renditions of tree myths and fertility rituals, would interpret this first section as a rite of passage from a patriarchal to a matriarchal sensibility, and a return to Catholicism's ancient roots. Near the beginning of his "historical grammar of poetic myth," Graves articulates a position Heaney has restated numerous times. "The popular appeal of modern Catholicism, is, despite the patriarchal Trinity and the all-male priesthood, based rather on the Aegean Mother-and-son religious tradition, to which it has slowly reverted" (1948, 61). The cutting of the bough initiates Heaney's renunciation of the father, and to a certain extent of his own masculinity, as he turns toward the mythic women. Graves explains that "the cutting of the mistletoe from the oak by the Druids typified the emasculation of the old king by his successor—the mistletoe being a prime phallic emblem," and that this castration recalls the "myth of the emasculation of Uranus by his son Cronus," which also recorded "the annual supplanting of the old oak-king" (65). Heaney sym-

bolically cuts down and supplants the patriarchal Sweeney who resides within
his own psyche because Sweeney threatens his devotion to the "shawled
women" in the field—the leaders of the pilgrimage. Taken together, they
constitute his Catholic muse, his sublimated Mother, a sybilline figure who
will direct him toward the ghostly underworld just as the Sybil at Cumae
directed Aeneas and, in similar fashion, Aeneas directed Dante. The symbolic castration, the repression of libido that precedes sublimation and that
will eventually substitute pen for penis, propels Heaney simultaneously into
language, tradition, and the unconscious. Heaney's therapeutic journey will
entail incorporating literary ghosts in the unconscious and writing his way
beyond them.

Heaney's first challenge comes when he encounters the ghost of William Carleton, whose experience at Lough Derg fueled his disenchantment
with Catholicism and his later conversion to Protestantism. Carleton's "The
Lough Derg Pilgrim," the first article he ever published, bristles with invective against all forms of pious devotion. He recalls the "superstitious absurdity" (Carleton 1881, 69) of trying to walk on water in a marl pit in
preparation for the same feat at Lough Derg. "It was really the first exercise
of that jealous spirit of mistaken devotion, which keeps the soul in perpetual
sickness, and invests the *innocent* enjoyments of life with a character of sin
and severity" (69). Although surprised by the endurance of the elderly
pilgrims, Carleton never deviates from his contention that the pilgrimage is
a "great and destructive superstition" (85). After one of the stations, he
declares, "There is not on earth, with the exception of the pagan rites . . . a
regulation of a religious nature, more barbarous and inhuman than this"
(85). He pulls no punches. "We know that nothing acts so strongly and so
fatally upon reason, as an imagination diseased by religious terrors" (85).

A chastising presence, Carleton insinuates himself into Heaney's affections. Heaney identifies with him and presents him as if he were his double.
He emphasizes similarities in their backgrounds: both grew up near "the
reek of flax," witnessed victims of Protestant and Catholic feuds, and as
adults fell into religious and political ambivalence. Still, differences remain.
Carleton repudiates the Ribbonmen, the Catholic peasants who became
secret vigilantes terrorizing unjust landlords and land-grabbing compatriots,
and denounces their Protestant counterparts, the "Orange bigots." Heaney
expresses fondness for the Mariolatry of contemporary Ribbonmen and
dreams of a state purified of feuds. Carleton's examples of purity and transcendence have all the thrust of a dagger's riposte. Of poetry's power to
redeem decadence by standing up to it and naming it for what it is, Carleton
hypothesizes, "All this is like a trout kept in a spring" to keep it free of bugs
and algae, or "maggots sown in wounds" to eat away infected flesh. This is

how "another life . . . cleans our element." This idea may seem blasphemous
coming from a pilgrim on his way to Station Island. Undaunted, Heaney
envisions this gruesome cleansing as he does Sweeney's earlier breaking of
the phallic boughs, as the physical act at the root of the mythical ritual. It is
the natural process of purgatory before it gets dressed up in symbolic garb.

Speaking for Carleton, Heaney again speaks for himself. He employs
other voices as well, so that echoes ricochet from past to present and back
again, conflicting and blending. In the next section Heaney's vestigial Catholic
self enunciates old decorums while performing a station in the island's
chapel. Earlier he describes the pilgrimage as a "drugged path," echoing
Marx's famous denunciation of religion as an opiate and Freud's as a consoling illusion. Now Heaney describes the pilgrimage as "habit's afterlife,"
the dead, perfunctory ritual of the church that can still offer vivid and
invigorating epiphanies. In the chapel's meditative hush Heaney has a vision
of "a seaside trinket," which, like Proust's madeleine or Robert Lowell's
china doorknob, stimulates childhood memories and uncanny poetic associations. Heaney remembers a mysterious "child invalid," who in fact was
his father's sister, Agnes Heaney, who died of tuberculosis in the 1920s. The
trinket, which acts as a metonymy in a long chain of associations, as he
explains in "Place, Pastness, Poems: A Triptych," "had obviously been bought
at the seaside as a present for her. A little grotto about four or five inches
tall, like a toy sentry box, all covered with tiny shells, a whitish gleaming
secret deposited in the family sideboard like grave-goods in the tomb of a
princess. To this day, I cannot imagine the ravages of disease in pre-inocula-
tion rural Ireland except in relation to the slight white fact of that trinket"
(1985–86, 34). Agnes resembles Petrarch's Laura and Dante's Beatrice and
for Heaney recalls the Catholic rites performed on her behalf. Shucking his
role as the grim naturalist, now he speaks for the religious 'supernaturalist'
entranced by mystic moments. Images of emptiness and absence recur and,
like Eliot's contemplative silences in *The Waste Land* and *Four Quartets*,
anticipate moments of fulfillment. He says,

> I thought of walking round
> and round a space utterly empty,
> utterly a source, like the idea of sound;
>
> like an absence stationed in the swamp-fed air.

Heaney focuses on the spirit of the young girl, an apotheosis of youthful
innocence preserved by early death. She becomes a metaphor for the goddess who guides his purgatorial journey upward. Transcendence, however, is

a temptation to be temperately resisted. Meditating on divine emptyings and ultimate sources, Heaney sobers himself with all-too-present smells of mortality. He matches his thoughts of gods with thoughts of dogs, as Joyce liked to do, comparing the girl's corpse irreverently in the last line to "the bad carcass and scrags of hair / of our dog that had disappeared weeks before."

His next portrait also joins spiritual devotion with bodily putrefaction. About to declare "I renounce" at one of the stations, he meets the ghost of a priest (Terry Keenan) who renounced the bourgeois religiosity of his homeland only to rot "like a pear" among "bare-breasted / women and rat-ribbed men" in a foreign jungle. The sacrificial renunciation of the martyr, Heaney's former friend intimates, is pointless and dangerous, impelled by blind faith rather than mature judgment. Having renounced the world in life, in death the disillusioned priest renounces the spirit in order to return to earth. He explains to Heaney in accents of Wallace Stevens that the religion he "thought was chosen was convention"; "god has . . . withdrawn." Stevens's "Asides on the Oboe" affirmed "that final belief / Must be in a fiction" and "it is time to choose" (Stevens 1972, 187). Heaney's priest abjures religious fictions, having been deceived by them once too often, and searches for hard facts. Why Heaney is "going through the . . . motions" of the pilgrimage baffles him. Heaney is not as deceived as he appears. He can believe in fictions and facts too. Devoted to conventions, he also complies with a poetic tradition that scrupulously and skeptically dissects those conventions. The priest, limited by his either/or philosophy, wonders if Heaney is "here taking the last look" at the ritual of a dying faith. For the poet the gods never die; they simply return in different linguistic guise.

Linguistic exercises are on Heaney's mind in the fifth section when he calls up the ghost of Master Murphy, who drilled him in Latin as a boy at the Anahorish School. Old artificers, old "fosterers" appear, mainly to remind Heaney of the deliquescence of their old institutions. Anahorish School has declined into ruins. Still, the past persists. Patrick Kavanagh surfaces to remind Heaney he is repeating religious and poetic exercises he completed forty-two years before. His own *Lough Derg* predicts Heaney's concerns with religious fictions, although Heaney usually avoids his satirical bitterness. Kavanagh suggests that an artist-god designed the pilgrimage as a lie to trap naïve believers while pretending to console them, and that "they come to Lough Derg to fast and pray and beg / With all the bitterness of nonentities, and the envy / Of the inarticulate when dealing with the artist" (quoted in Kennelly 1970, 344). At the end of the third section he compares the "routine and ritual" enacted at Station Island to "a novel [that] refuses nothing," in which "no truth oppresses" the characters (345). The illusion of "a marvellous beauty" in heaven, the poet states sardonically, "leads / These petty mean people" on (345). "Convention" is a deceptive, entangling forest "where Adam wanders deranged with half a memory" (349). Tentative relief comes to those few who recognize the pilgrimage for what it is. The poem ends, "And three sad people had found the key to the lock / Of God's delight in disillusionment" (362). God remains, in Kavanagh's view, either to take sadistic pleasure from the pilgrims' loss of faith, or to share the irreverent joy of those who no longer believe in Him or His fictitious rituals.

Absorbing Kavanagh's satirical jabs, the latter-day pilgrim Heaney re-frains from a pugilistic confrontation. He lets his precursor speak and moves on, imitating Kavanagh's litany of sonnets in sections 6 and 9, but not without transforming them. He partially agrees with Kavanagh's remark, "In my own day / the odd one came here on the hunt for women." He shows that women lead him on too, in the form of mythic personages. In section 6 he makes his childhood game of "secrets" with a young girl mythic by comparing it to prehistoric and pagan adventures. The girl who visits him in his dream is catholic in the sense of being universal; she is a vegetation goddess in modern dress (Heaney calls her "pod of the broom, / Catkin-pixie, little fern-swish"). She is also a young playmate, the legendary garrulous wife of ass-eared Midas, and embodies characteristics of the Virgin Mary as well as the poet's wife (whose name is Marie). Having abandoned the young man's voyeuristic gaping through keyholes and vain attempts to purge sexual love altogether in confessionals, Heaney glimpses the good life of healthy sexuality. He compares his newfound happiness to Horace's contentment on his Sabine farm and Dante's renewed inspiration in the *Inferno* after visits by Lucy and Beatrice. When his wife modulates into Demeter, the "wheatlands of her back" prompt the poet to Eleusinian devotion. He ends his eulogy with an apt translation of a few lines from the second Canto of *The Divine Comedy*, where Dante compares himself to flowers rejuvenated by Lucy's radiance.

It may seem odd for Heaney to indulge in visions of pastoral farms and fulfilling sexuality while traversing the *via negativa* of the Lough Derg pilgrimage. *In extremis*, he considers Horace, for whom extremes were anathema. On the island's grueling rocks he savors Horace's Ode (Book 3, Ode 21) that praises the resuscitating virtues of a jar of Massic wine. Heaney contradicts himself, and he does so to reveal the validity of contradictions. His earnest asceticism engenders an equal and opposite hedonism, just as his figurative castrations and maternal devotions lead healthily to an oedipal resolution in which he becomes a father capable of libidinal and linguistic fulfillment. Like "Chekhov on Sakhalin," the title of an early poem in *Station Island*, who "drank cognac by the ocean / With his back to all he travelled north to face" (i.e., a penal colony), Heaney enjoys moments of sensuous ecstasy in the midst of, and because of, his ordeals of deprivation. As he vacillates between emptiness and plenitude, absence and presence, he mortifies the flesh not to abandon it but to condition its sensitivity for future pleasures.

Such lyrical interludes, however, are fleeting and, like the Massic wine, a long way from Station Island and the political turbulence that surrounds it. After translating the passage from Dante, Heaney follows his tutelary shade toward ghosts of a specifically Irish inferno. The first to accost him is a friend with whom he played football, William Strathern, who was murdered by two policemen. The second ghost to speak is an archaeologist (Tom Delaney), a friend and fellow digger "dead at thirty two," who leads Heaney deeper into the "muck of bigotry under the walls / picking through shards and Williamite cannon balls." As Heaney approaches the nadir of his journey, a second cousin (Colum McCartney), murdered by Protestants, materializes and delivers the harshest attack so far. His nightmare vision, bewildered by invective from both sides, accepts culpability for his "timid circumspect involvement" in Northern Ireland's affairs, for his unintentionally condoning rather than actively deterring atrocities.

For Heaney the age-old debate between isolationism and interventionism is an intensely private one. It is all the more painful because he fails to decide on a consistent policy. His pilgrimage, at the end, turns into a penitential exercise to purge the anxiety of tergiversation. Heaney's ninth section traces his descent to a ninth circle of tenebrous gloom where he confesses his "blanching self-disgust." An ascent follows and, as in the ritual of Tenebrae commemorating Christ's resurrection from the harrowing of hell, Heaney follows a candle out of darkness toward the resurrected light of day. He turns from old ways, even while affirming their inevitable continuity. Like a stone whirled by a cascade, he cannot grind himself "down to a different core," even though he desperately wants to. "The tribe whose dances never fail / For they keep dancing till they sight the deer" reminds him that his perceptions of salvation may be illusions bred out of exhaustion, like the visions of the other fasting, sleepless pilgrims on Station Island. He suggests that only those who, in Rimbaud's words, engage in a systematic deregulation of all their senses finally believe in *la vita nuova*. In a characteristic turn, Heaney submits his laborious progress to withering psychological and anthropological scrutiny, and concludes that he has circled back to the same old divided ground.

His next progression, however, records real gains. Heaney, who has described himself halfheartedly as "Jungian in religion," ends his descent into the underworld with a classical Jungian revelation. According to Jung, after encountering archetypal mothers and fathers on the journey of 'individuation,' the mythical hero plunges into 'the shadow,' the 'collective unconscious,' and on ascending envisions an emblem of wholeness, a mandala. For Heaney the mandala is a mundane cup "patterned with cornflowers," its design suggesting the resurgent energies of his purged imagination. In his tale of ablution and absolution (he compares the cup to "Ronan's psalter / miraculously unharmed, that had been lost / a day and a night under lough water"), the cup comes to represent his own sense of fulfillment. Having completed the perilous journey, he receives the boon (the holy grail demystified) and the power to dispense fructifying waters and words to his audience.

As his poem and pilgrimage wind toward an end, Heaney stresses again his religious sense of poetry and his poetic sense of religion. He reminds us that "the root of the word in *religare* [is] to bind" (1980a, 133), and here, when a monk tells him to "read poems as prayers," he translates a poem by Juan de la Cruz ("Song of the Soul that Rejoices in Knowing God through Faith") that dramatizes the bond between questor and his source of spiritual inspiration. St. John's "eternal fountain" is one of many forms water takes in the poem and has sacred as well as profane implications. The fountain is both poetic and Christian *spiritus*, both origin and destination, like Frost's spring at the end of "Directive." "The eternal fountain hides and splashes / within this living bread that is life to us / although it is the night." The dark night of meditative withdrawal, the soul's *via negativa*, precedes the soul's communion with the divine spirit, just as Heaney's withdrawal to Station Island preceded his ghostly communications with writers and friends.

The last section of "Station Island" offers another night journeyer whose darkness is physiological rather than religious. Heaney pays homage to Dante here with a virtuoso display of *terza rima* in which the familiar ghost is Joyce. Blind Joyce, like blind Tiresias for Eliot, is the prophetic master, the final guide out of the waste land. He bestows boons in the form of advice regarding the artist's vocation and badgers Heaney about his fastidious devotions. "And don't be so earnest," he commands. "Let others wear the sackcloth and the ashes." He wants Heaney to think of art as a rigorous game played for erotic prizes rather than as a vendetta against English precursors or a dizzying exercise in martyrdom. "His voice eddying with the vowels of all rivers" recalls Anna Livia Plurabelle's discursive "riverrun" at the end of *Finnegans Wake*. He instructs Heaney "to swim / out on your own and fill the element / with signatures." After spells of self-loathing and spiritual dryness ("my brain dried like spread turf"), Heaney encounters an abundance of water in the form of rivers, sea, and rain that suggests a new determination to rejuvenate the land wasted by strife.

The central conflict in *Station Island* between the artist's devotion to his craft and the political demands of his conscience struggles toward resolution in the final watery inundation. Content to remain in the safe confines of his home where he can mull over poems, at the same time Heaney feels torn away by obligations to the community. His temperamental disaffection with "the angry role" does not preclude a militant desire to right the wrongs around him. Reflecting on *Station Island* in his essay on Dante, he reveals, "The main tension is between two often contradictory commands: to be faithful to the collective historical experience and to be true to the recognitions of the emerging self" (1985, 19). Another Hamlet (a character he identifies with in "Viking Dublin: Trial Pieces"), he is wracked by indecision. Should he take arms against his sea of Irish troubles and by opposing end them or is it nobler to suffer his nation's misfortunes and simply write them out in verse? In the end he chooses the path of suffering and writing, redressing the Troubles by addressing them in dramatic lyrics.

Poetry may make nothing happen and only persist in the isolated valley of its making, as Valéry and Auden suggested. Nevertheless, Heaney attacks the notion of the poet as otherwordly recluse, as shunner of the tribe. His article "Current Unstated Assumptions About Poetry" praises Robert Lowell and Osip Mandelstam for heroically standing up to the political terrors of their time, suffering for their beliefs, and remaining sacrificially devoted to their poetic vocations. He ends with a eulogy to Mandelstam. "No poet was more literary, yet no poet was more aware of poetry's covenant with life. That covenant was sealed by a reverence for the word as the ratifying bond between the poet and 'the reader in posterity' " (1981, 650). Skeptical of religious rituals commemorating God's Word, Heaney celebrates poetic rituals committed to poetic words. Written communication, which binds together past, present, and future, becomes his substitute communion. Deeply preoccupied with private matters, Heaney's final direction is always toward the community, and to the painful issues that sunder it. A Lough Derg pilgrim pushed and pulled by contradictory impulses, he returns to the troubled land he started from to tackle its problems with pen rather than sword.

10

DECONSTRUCTIONS

CRITICS WHO EXPECTED from Seamus Heaney a rhetoric as consistently dense and pungent as his peat bogs and potato drills were startled by the lighter feel of *The Haw Lantern*. J. D. McClatchy predicted in *The New Republic* that Heaney's audience would "find *The Haw Lantern* something of a disappointment." Earlier volumes had been written with pyrotechnic flare, he observed, the latest "with damp powder" (1987, 38). Focusing on Heaney's elegiac sonnet sequence to his mother and its "reluctance to reach for anything that might be thought of as poetic grandeur," Ian Hamilton complained that " 'silence' and 'emptiness' are what these sonnets register, and one senses that silence and emptiness are at the emotional centre of this book. Weariness, also" (1987, 11). A vacuum, according to Hamilton, had replaced the abundant sensuality and music of earlier volumes. Helen Vendler, one of Heaney's staunchest supporters, also voiced uncertainties about his new stylistic *askesis*. "As the earth loses for him the mass and gravity of familiar presences—parents and friends taken by death—desiccation and weightlessness threaten the former fullness of the sensual life" (1988, 41). For Herbert Lomas, writing in the *London Magazine*, this threat had already taken its toll and the result was a poetry full of dead abstractions and empty verbiage. "Stodge, if not actually on stage, is certainly hovering in the wings" (1987, 94). As a cure he prescribed a dose of "Yeats's wildness and wickedness," as if the old poet's earthiness could revive Heaney's moribund naturalism.

Oddly enough, Yeats's example informs much of *The Haw Lantern*, in a way unaccounted for by Lomas and others. As Heaney surely knows, Yeats's bodily fervor in old age was impelled by and toward an equally fervid asceticism. Contemplative hermit and raving sensualist jockeyed for command and ultimately were masks Yeats donned in his dialectic pursuit of the truth. Loath to stand still on apex or base of his interpenetrating gyres, he

175

rode antithetically between them, declaring that vacillation *was* the truth. Yeats's later poetry embraced bodily energy usually for an ascetic, philosophical end. Yeats-the-wildman, like Heaney in the role of Sweeney or Diogenes the Cynic (who wanted to live like an animal), proposed to demolish his masterful images, allegorical dreams, and painted stages in order to reveal the "rag and bone shop" ("The Circus Animals' Desertion," Yeats 1983, 348) beneath them. A letter written by Yeats in 1914 outlined this paradoxical quest. "The poet seeks truth, not abstract truth, but a kind of vision of reality which satisfies the whole being. It will not be true for one thing unless it satisfies his desires, his most profound desires. . . . I think the poet reveals the truth by revealing those desires" (1955, 586). The relationship between reality and vision inspired some of Yeats's most powerful meditations and culminated in the elaborate system of rotating gyres and lunar phases—those "stylistic arrangements of experience"—that helped him "to hold in a single thought reality and justice" in *A Vision* (1937, 25). *The Haw Lantern* yearns just as passionately for a vision of reality and justice but chooses to delineate it through allegories that seem simple beside Heaney's countryman's boggling array of symbols and systems.

The impassioned silences and emptinesses that haunt Heaney's new book also resemble the wintry, analytical atmospheres of Wallace Stevens, a poet he was rereading at the time. Heaney also cuts through fictive obfuscations with a "mind of winter" to "return / To a plain sense of things" (Stevens 1972, 54, 82). For these wintry meditators, mystic illumination demands a purgatorial emptying or clearing. Heaney sketches this psychological state emblematically in his title poem.

> The wintry haw is burning out of season,
> crab of the thorn, a small light for small people,
> wanting no more from them but that they keep
> the wick of self-respect from dying out,
> not having to blind them with illumination.

The red berry of the hawthorn is Heaney's symbol for the mind's tough, enduring clarity and integrity. It represents a principle of revelation and judgment that he and his nation must strive to uphold even when menaced from all sides. Yeats called for a fullblown pagan or biblical apocalypse—heaven blinding and blazing into the heads of the tragic Irish, judging them for their sins, and impregnating them with a new heroic energy; Heaney's apocalypse is more subdued, more like Stevens's chilly auroras of autumn. His luminous berry resembles Christ more than Zeus or Jehovah. It stands for Yeats's "unity of being" (pith bonded to stone), though it possesses little of the other poet's judgmental rapacity (as in "Leda and the Swan" or "Under Ben Bulben"). It is more victim than victimizer; it judges more by example than by violent annunciation. Heaney declares, "You flinch before its bonded pith and stone, / its blood-prick that you wish would test and clear you, / its pecked-at ripeness that scans you, then moves on." Cooling Yeats's apocalyptic heat and his penchant for bellicose slogans like "Send war in our time, O Lord" ("Under Ben Bulben," Yeats 1983, 326), Heaney bears witness to a vision of reality and justice that is always on the verge of collapse. His affirmation is all the more moving because it is made in the teeth of obliteration.

As Heaney's recent collection of essays, *The Government of the Tongue*, attests, other poets than Yeats and Stevens helped formulate his new philosophical style. Among them, the Polish writer Zbigniew Herbert was crucial in demonstrating how, through lucid, pared-down parables and myths, Heaney could achieve a mode as simple as it was profound. Herbert's poetry, Heaney argues, is Socratic in its search for self-knowledge. "In the exactions of its logic, the temperance of its tone, and the extremity of its recognitions, it . . . resemble[s] what a twentieth-century poetic version of the examined life might be" (1988a, 54). Greek philosopher and Polish poet "expose the shape of things" (54) behind the painfully bewildering flux. The later poetry of Patrick Kavanagh is similarly revealing and influential. Heaney could be mapping his own stylistic evolution when he says, "The early Kavanagh poem . . . is supplied with a strong physical presence and is full of the recognitions which existed between the poet and his place; it is symbolic of affections rooted in a community life and has behind it an imagination which is not yet weaned from its origin, an attached rather than a detached faculty" (4). Throughout the later work, "the world is more pervious to his vision than he is pervious to the world. When he writes about places now, they are luminous spaces within his mind. They have been evacuated of their status as background, as documentary geography, and exist instead as transfigured images, sites where the mind projects its own force" (5). Likewise, Heaney's later landscapes become more overtly psychological than geographical, more *paysage moralisé* than simply *paysage*.

His quest for luminous moments also draws supportive examples from Philip Larkin. Like Larkin, he struggles to overcome an early predilection for unguarded romanticism. He obviously sympathizes with Larkin's transcendent moments that use their heightened perspectives to double back on transcendentalism and the abstractions it fosters. If both fly off like Shelley's skylark, they also plummet into the world's ludicrous events and terrible beauties. Heaney says, "We respond constantly to the melody of intelligence, to a verse that is as much commentary as it is presentation," and to

Larkin's "compassionate, unfoolable mind" (1988a, 15) that candidly dissects our predicaments. Romanticism's glassy-eyed notions of nature, eros, and self in Larkin's poetry are dispelled by a countervailing "need to imagine 'such attics cleared of me, such absences' " (22). The modern poet, Heaney would argue with Larkin, must abandon the egotistical sublime and tradition's attic of derelict symbols in order to see "things as they are."

Unlike the xenophobic Larkin, however, Heaney's search for fellow iconoclasts is international in scope. He finds another ally in the Czech poet and scientist Miroslav Holub, who almost literally applies "the knife of intellect" to romanticism's enticing corpse. "Poetry in English has not moved all that far from the shelter of the Romantic tradition," Heaney claims (1988a, 45), but Holub shows one way of avoiding it. His cool, surgical verse mocks the belated romantic "dandies who pirouette to a narcotic music." It cuts through romantic obsessions with "inwardness, yearnings and mergings of the self towards nature" (45) and exposes them as infantile. Holub is yet another tutelary guide who helps Heaney shed the continually seductive romanticism of his youth for a more candid style.

Heaney is most revealing about his ambivalent transition from a poetry governed by romantic principles of passion and spontaneity to a more classical mode governed by intellect and design in his essay "Sounding Auden." Too much intelligence can be a bad thing, he argues, and while criticizing the late Auden he could be posting warning signs for himself. "The price of an art that is so faithfully wedded to disenchantment and disintoxication, that seeks that heraldic shape beneath the rippling skin, that is impelled not only to lay down the law but to keep a civil tongue, the price of all this is a certain diminution of the language's autonomy, a not uncensorious training of its wilder shoots" (1988a, 126). The government of the tongue, Heaney explains, can be a private or public censoring of linguistic freedom: the intellect's repression of the poet's lyric cry or the dictator's oppression of poetic expression in general. The most moving poetry is that which moves back and forth between formal design and the kind of emotional exclamation that disrupts design, between the governed and ungoverned. Speaking of similar antinomies and tensions, Helen Vendler astutely observes, "*The Haw Lantern,* posed between these contradictory imperatives of adult life, is almost penitentially faithful to each, determined to forsake neither" (1988, 41). What is so startling about Heaney's recent poetry and criticism is his readiness to side with the intellect brooding in silence, as if only in the calm of a monk's cell, scientist's laboratory, or philosopher's carrel can the mind free itself from its romantic yearnings. What saves the poetry from dusty abstractions is its contradictory urge to break out of these enclosures and test its principles in reality.

Heaney has orchestrated a brilliant career around his uncanny ability to cross back and forth between different enclosures, whether they be Irish or English, British or American, Protestant or Catholic, Romantic or Classic. To what extent these different factions can be united peacefully and to what extent simply suspended in tense or bloody proximity is a problem Heaney returns to obsessively. Yoking binary oppositions in a text may be easy enough for a linguist or literary critic, but it is a different matter when the oppositions are wielding assault rifles and plastic explosives in the street. Although Heaney dramatizes the moral debate between artistic and political commitments, his resolutions are almost always provisional. His quests characteristically end in cul-de-sacs or, as he says in "North," "exhaustions nominated peace," which in turn generate new questions, new anxieties, new debates. He seems damned not only by Auden's contention (inspired by another meditation on Irish art and politics) that "poetry makes nothing happen," but also damned because he wants poetry to be politically compelling.

Northern Ireland's perennial Troubles simmer under the wintry sangfroid of *The Haw Lantern*. When Heaney paraphrased Yeats, "Poetry is out of the quarrel with ourselves and the quarrel with others is rhetoric" (1980a, 34), he did not quite admit that his poetic rhetoric issued from political *as well as* private quarrels. Like the deconstructionists with whom he is familiar (he refers to "deconstructionist tools [that] yield many excellent insights" [1988a, 120] in his Auden essay), Heaney focuses on hierarchical values institutionalized in his culture that, because of their violent consequences, cry out for reevaluation and reformation. Earlier poems expressed a similar awareness of the history of sexual and sectarian differences embedded, fossil-like, in language. In these allegories he subverted Britain's patriarchal powers so that the silenced, matriarchal voices of his heritage could speak. In *The Haw Lantern* Heaney again summons the British power brokers to the debating table, and, although the talk is perhaps more metaphysical in tone and subject than in previous volumes, the underlying political and linguistic issues are the same. Heaney's deconstructionist slant may seem novel, but other critics have detected it from the start. Blake Morrison, for example, set Heaney squarely in the postmodernist camp of such deconstructionist writers as Derrida and Barthes, arguing that Heaney's central preoccupation had always been the political impulses behind speech, writing, and silence. Surveying Heaney's early poems, Morrison concluded, "The cumulative effect of these poems is to suggest that as a young poet Seamus Heaney found himself in the position of valuing silence above speech, of defending the shy and awkward against the confident and accomplished, of feeling language to be a kind of betrayal" (1982, 23). Torn between rural outback and urban center, between a close-knit, semi-literate Irish Catholic agricultural community and the highly literate British-dominated culture of Queen's University in Belfast, Heaney tried to govern his tongue so he could thrive in both regions. To cross back and forth required the skill of a chameleon. His poems registered the perils of playing the camouflaged "double-agent," as he calls himself in *Stations*, as well as the kind of shuttle diplomacy needed to tear down old barricades and live peacefully with factions.

In a review of Richard Kearney's work in the *TLS* (which mentions Heaney several times), Terry Eagleton points out that for the Irish deconstruction comes with the territory. Its tenets were laid down *avant la lettre* by Joyce and Beckett. "That post-structuralism should strike a responsive resonance in a post-colonial society is really not at all that surprising: it is not irrelevant that the founder of deconstruction grew up as an Algerian colonial. . . . The fracturing of identity, the hankerings of desire, the clash of cultural codes, the collapse of triumphalist teleologies: all of these are motifs to which the experience of subcultures or the post-colonial peripheries is likely to prove more hospitable than the doctrinal assurances of the metropolitan centers" (1989, 132). Referring to deconstruction in a letter, Heaney comments, "It is impossible not to have inhaled the new awareness of writing as writing rather than 'communication,' and impossible not to recognize the useful truths underlined by those who point out the connivance between the promotion of art and the prevailing structures of capitalist society + the economy: i.e., the Marxist suspicion of pure aesthetic value is salutary, even tho' I resist the notion that the work of art is a sort of determined product" (letter to the author, 17 February 1989). Heaney's *Haw Lantern* is a miniature but probing grammatology that attacks 'logocentric' preferences for the spoken word that dominate Western metaphysics from Socrates to the present. As Derrida puts it, "Writing, the letter, the sensible inscription, has always been considered by western tradition as the body and matter external to the spirit, to breath, to speech, and to the logos" (1974, 35). In the dialectic approach to truth exemplified by Socrates in Plato's *Dialogues*, writing is dismissed as a re-presentation or approximation of the truth, an aid to memory that in fact encourages forgetfulness, an abolition of authorial presence. Socratic tradition (and of course there would be no Socratic tradition if Plato had never written!) proposes that writing is flawed with absences; speech is blessed with presences. Writing is an opaque encumbrance to meaning, something dead and unanswerable as a pottery shard; speech is the spirit of truth itself, the transparent medium through which the message flows, a living and breathing oracle that divine reason uses to communicate (His) eternal verities. The philosopher who *speaks* truth will be king of Plato's Republic; the poet who *writes* fictions and traffics in myths will be exiled from its sacred groves.

Plato records Socrates' linguistic biases in the *Phaedrus*. Socrates, we learn, favors a discourse untainted by myth and writing. Ironically he invokes the myth of the Egyptian god Theuth who argued that writing was a positive aid to memory only to conclude, "Anyone who leaves behind a written manual on the superstition that such writing will provide something reliable and permanent, must be exceedingly simple-minded" (Plato 1961, 521). Socrates, as it turns out, refuses to repudiate writing altogether. He asserts cryptically that "the sort [of writing] that goes together with knowledge, and is written in the soul of the learner," is close to the true *logos*, presumably because it is inscribed by the reasoning mind. When Phaedrus responds, "You mean no dead discourse, but the living speech, the original of which the written discourse may fairly be called a kind of image," Socrates replies, "Precisely" (521). Here speech is patently the primary or privileged vehicle of the gospel according to Socrates; writing is secondary, an adulterated transcription of the original *logos*. Precision, however, is not what Socrates achieves because he actually assumes what he intends to dismiss. His soul-writing is, after all, writing: an "archi-writing" as Derrida calls it, a fundamental system of differences from which writing and speech and indeed all forms of meaning derive.

Heaney mounts his own critical assault on the Greek philosopher in his poem "A Daylight Art." He goes to another *Dialogue*, the *Phaedo*, and uses Socrates's anxious revelations before he died to show how uncertain the philosopher was about his denigration of writing. About to take the poison, Socrates confides to his disciples,

In the course of my life I have often had the same dream, appearing in different forms at different times, but always saying the same thing, 'Socrates, practice and cultivate the arts.' In the past I used to think that it was impelling and exhorting me to do what I was actually doing. . . . But ever since my trial. . . . I have felt that perhaps it might be this popular form of art [poetry] that the dream intended me to practice. . . . I thought it would be safer not to take my departure before I had cleared my conscience by writing poetry and so obeying the dream. I began with some verses in honor of the god whose festival it was. When I had finished my hymn, I reflected that a poet, if he is to be worthy of the name, ought to work on imaginative themes, not descriptive ones, and I was not good at inventing stories. So I availed myself of some of Aesop's fables which were ready to hand and familiar to me, and I versified the first of them that suggested themselves. (Plato 1961, 43–44)

At the end of his life Socrates foregoes speech, truth, and presence as he had formerly defined them in order to rewrite fictions, to represent representations as he versifies already written fables. Perpetuating the series of retellings and rewritings, and showing how complex the business of representing an 'original' truth really is, Plato then writes down the story of Socrates telling his story of writing to his disciples, and no doubt fictionalizes the actual dialogue as he does so.

In Heaney's rendition of all this, Irish poet plays interrogatory foil to Greek philosopher, chiding Socrates for his hypocrisy on the issue of writing and speech. If Socrates never reconciled poetry with philosophy, Heaney intends to outdo his opponent by merging them. Questioning the principles that governed all but the last hours of Socrates's life, Heaney underscores the alliance rather than the antagonism between the different 'arts.' His version reveals,

> On the day he was to take the poison
> Socrates told his friends he had been writing:
> putting Aesop's fables into verse.

> And this was not because Socrates loved wisdom
> and advocated the examined life.
> The reason was that he had had a dream.

Indeed, 'reason' or *logos* is the issue here. Reluctant to obey the mind's highest faculty, Socrates succumbs to voices from his lower 'poetic' faculties, to dreams bubbling up from the irrational unconscious. He is the inspired, possessed poet he describes in the *Ion* who "is beside himself, and reason is no longer in him" (Plato 1961, 220). His obsessive anxiety about his vocation has led to an ecstatic breakdown of old attitudes and his partial conversion to poetry.

Reminiscent of the Shakespearean scene in Yeats's "Lapis Lazuli," where the "drop scenes drop" and "tragedy wrought to its uttermost" (1983, 294) blacks out the heroes and illuminates them with heavenly visions, Heaney's drama ironically compares Socrates to real and fictitious autocrats whose sins are the tragic flaws that finally lead toward redemption.

> Caesar, now, or Herod or Constantine
> or any number of Shakespearean kings
> bursting at the end like dams

where original panoramas lie submerged
which have to rise again before the death scenes—
you can believe in their believing dreams.

But hardly Socrates. Until, that is,
he tells his friends the dream had kept recurring
all his life, repeating one instruction:

Practise the art, which art until that moment
he always took to mean philosophy.

Approaching death, Socrates experiences an epiphany that judges and rear-
ranges his priorities. To Heaney's syncretic view, philosopher, politician, and
poet practice one art and in a way are determined by art. Tragic or comic
heroes, they follow traditional plots, encountering their allotted share of
revelations and reversals as they strut and fret across their different stages.
      Heaney ends his disquisition on writing with an echo of Horace's
famous "happy the man" refrain. Like the Roman poet, he aims for equanimity, a leveling of hierarchies, and the sort of balanced life that Horace
achieved on his Sabine farm. Both poets are familiar with the extremes of
social stratification and civil war (Horace, the son of a freed slave, was later
invited to serve as Octavian's secretary; Heaney, the son of a cattle farmer,
has become a poet of international renown). Both choose to distance themselves from the centers of imperial power and thereby avoid a Socratic fate.

Happy the man, therefore, with a natural gift

for practising the right one from the start—
poetry, say, or fishing; whose nights are dreamless,
whose deep-sunk panoramas rise and pass

like daylight through the rod's eye or the nib's eye.

Heaney usurps Socrates's position as wise philosopher by imitating, chastising,
and finally outdoing him. His own versified fable, which revises the adage
about the difficulty of the rich man getting to heaven through the needle's
eye, proposes that it is easier for a poet who is philosophically and politically
'balanced' to get to heaven than it is for the camel-like philosopher 'unbal-
anced' by his cumbersome biases.
      Deconstructing Socrates, Heaney also deconstructs himself. After all,
for the first half of his career he was the poet of the dark soil, of the "door

into the dark," of the nightmarish darkness of history. Now he wants to absorb that rational Mediterranean light that Socrates and Horace purveyed and turn it back, mirrorlike, on his as well as their political and poetic assumptions. One of the most intriguing poems in *The Haw Lantern*, "Alphabets," returns to the Greek and Latin sources of his education and culture and again appropriates a humanistic light to illuminate them. The poem tells a complex story of reading and writing in which Heaney reads himself back through his writing career to a moment of entranced, fateful reading during which, as it turns out, he discovers his vocation as a writer. He literally receives a sign by reading a sign with his name on it. The moment comes when, as a child, he trains his "wide pre-reflective stare / All agog at the plasterer on his ladder / Skimming our gable and writing our name there / With his trowel point, letter by strange letter." Coming at the end of the poem, this recollection of an early enchantment with reading and writing is particularly significant, primarily because of the way it demystifies the original mysterious aura that he projected around his name, his authorial signature—an aura that clamoring audiences now project around it with the same prereflective abandon. The poem meditates on the strange phenomenon of fame in which the complexities of a flesh-and-blood human get reduced to a 'name,' a sign that attracts customers like an advertisement to a product. "Alphabets" is another self-portrait of the artist as a young man and, with Joyce, Heaney aims to expose and quietly mock the egocentricity and prereflective naïveté behind adolescent love affairs with authorial status. The boy's narcissistic gaze is as far from the truth about writing as is the famous poet's audience. To the question "What's in a name?" Heaney would reply: alienation, falsity, absence, and also economic as well as political power. His whole poem reenacts his long struggle to root the writerly ego in the domestic and cultural background from which it has grown estranged. While it accepts the fact of the artist's alienation and exile, it resists the fate of the "inner émigré" by attempting to restore known presences to strange representations, ground foreign languages in native experience, fill absences (the *o*'s that appear throughout the poem) with familiar objects, and marry art to nature so that word and world at least appear to be one.

Heaney traces the original wordsmith and namegiver to the father who named him and taught him how to 'name' (in Heaney's case) by making shadowy representations of animals on the wall. School teaches him more sophisticated languages—Latin and English—that are just as patriarchal. For him writing is embroiled in gender politics and international politics from the start. When he studies Latin, the signs of ancient empire and religion (Roman Catholicism) are confounded with the patriarchal military forces used to impose them on resistant populations (e.g., the Irish).

> Declensions sang on air like a *hosanna*
> As, column after stratified column,
> Book One of *Elementa Latina*,
> Marbled and minatory, rose up in him.

Out of the inchoate shadow and smoke of Heaney's linguistic origins (the 'ghost-writing' on family wall and school blackboard) stratified Roman institutions assert themselves like God's words in chaos. The departure in 1951 for St. Columb's College from Anahorish School, recorded in the middle of the poem, amounts to an abandonment of this patriarchal writing and a return to the maternal pagan goddess of nature and Gaelic Ireland.

> he left the Latin forum for the shade
>
> Of new calligraphy that felt like home.
> The letters of this alphabet were trees.
> The capitals were orchards in full bloom,
> The lines of script like briars coiled in ditches.
>
> Here in her snooded garment and bare feet,
> All ringleted in assonance and woodnotes,
> The poet's dream stole over him like sunlight
> And passed into the tenebrous thickets.
>
> He learns this other writing.

In short, he reads and writes his way toward the White Goddess of the Celts and away from the imperially male Jehovah figures of Roman and English Christians. "He alludes to Graves," he says in the next section, and here he refers to Graves's polemical eulogy for the poetic muse in *The White Goddess*. The Celtic poems that interested Graves were riddles of alphabetic secrets in which trees stood for letters ("in all Celtic languages *trees* mean *letters*," he reveals [1948, 38]) and "the answer to the conundrum [of Gwion's poem, "The Tale of Taliesin"] is a bardic alphabet" (126). The alphabetic secret spells out the name of a vegetation god, although Graves persistently defers to the goddess, the inspiring lunar muse.

Siding with Graves's matriarchal preferences, Heaney also welcomes Christian "self-denial, fasting, the pure cold" as an antidote to Celtic excess.

The last section of the poem is an elegiac acceptance of emptiness and absence, of Christian asceticism and writerly *askesis*. His "script grows bare and Merovingian," just as Clovis, the first king of the Merovingians, agreed to shed his pagan trappings through Christian baptism (in A.D. 496 or 506). Later he says, "Constantine's sky-lettered IN HOC SIGNO / Can still command," as if the vision of Christ and His accompanying edict, "In this sign conquer," which spurred Constantine in his conquest of Rome and personal conversion to Christianity, also spurs Heaney in his linguistic assault on pagan romanticism. When Heaney returns to Anahorish School, he does not come back as a broken king mourning "the vanished power of the usual reign," but rather as a mature poet thoroughly aware of the way institutions (schools, churches, governments) maintain power by oppressing native languages and values while inculcating their own. Heaney is not altogether forlorn when he surveys the bulldozed ruins because the landscape, once bristling with foreign (Greek) signs, has been partially reclaimed by indigenous Irish growths. Here Heaney reaffirms his commitment to artifice that revivifies the dead and gathers the fragmentary past into new emblems of unity, such as the strange, talismanic

> necromancer
>
> Who would hang from the domed ceiling of his house
> A figure of the world with colours in it
> So that the figure of the universe
> And 'not just single things' would meet his sight
>
> When he walked abroad.

The necromancer is Heaney's alter ego, a Lazarus figure who comes back from the dead to write rather than tell us all.

The paradoxical end of "Alphabets" is especially interesting in the way it reinterprets Heaney's stylistic beginnings. The dead naturalist and naturalist of death in his first books coalesce in the figure of the necromancer. This compound ghost also embraces the astronaut in outer space looking back on the natural world, who "sees all he has sprung from, / The risen, aqueous, singular, lucent O / Like a magnified and buoyant ovum." To add more masks to his persona, Heaney aligns him with the child looking up at the sign inscribed with his family name. The final figure of the O suspended in space brilliantly 'rounds up' the different oppositions that constitute "Heaney" and his work. It unites the older poet reflecting back on his womblike beginnings (the fetal Dedalus before learning to fly on artistic wings) with the young boy looking forward to his future as a high-flying artificer or sign-maker. Male and female principles unite in the feminine ovum, Mother Earth, womb of imagination, and the O that signifies both empty zero and infinite plenitude. Heaney's Joycean story of the artist-god's genesis, however, resists the temptation of positing an absolute, mono-theistic origin. By renouncing a singular creative force it emphasizes the productivity of different forces. Both male and female, ovum and semen, reflection and prereflection, natural object and written subject, sign and signified, presence and absence, speech and writing, living and dead, colony and empire make up the fundamental theatre, the multifaceted Shakespearean 'globe,' as Heaney punningly suggests, in which significance flourishes.

As boy looks up and man looks down in "Alphabets," the various oppositions seem to mingle in consciousness itself. Consciousness and con-science, in fact, play leading roles in *The Haw Lantern*, and ones that are both self-inculpating and self-exculpating. With his personality and culture in court, Heaney plays both plaintiff and defendant, victor and victim, British interrogator and Irish suspect, masterful English poet and obedient Irish citizen, a collaborator who admires as well as despises empire's majestic forms. His deconstructionist style of adjudication uncovers and then under-mines the invidious systems of privilege forced upon him by ancient and contemporary history. Combative in a moral rather than in a military way, he nevertheless imagines stealing weapons from his enemies and turning them on himself and his enemies too. This ironic process is searingly docu-mented in "From the Frontier of Writing," where the first four quatrains depict a literal interrogation in Northern Ireland in which Heaney is stopped and questioned by British soldiers, and the last four quatrains depict an internalized interrogation, where Heaney is the soldier and his writing the target. While Heaney's wrongdoing is as hauntingly vague as K's in *The Trial*, his inclusionary strategies ultimately indict the exclusionary ones be-ing practiced around him.

Heaney's literary court proves both sides are guilty, but after sufficient penitence they are allowed to go free. In "From the Frontier of Writing," after the "marksman training down / out of the sun upon you like a hawk" (the maker of marks—Heaney—and the hawklike maker, the Joycean artist-god) fades behind him, Heaney is "arraigned yet freed." "The Haw Lan-tern" offers the luminous icon—the hawthorn berry and its thorn—to administer a kind of poetic and moral blood test. Here Heaney wants to pass a similar test. And he does. He

> passed from behind a waterfall
> on the black current of a tarmac road

> past armour-plated vehicles, out between
> the posted soldiers flowing and receding
> like tree shadows into the polished windscreen.

His cunning conceit of "the polished windscreen" inscribed with shadows is a figure for the politicized poem (recalling the wall inscribed with his father's shadow-play in "Alphabets"). It reflects outer and inner differences in its shadowy marks, passing judgment on the sectarian divisions in the state by documenting their violence in poetic statements.

To illuminate and reflect, to be both haw lantern and windscreen, ethical lamp and aesthetic mirror, conscience and consciousness, Heaney strives for a poetic epiphany comparable to those he praised in Philip Larkin's poetry. The epiphany is writing itself, not a still-point or stationary end so much as a fleeting moment of inscription in history's flux. Stasis and movement, end and beginning, presence and absence collide, fuse, and regenerate as irrepressibly as the sectarian factions they represent. His elegy for his former Harvard colleague, Robert Fitzgerald, cannot help but depict Irish history (perhaps because of his friend's Irishness) as a bloody and continuous cycle comparable to the adventures of Odysseus that Fitzgerald memorialized in his translations of Homer. Since history has no final, apocalyptic resolutions, Heaney argues, poetry should renounce them as well. "There is no last door, / Just threshold stone, stone jambs, stone crossbeam / Repeating *enter, enter, enter, enter.*" The passage-grave from Neolithic or Bronze Age Ireland, constructed so that the hero's spirit could pass through this world to the next, begins Heaney's series of elisions in which Greek, Irish, and American figures merge. Fitzgerald's spirit is equated with the arrow Ulysses shoots through the axes upon his homecoming. It is something material—history's arrow as well as writer's pen—and traces a bloody, dialectical struggle that shows no sign of ever permanently ending. Corresponding with Odysseus's 'end' in Ithaca, which is actually a stopping point before a new faring forth, Fitzgerald's 'end' in death is similarly impermanent; his spirit remains in his work. As Heaney paradoxically affirms, the endless journey *is* the end of life as well as art.

> After the bowstring sang a swallow's note,
> The arrow whose migration is its mark
> Leaves a whispered breath in every socket.
>
> The great test over, while the gut's still humming,
> This time it travels out of all knowing
> Perfectly aimed towards the vacant centre.

Meditating on the mortal artist's immortality in art, Heaney recalls Zeno's paradox of the arrow that seems stationary at each moment of its flight. As Heaney tells the story of Fitzgerald retracing original Greek texts in his *Iliad* and *Odyssey*, which in turn are retracings of Homer's "whispered breath" and the breaths of the storytellers before Homer, he deconstructs the old hierarchies by emphasizing that writing and speech, textual tradition and oral tradition, inscribing arrow and whispered breath, presence and absence, end and origin, known world and unknown underworld, issue from the same "vacant centre," which could be the mysterious source of all being as much as the indeterminate structure of differences out of which history, story, and all other significant forms struggle to assert their meanings.

By rearranging archaic systems of privilege and discrimination, of centrality and marginality (as when, in the Fitzgerald elegy, he grants priority to ancient Irish history, transporting 'central' American and Greek figures to a passage-grave), Heaney's poems highlight the way displacements and differences make it possible for language to signify. According to his own account, "The function of language in much modern poetry, and in much poetry admired by moderns, is to talk about itself to itself. The poem is a complex word, a linguistic exploration whose tracks melt as it maps its own progress" (1980a, 81). A poem like "Hailstones" unflaggingly draws attention to the poem as a linguistic map of its own genesis and deconstructive journey. Cultural discriminations in this case are literally their own undoing. They impel the poem toward a denouement, an untying of the very discriminations that are knotted (or, as it turns out, frozen) in the language from which it is made. "My cheek was hit and hit," he begins, just as he is hit in school with "a ruler across the knuckles" by authorities determined to knock some British sense into him. The hailstones, like the terrible hailstones in John's Apocalypse, are objective correlatives for an authoritarian system of godlike 'rulers' who transmit their established values by inflicting punishment. To redeem or revalue, to initiate his own counter-Apocalypse in which he perfects the imperfections in himself and his culture, he makes something out of what originally oppressed him—something he can use as a weapon against his oppressors.

> I made a small hard ball
> of burning water running from my hand
>
> just as I make this now
> out of the melt of the real thing
> smarting into its absence.

"Hailstones," like Frost's metaphoric "piece of ice" (Heaney 1980a, 80), melts away what constitutes it. It "rides" on the hierarchical differences between "real thing" and fictive thing, presence and absence, dissolving them as it goes. A self-consuming artifact, it traces the author's troubled, self-conscious relationship with all authorities, including himself. And what good is all this pain, this hail of repression and oppression from inside and outside that Heaney felt so viscerally early on? He asks,

> For what? For forty years
>
> to say there, there you had
> the truest foretaste of your aftermath—
> in that dilation
>
> when the light opened in silence
> and a car with wipers going still
> laid perfect tracks in the slush.

The car's windscreen again is a metaphor for the poet's vision and text, which try to see through and clear up old differences. Car and poem move forward on the melting slush that delineates their paths.

Exposing the institutionalized values frozen in the slush of language is one of *The Haw Lantern*'s wintry obsessions. Yet if Heaney deconstructs his cultural heritage coded in language, he also protests against deconstruction as if all it can do is annihilate. His inaugural lecture as professor of poetry at Oxford underscores this complaint. "The deconstructionist critics, with their unmaskings and destablizings, are prolonging by other means the political and intellectual wars that have marked modern times, most especially the war between the shorers up and the tearers down. Yet the poetic intelligence is not absolved of its old responsibility to find bearings just because it wakens in a quandary, in a quagmire where it can touch no solid linguistic ground" (1989, 1412–18). "The Stone Grinder" reinforces this sentiment when it distinguishes between two kinds of writer: the deconstructionist poet who destroys in order to remake and the deconstructionist per se who merely destroys so others can remake. The first actually produces; the second only reduces. Penelope unweaves and reweaves her text (her "textile," which derives from a Latin root meaning to weave or to construct); her counterpart, the lithographer's helper, subserviently erases the lines printed on his textual stone so that his masters can make new maps and new prints. Penelope resembles Robert Lowell as Heaney describes him in "Lowell's Command," "facing into his forties and knowing that it [his old style] will all have to be done again" (1988a, 137). She also resembles Heaney, facing into his forties as he tries to overhaul his style in *The Haw Lantern*. As Heaney knows, Lowell embraced the revisionary process with intense ambivalence.. His "Fishnet" declares, "I know I've gladdened a lifetime / knotting, undoing a fishnet of tarred rope" (1973, 15), but his "Epilogue" near the end of his last book, *Day by Day*, betrays his readiness to throw the net into the sea. "Those blessèd structures, plot and rhyme— / why are they no help to me now . . . ?" he asks (1977, 127). Heaney is similarly ambivalent about both the stylistic and ideological ramifications of his deconstructions.

If Penelope, the happy unmaker and remaker of texts, is his ideal, it is the stone grinder and his complaints that dominate the poem. While "Penelope worked with some guarantee of a plot," embracing her undoings with tragic gaiety, the stone grinder rankles with tragic sarcasm. He is Sisyphus "coming full circle," a serving man bitterly aware that he will have his nose pushed to the grindstone for the rest of his creative life. He has a powerful nostalgia for being one of the artist-gods who can produce something truly original and complains,

> I ground the same stones for fifty years
> and what I undid was never the thing I had done.
> I was unrewarded as darkness at a mirror.
>
> I prepared my surface to survive what came over it—
> cartographers, printmakers, all that lining and inking.
> I ordained opacities and they haruspicated.
>
> For them it was a new start and a clean slate
> every time. For me, it was coming full circle
> like the ripple perfected in stillness.

At this point, the darkness and perfect stillness are a partial consolation, like the mystical 'dark night' bred out of exhaustion and promising religious and poetic divination or "haruspication" (as in the meditational poems in *Door into the Dark*). But defacing one's past images is like cutting off one's nose to spite one's face. The stone grinder responds, "To commemorate me. Imagine the faces / stripped off the face of a quarry. Practise / *coitus interruptus* on a pile of old lithographs." Heaney's stone grinder is no doubt dreaming of Yeats's golden smithies in Byzantium who break up the marmoreal images of the past to joyously beget new ones, and who live by the principle expressed by their artistic cohorts in "Lapis Lazuli." "All

things fall and are built again / And those that build them again are gay"
(1983, 295). Heaney's stone grinder, however, never attains requital for his
artistic desires. Ultimately he is neither productive nor reproductive. He
yearns like Pygmalion for his stone to turn into a living, speaking presence
and is left with only absences, print, bare stone. Unlike Roland Barthes who
viewed the text as a seductive body, this deconstructionist views it as a naked
corpse.

Moving from prosecution to defense, Heaney stands up for the necessary rigors of the writing life and rebuts some of the stone grinder's more
vociferous complaints. "The Stone Verdict" and "From the Land of the
Unspoken" similarly advocate the "death-in-life" and "life-in-death" (Yeats
1983, 248) in which, as Yeats indicated in "Byzantium," writers work most
intensely. Again Heaney attacks the sociopolitical institutions that would
privilege 'living' speech over 'dead' writing, which he compares to the
writer's gravestone and engraved stone. Hermes, the tutelary god of speech
and writing, for Heaney in "The Stone Verdict" is preeminently the writer
who has "an old disdain of sweet talk and excuses," that is, for the cant and
recantations of politicians. Civilized writing from his Freudian perspective is
repressed, sublimated speech, but here he is one of civilization's advocates
rather than one of its discontents. His conscience calls for a written 'sentence' or censorious silencing of the political 'blab of the pave,' as Whitman
called it in "Song of Myself" (1. 154), so that writing can predominate. He
asserts, "It will be no justice if the sentence is blabbed out. / He will expect
more than words in the ultimate court / He relied on through a lifetime's
speechlessness." The stones hurled at the hermetic writer are not so much
"the stones of silence" mentioned in Heaney's "Punishment" as the stones
of speech. Hermes, who stands "waist deep in the cairn / Of his apotheosis" (his name derives from the Greek, *herma*, a stone heap, and he was
often memorialized with a pile of stones along roads), by poem's end is any
writer whose writing pains have become his monument. Heaney in this
instance embraces authorial solitude "where hogweed earths the silence"
and distances himself from the political speechmaker and even the laudatory
reader of posterity. The vocal majority and politicians who lead them on for
Heaney are not the great communicators but the great desecrators because
they willfully abuse language by mining its sentimental clichés and perverse
stereotypes. They are like graverobbers spoiling the graven images and
magnificent monuments in the "singing schools" of tradition, as Heaney
would say with Yeats. As it is for Heaney's other countryman, Samuel
Beckett, speech is here a desecration of silence.

Heaney often proscribes the logocentric preference for the spoken
word and all it represents. Still, he is rarely as confident or dispassionate in

his deconstructions as Derrida. He shares the philosopher's conviction that an "archi-writing" or fundamental system of differences exists at the indeterminate center of all discourse, but his attitudes toward endless differings and deferrings vacillate. One of his most forthright allegories of speech, writing, and logocentricity, "From the Land of the Unspoken," anxiously addresses the marginal status of writers and writing in rich, capitalist, speech-oriented countries (like America). Nevertheless, it resists a decentering jeremiad or reevaluation (like Allen Ginsberg's in "America"). It condones a capitalist center or "hub" (for part of every year Heaney lives in the capital called the Hub, Boston). After all, Heaney is valued by many as *the* central poet in the English-speaking world, and through his talks and readings, through his spoken poems, he has made his writing a highly remunerative enterprise. Why bite the platinum hand that feeds him? How can he pretend to be a homeless exile when he seems perfectly at home in all the logocentric capitals? He admits,

> I have heard of a bar of platinum
> kept by a logical and talkative nation
> as their standard of measurement,
> the throne room and the burial chamber
> of every calculation and prediction.
> I could feel at home inside that metal core
> slumbering at the very hub of systems.

Residing in a center where money talks, and the logic of the traditional *logos* (reason, God, the spoken word, truth) resists ambiguities and wants to turn all issues into definite, measurable quantities, may have its soporific consolations. Heaney, with some effort, finally renounces the temptations of this "slumbering" dream. He expresses nostalgia for one standard of measurement, like the one-kilogram cylinder of platinum-iridium alloy established by the imperial Napoleon and kept by the International Bureau of Weights and Measures near Paris (a duplicate is kept in America by the National Bureau of Standards), but he is a relativist at heart. Different people, he knows, have different standards. One god, one truth, one language, one authority are figments of an authoritarian sensibility in which he no longer believes. Although some would argue that you need to burrow into the power structure's center in order to take it apart and rectify it, Heaney nevertheless resigns himself to his vocational commitment to outcasts on the peripheries.

It should therefore come as no surprise that Heaney declared to the Boston reporter after completing *The Haw Lantern*, "Everybody's in exile to start with, everybody who writes" (RD 1987, sec. 3.3). "We are a dispersed people," he says in the poem; "when or why our exile began / among the speech-ridden, we cannot tell / but solidarity comes flooding up in us / when we hear their legends." Exiled to the land of the unspoken, which recalls Lowell's "land of unlikeness" (although there the exiles were estranged from the *logos*, God), Heaney glances over his shoulder at logo-centric forms that obviously attract him, like the stylized literary speech of oral traditions that produced such legendary figures as Moses, Scyld, Beowulf, and numerous Gaelic heroes, "floating in coracles towards destiny / or . . . [in] kings' biers heaved and borne away / on the river's shoulders or out into the sea roads." In the contemporary wasteland of the unspoken, the no-madic writers who no longer receive patronage from rich aristocrats in urban centers (but who are patronized by universities, as Heaney is by Harvard and Oxford) roam around the world like the old epic heroes.

This dispersed international community is a kind of government in permanent exile. It represents Heaney's government of the tongue, a body whose members are "unacknowledged legislators of the world" because the powers that be refuse to acknowledge them. Heaney himself is hesitant to acknowledge the political poets' voice, and perhaps he is right, considering the politics of the 'great' poets of the past. Obviously drawn to legendary political leaders (Moses, Beowulf), by the end of "From the Land of the Unspoken" he stigmatizes the openly political poet as a traitor to language, as if by participating in democracy and the demagogic rhetoric that saturates it he will inevitably flounder in linguistic corruption. The silent introspective life in which private intuition reigns above public discourse, for Heaney seems the only alternative for the poet susceptible to indiscretions commit-ted against language in the marketplace. Speaking for the apolitical poets, he declares,

> Our unspoken assumptions have the force
> of revelation. How else could we know
> that whoever is the first of us to seek
> assent and votes in a rich democracy
> will be the last of us and have killed our language?
> Meanwhile, if we miss the sight of a fish
> we heard jumping and then see its ripples,
> that means one more of us is dying somewhere.

The private revelations of poets, like the Gospels and the Book of Revela-tion, are born out of a love of the word (or Word) and a hatred of the imperialistic political world that tends to crucify language as it once crucified the Christ-Word. Although the writers with their "unspoken assumptions" are dangerously above the law in their covert, antidemocratic operations, Heaney risks the charge of smugness in his attempt to articulate the writers' ambiguous position in a modern society whose popular, 'democratic' media have swept the poets aside. Logocentric spokespersons engulf Heaney with their spurious appeals to truth, reason, God, and spirit. From "the very hub of systems" and from the peripheries as well, Heaney mounts his campaign in which he demands fair time for the writers whose audience has slowly eroded before the advancing army of other media.

Having excoriated the simplistic rhetoric of politics and mass media in "From the Land of the Unspoken," in "Parable Island" he turns his attention to Northern Ireland and once again undermines his nostalgia for one authoritarian standard (such as a homogenous one-island culture, perhaps like Japan's) by recognizing the hard facts of dispersal and difference. His parable proclaims that cohesive cultural communities and original, innocent, unified languages are myths. He returns to the entanglement of linguistic and sectarian divisions in his homeland, mocking both "the subversives and collaborators" (the nationalists like the I.R.A. and Anglophiles like the unionists) for arrogantly presuming their version of Ireland's history and destiny is the *only* one. Their absolutist beliefs hark back to the story of the "one bell tower / which struck its single note" to "the one-eyed all creator"; they are ideological fictions or 'Irish facts,' as Hugh Kenner would say. Differences abound in Ireland, whether between Celtic past and Christian present, British Protestant and Irish Catholic. These differences are so unpalatable to the paramilitary groups and sectarian bigots that, as Heaney tells it,

> the forked-tongued natives keep repeating
> prophecies they pretend not to believe
> about a point where all the names converge
> underneath the mountain and where (some day)
> they are going to start to mine the ore of truth.

The one "ore of truth" recalls the previous "bar of platinum," that Heaney exposed as an authoritarian standard devoted to elevating its system above others.

As "archaeologists begin to gloss the glosses," reading their way back into Irish history and rewriting the evidence they find, they disseminate fictions and half-truths with the partisan abandon of their cousins, the political mythmakers. "Always vying with a fierce possessiveness / for the right to set 'the island story' straight," they claim there is one story and one story only in the debate over whether Northern Ireland is an island in itself, part of the Irish island, or part of the British Isles. The different factions together embody the truth, Heaney suggests, although they do not know it. Their versions of historical 'truth,' like Heaney's verses, are partial in more ways than one. They grind the stones and axes of their competing ideologies, scattering "Irish facts" that reveal as much as they conceal. Heaney's own parable moves toward a concluding revelation that highlights the absurdity of all the previous culture-bound claims to single origins and absolute truths. His final story of the man who "died convinced / / that the cutting of the Panama Canal / would mean the ocean would all drain away / and the island disappear by aggrandizement" mocks all absolutist myths.

How can this delusion of the paranoid, senile, xenophobic old man who is afraid his nationalist and isolationist values are going to be destroyed in the coming apocalypse point to a better world? As with most apocalypses, the blind madman is also a seer unaware of how insightful his horrific scenario is. For Heaney he reiterates Donne's aphorism, "No Man is an *Iland*, intire of it selfe; every man is a peece of the *Continent*, a part of the *maine*" (Donne 1975, 87). Following the prophetic example of the old man, Heaney offers a final revelation that is also a last judgment. He deconstructs the politically motivated stories that claim to possess the one true answer to 'the island question,' pointing out that, like the forbidding sea around Ireland, the stormy ideologies actually define the island. By figuratively draining away the sea, Heaney reveals that below there is only earth, the literal 'ground' of all the raging differences above. Related to his historical bog "composing / the floor it rots into" in "Kinship," this sub-aqueous composition or subtext produces the differences that constitute it. With Whitman, who implores us to look under our boot soles to find him, Heaney holds up the earth as a moral example of differences creatively rather than destructively engaged.

Heaney's allegorical technique roots linguistic, political, religious, and indeed all differences in this 'ground' because that is where one cure of the internecine fighting lies. By bringing inflammatory abstractions down to earth he hopes to expose and defuse them. His parable poetry has been traced to Eastern European models; it also derives its impetus from Auden, especially from his elegy to Yeats which allegorically grounds the psychological and political oppositions of "mad Ireland" in body and earth. Once Yeats is dead, his body actually becomes bifurcated Ireland.

> The provinces of his body revolted,
> The squares of his mind were empty,

Silence invaded the suburbs,
The current of his feeling failed.

(Auden 1971, 52)

Heaney extends this technique in *The Haw Lantern* to tease out all the possibilities of a revolt in the provinces of the Irish body politic.

For example, in "From the Republic of Conscience" the 'revolting' provinces are the counties of Northern Ireland from which Heaney flies by plane to the Republic of the South. Or the "Republic of Conscience" could be Ulster where, because he is a member of the Catholic minority, his "symptoms of creeping privilege disappeared." Heaney does not specify his geographical territories so much as establish a *paysage moralisé* across which he makes an allegorical journey. As he crosses political, religious, and linguistic boundaries, he declares the burden of his guilt to customs officials who represent his ever-vigilant conscience. He tries to atone for the system of privileges that has afflicted Ireland for centuries, and that has appropriated him as a privileged national hero (bestowing upon him the jocular but also enviable title, "Seamus Famous"). In this imaginary country where conscience rules and the government of the tongue tacitly legislates, "At their inauguration, public leaders / must swear to uphold unwritten law and weep / to atone for their presumption to hold office." Heaney persistently writes "the uncreated conscience of his race" into being. More home-minded than his precursor, Joyce, who rigorously distanced himself from the actual Irish Troubles, almost never returning to his homeland, Heaney returns in word *and* deed. Although his conscience is private, withdrawn, writerly (Heaney identifies its 'country' as "noiseless," one where "lightning spells" and people worship the craft of the "stylized boat" with its "sloping pen" for mast), his symbolic plane flight to this secluded island is not one-way. He returns to the harsh politicized world beyond his solitary conundrums. His conscience, in the form of the old man, implores him to be a political representative and speechmaker rather than simply a writerly representer and bookmaker.

> He therefore desired me when I got home
> to consider myself a representative
> and to speak on their behalf in my own tongue.
>
> Their embassies, he said, were everywhere
> but operated independently
> and no ambassador would ever be relieved.

Heaney registers here the moral imperative to speak out against the Troubles. He also registers his anxiety that, as a writer, he does not do enough, and

that the writing life somehow renders him impotent when it comes to
political speeches and political acts. With a glance at Yeats he wonders if
knowledge and power, moral conviction and passionate intensity, can ever
be yoked in a civilized way.

To those critics who complained that *The Haw Lantern* heralded a
wintry withdrawal from sensuality and was more private than the overtly
political books like *North*, many counter examples could be given. Even in
the much-acclaimed "Clearances," where Heaney elegizes his mother and
articulates the most intimate relations between them, the domestic drama is
played out on a much larger political stage (the title, for example, recalls the
eviction of Gaels from the Scottish Highlands in the middle of the nineteenth century). His memories of peeling potatoes, folding sheets, and
attending mass with his mother are overshadowed by an awareness of the
tricky political maneuvering needed to keep the peace in home and nation.
Both mother and son have to humble themselves and in effect lie in order
to carry on a dialogue. The family hierarchy is inverted; the mother who
feels inadequate around the scholarly boy abases herself and challenges her
son to do the same. This mutual brinkmanship appears in a discussion of
Bertold Brecht where the German author who vowed to break down the
authoritarian relationship that alienated actor from audience ironically gets
broken down so Heaney can overcome his alienation from his mother.

> Fear of affectation made her affect
> Inadequacy whenever it came to
> Pronouncing words 'beyond her.' *Bertold Brek.*
> She'd manage something hampered and askew
> Every time, as if she might betray
> The hampered and inadequate by too
> Well-adjusted a vocabulary.
> With more challenge than pride, she'd tell me, 'You
> Know all them things.' So I governed my tongue
> In front of her, a genuinely well-
> adjusted adequate betrayal
> Of what I knew better. I'd *naw* and *aye*
> And decently relapse into the wrong
> Grammar which kept us allied and at bay.

The cost of this alliance is high. Both parties have to act like provincial
bunglers to keep from fighting.

Their game of concession making is full of paradoxical betrayals. They
affect to avoid affectation. They govern their tongues in order to appear
ungoverned. To reestablish solidarity with family and minority cultures,

Heaney, who even as a student is a citizen of national and international cultures, has to court impropriety and idiosyncrasy. The government of the tongue, in this case, requires that the scholarly boy curb his tongue. As the writer and his writing are censored and disfigured, Heaney can only try to talk his way out of the impasse.

Death and writing ultimately settle the differences between mother and son. The absence of his mother affects him so powerfully that she becomes a presence, a representation. "The space we stood around has been emptied / Into us to keep, it penetrated / Clearances that suddenly stood open." This is how writing has always taken place for Heaney. Imitating nature, Heaney's imagination abhors a vacuum. When presences turn in- eluctably to absences, representations rush in to replace them. The final sonnet in "Clearances," which tells of the mythical mother tree's demise, repeats a similar scene of writing, of absences translated into presences, and it specifically recalls the third section of "Station Island" where Heaney elegized his father's sister, Agnes, who died as a young girl. In "Clearances," the tree becomes Heaney's compound ghost, a symbol of his womblike and tomblike imagination, as well as the goddess and muse who inspire it with new conceptions. Following the young man in Frazer's *Golden Bough* who breaks the mythical bough and transfers power to himself by killing the old king, Heaney breaks away from his mother, absorbing her power as she dies.

Heaney's relations with his mother are ambivalent, marked like most mother/son relationships by love and disagreement. His family romance passes through what the poet calls their Lawrentian "*Sons and Lovers* phase" and possesses some of the violent, oedipal melodrama characteristic of the vegetation rituals and lunar myths that fascinated Frazer, Freud, and Graves. In the end, though, tree and mother are victims of an alien reaper's axe- wielding force, and Heaney is more a redeemer resurrecting the mother tree in "the placeless heaven" of his imagination than matricidal son or oedipal lover. After "the hatchet's differentiated / Accurate cut," he says, "I thought of walking round and round a space / Utterly empty, utterly a source / Where the decked chestnut tree had lost its place / . . . . Its heft and hush become a bright nowhere, / A soul ramifying and forever / Silent, beyond silence listened for." The "bright nowhere" or "luminous emptiness" recalls those moments of transcendence Heaney cherished in Larkin's poetry. In this 'clearance' his longstanding oedipal struggle with his mother will be temporarily resolved. The poem has traced a branch of Heaney's family tree, deconstructing as well as reproducing the hierarchical relations within it. With Yeats's "Among School Children," which focuses on a similar "great- rooted blossomer" (1983, 217), Heaney acknowledges writing as both a bruising and redemptive enterprise.

To detect the transcendent silence of artistic resolution Heaney has had to tap the silences of memory in which painful differences, once repressed, reassert themselves. The memorial address at the beginning of the sequence compares his writerly memory to a hammer used to split blocks of coal. His mother is his tutelary muse who "taught me to hit, taught me to loosen, / / Taught me between the hammer and the block / To face the music." He implores, "Teach me now to listen, / To strike it rich behind the linear black." The hatchet at the end that "differentiates" recalls the earlier hammer that, like Heaney's other metaphoric writing instruments, grafts together and splits apart, divides differences and demonstrates their necessary connection. Recording writing's iconoclastic violence against the mother, Heaney recodes it as a propitiatory silence, a unifying absence full of heavenly presences. Beginning and end merge, as do mother and son and all the other differences in the poem. His elegy to his mother is also a eulogy to the artistic imagination as motherly *omphalos*, as androgynous source, and to Heaney's own 'maternal' imagination biologically engendered by his mother. In his continual debate over "the government of the tongue," his deconstructive maneuvers rearrange traditional boundaries between man and woman, presence and absence, speech and writing, so that a matriarchal tongue becomes the fundamental matrix of meaning.

The argument Heaney wages with his patriarchal self and logocentric culture understandably focuses on the hierarchical attitudes that have invaded, disfigured, and divided Ireland for centuries. Heaney's private investigations into writing always return to the public struggles in Northern Ireland. They strive to reveal truth—the way things are in the present and have been in the past—and reveal justice—the way things should be in the future. They also admit to the indeterminate, differential nature of truth and justice. Through parable and allegory Heaney creates grammatological dramas in which the writer wrestles with his artistic and political commitments and the furies that drive him toward confession and penitential exile. From his inner turmoil, in spidery fashion he spins his gossamer lines. Even in the bleakest moments language does not abandon him: it generates more language. He contends at the end of "Shooting Script" that the script never ends. It continues to loop back, examining its own linguistic hopes and failures, erasing its past as it writes its way into the future.

> And just when it looks as if it is all over—
> Tracking shots of a long wave up a strand
> That breaks towards the point of a stick writing and writing
> Words in the old script in the running sand.

Heaney's self-conscious poetry is rife with self-perpetuating energies. His mystic way is negative only to be affirmative. Questing for new words and new poems, he dismantles past words and past poems, and then these deconstructions, like his melted hailstones, become the substance of new poems. "Every phrase and every sentence is an end and a beginning, / Every poem an epitaph," Eliot said in "Little Gidding" (1969, 197). While the brilliant rhetoric of yesterday turns into the hollow clichés of today, writing preserves even what the contemporary poet must exclude or transform, just as Heaney's film preserves the writing in the sand obliterated by wind and water. Without this stored deposit of traces called 'tradition' or 'language,' new forms would be like Macbeth's shadow strutting and fretting across the stage, full of sound and fury but signifying nothing. Pushing ever closer toward silence, absence, erasure, and empty space, Heaney's poetry paradoxically offers an eloquent cry for new language to fill the void. Poem after poem bears witness to the sort of scrupulous conscience needed to expose and rectify the cultural forces embedded in language that define and, to a certain extent, determine the way we live.

WORKS CITED
INDEX

WORKS CITED

Aarsleff, Hans. 1983. *The Study of Language in England, 1780–1860*. Minneapolis: Univ. of Minnesota Press.

Alvarez, A. 1980. "A Fine Way with the Language." *New York Review of Books,* 6 Mar., 16–17.

Auden, W. H. 1971. *Selected Poetry of W. H. Auden.* New York: Vintage.

Barfield, Owen. 1924. *History in English Words.* London: Faber and Faber.

Barrell, John, and John Bull, eds. 1975. *A Book of English Pastoral Verse.* New York: Oxford Univ. Press.

Barthes, Roland. 1976. *Sade, Fourier, Loyola.* Translated by Richard Miller. New York: Hill and Wang.

Bernheimer, Richard. 1970. *Wild Men in the Middle Ages.* New York: Octagon.

Braidwood, John. 1969. *The Ulster Dialect Lexicon, An Inaugural Lecture.* Belfast: Queen's Univ.

Broadbridge, Edward, ed. 1977. *Seamus Heaney.* Copenhagen: Danmarks Radio.

Brownjohn, Alan. 1973. "Berryman Agonistes." *New Statesman.* 16 Feb., 238–39.

Buttell, Robert. 1975. *Seamus Heaney.* Lewisburg, Pa.: Bucknell Univ. Press.

Campbell, Joseph. 1949. *The Hero with a Thousand Faces.* Princeton: Princeton Univ. Press.

Carleton, William. 1881. *Traits and Stories of the Irish Peasantry.* London: Ward, Lock and Co.

Carson, Ciaran. 1975. "Escaped from the Massacre?" *The Honest Ulsterman,* no. 50 (Winter): 183–86.

Chadwick, Nora. 1961. *The Age of Saints in the Early Celtic Church.* London: Oxford Univ. Press.

———. 1971. *The Celts.* Harmondsworth, England: Penguin.

Clines, Francis X. 1983. "Poet of the Bogs: Seamus Heaney, Ireland's Foremost Living Poet Commands a Growing Audience." *New York Times Magazine*, 13 Mar., 42–43, 98–99, 104.

The Cloud of Unknowing. 1961. Translated by Clifton Wolters. Harmondsworth, England: Penguin.

Conrad, Joseph. 1989. *Heart of Darkness.* Edited by Ross Murton. New York: St. Martin's Press.

Coogan, Tim Pat. 1987. *The IRA.* Glasgow: Fontana/Collins.

Corcoran, Neil. 1986. *Seamus Heaney.* London: Faber and Faber.

Culler, Jonathan. 1982. *On Deconstruction.* Ithaca, N.Y.: Cornell Univ. Press.

Davis, Dick. 1982. "Door into the Dark." In *The Art of Seamus Heaney,* edited by Tony Curtis, 29–34. Bridgend, Wales: Poetry Wales Press.

Deane, Seamus. 1976. "The Appetites of Gravity." *Sewanee Review* (Winter): 199–208.

———. 1982. "Postscript." In *The Crane Bag Book of Irish Studies,* edited by Richard Kearney. Dublin: Blackwater Press.

———. 1985a. *Celtic Revivals.* London: Faber and Faber.

———. 1985b. "A Noble, Startling Achievement." *Irish Literary Supplement* (Spring): 1, 34.

de Man, Paul. 1983. *Blindness and Insight.* Minneapolis: Univ. of Minnesota Press.

Derrida, Jacques. 1974. *Of Grammatology.* Translated by Gayatri Chakravorty Spivak. Baltimore: Johns Hopkins Univ. Press.

Devlin, Polly. 1983. *All of Us There.* London: Weidenfeld and Nicolson.

Dineen, Francis P. 1967. *An Introduction to General Linguistics.* New York: Holt, Rinehart and Winston.

Donne, John. 1975. *Devotions Upon Emergent Occasions.* Edited by Anthony Raspa. Montreal: McGill-Queen's Univ. Press.

Donoghue, Denis. 1984. "A Mad Muse." *The New Republic,* 30 Aug., 27–29.

Eagleton, Terry. 1989. "Turning Towards Europe." *Times Literary Supplement,* 10–16 Feb., 132.

The Earliest English Poems. 1966. Translated by Michael Alexander. Harmondsworth, England: Penguin.

Eliade, Mircea. 1954. *The Myth of the Eternal Return.* Princeton: Princeton Univ. Press.

Eliot, T. S. 1969. *The Complete Poems and Plays.* London: Faber and Faber.

Emerson, Ralph Waldo. 1940. *The Selected Writings.* New York: Modern Library.

Empson, William. 1935. *Some Versions of Pastoral.* London: Chatto and Windus.

Ewart, Gavin. 1972–73. "Chicken Soup." *London Magazine,* Dec./Jan., 132–35.

Foster, John Wilson. 1974. "The Poetry of Seamus Heaney." *Critical Quarterly* 16 (Spring): 35–48.

Frazer, James. 1922. *The Golden Bough*. Abridged ed. New York: Macmillan.

Fredman, Stephen. 1983. *Poet's Prose*. Cambridge: Cambridge Univ. Press.

Freud, Sigmund. 1918. *Totem and Taboo*. New York: Vintage.

Frost, Robert. 1972. *The Poetry of Robert Frost*. Edited by Edward Lathem. London: Jonathan Cape.

Glob, P. V. 1969. *The Bog People*. London: Faber and Faber.

Graves, Robert. 1948. *The White Goddess*. New York: Farrar, Straus and Giroux.

Haffenden, John. 1981. *Viewpoints: Poets in Conversation with John Haffenden*. London: Faber and Faber.

Hamilton, Ian. 1987. "Excusez-moi." *London Review of Books*, 1 Oct., 10–11.

Hardy, Barbara. 1982. "Meeting the Myth: *Station Island*." In *The Art of Seamus Heaney*, edited by Tony Curtis. New ed. Ogmore by the Sea, Wales: Poetry Wales Press.

"Harvard Portrait: Seamus Heaney." 1985. *Harvard Magazine*, Nov./Dec.: 88.

Heaney, Seamus. 1959a. "Nostalgia in the Afternoon." *Gorgon*, no. 3 (Nov.): 17.

———. 1959b. "October Thought." *Q*, no. 17: 27.

———. 1959c. "Reaping in Heat." *Q*, no. 17: 27.

———. 1960. "Aran." *Gorgon*, no. 4 (Feb): 7.

———. 1961. "Song of My Man-Alive." *Gorgon* (Hilary Term): 19.

———. 1965. "Lint Water." *Times Literary Supplement*, 5 Aug.

———. 1966a. "Prospero in Agony." *Outposts* 68 (Spring): 21–23.

———. 1966b. *Death of a Naturalist*. London: Faber.

———. 1967. "Irish Eyes." *The Listener*, 28 Dec.

———. 1968. "Old Derry's Walls." *The Listener*, 24 Oct.

———. 1969. *Door into the Dark*. London: Faber.

———. 1970a. "Boy Driving His Father to Confession." Surrey: Sceptre Press.

———. 1970b. "Views." *The Listener*, 31 Dec.

———. 1971. "Belfast's Black Christmas." *The Listener*, 23 Dec.

———. 1972a. "The Labourer and the Lord." *The Listener*, 28 Sept.

———. 1972b. "Mother Ireland." *The Listener*, 7 Dec.

———. 1972c. "A Political Stance." Talk with Elgy Gillespie. *Irish Times*, 19 May.

———. 1972d. *Wintering Out*. London: Faber.

———. 1973a. "Lost Ulsterman." *The Listener*, 26 Apr.

———. 1973b. "Poets on Poetry." *The Listener*, 8 Nov.

———. 1975. *Stations*. Belfast: Ulsterman Publications.

———. 1975b. *North*. London: Faber.

———. 1977. "Unhappy and at Home: Interview with Seamus Heaney." With Seamus Deane. *The Crane Bag* 1 (Spring): 61–67.

———. 1978a. "The Interesting Case of John Alphonsus Mulrennan." *Planet*, no. 41 (Jan.): 34–40.

———. 1978b. "On Robert Lowell." *New York Review of Books*, 9 Feb., 37–38.

———. 1979a. "An Interview with Seamus Heaney." With James Randall. *Ploughshares* 5, no. 3: 7–22.

———. 1979b. "A Raindrop on a Thorn: An Interview with Robert Druce." *Dutch Quarterly* 9, no. 1: 24–37.

———. 1979c. *Field Work*. London: Faber.

———. 1980a. *Preoccupations*. London: Faber and Faber.

———. 1980b. "Treely and Rurally." *Quarto*, no. 9 (August): 14.

———. 1981. "Current Unstated Assumptions About Poetry." *Critical Inquiry* (Summer): 645–51.

———. 1982a. "Artists on Art: An Interview with Seamus Heaney." With Frank Kinahan. *Critical Inquiry* 8 (Spring): 405–14.

———. 1982b. "Pastoral." In *Seamus Heaney, Poems and a Memoir*, edited by Henry Pearson. New York: Limited Editions.

———. 1982–83. "Bennet Award Acceptance Speech, 1982." *Hudson Review* (Winter): 519–20.

———. 1983. *Sweeney Astray*. Derry, Ire.: Field Day.

———. 1984a. *Place and Displacement*. Cumbria, England: Frank Peters.

———. 1984b. *Station Island*. London: Faber and Faber.

———. 1985. "Envies and Identifications: Dante and the Modern Poet." *Irish University Review* 15 (Spring): 5–19.

———. 1985–86. "Place, Pastness, Poems: a Triptych." *Salmagundi* (Fall/Winter): 30–47.

———. 1987. "The Impact of Translation." *Yale Review* 76 (Autumn): 1–14.

———. 1987b. *The Haw Lantern*. London: Faber.

———. 1988a. *The Government of the Tongue*. London: Faber and Faber.

———. 1988b. "An Interview with Seamus Heaney." With Randy Brandes. *Salmagundi* (Fall): 4–21.

Hemingway, Ernest. 1929. *A Farewell to Arms*. New York: Charles Scribner's Sons.

Henry, P. L. 1966. *The Early English and Celtic Lyric*. London: George Allen.

Hill, Geoffrey. 1984. *The Lords of Limit*. London: André Deutsch.

———. 1985. *Collected Poems*. Harmondsworth, England: Penguin.

Hughes, Ted. 1982. *New Selected Poems*. New York: Harper.

Ignatius Loyola, Saint. 1963. *The Spritual Exercises*. Translated by Corbishley. London: Burns and Oates.

Jackson, Kenneth. 1940. "The Motive of the Threefold Death." In *Essays and Studies Presented to Professor Eoin MacNeill*, edited by John Ryan, 535–50. Dublin: At the Sign of the Three Candles.

John of the Cross, Saint. 1973. *The Complete Works*. Translated by Kieran Kavanaugh and Otilio Rodriguez. Washington, D.C.: Institute of Carmelite Studies.

Johnson, Samuel. 1973. *Johnson as Critic*. Edited by John Wain. London: Routledge and Kegan Paul.

Jones, David. 1978. *The Dying Gaul*. London: Faber and Faber.

Joyce, James. 1939. *Finnegans Wake*. New York: Viking.

———. 1961. *Ulysses*. New York: Vintage.

———. 1968. *A Portrait of the Artist as a Young Man*. Edited by Chester G. Anderson. Harmondsworth: Penguin.

Kearney, Richard. 1982. *The Crane Bag Book of Irish Studies*. Dublin: Blackwater Press.

———. 1986. "Myth and Motherland." In *Ireland's Field Day*, edited by Field Day Theatre Company. Notre Dame: Univ. of Notre Dame Press.

Kennelly, Brendan. 1984. "Soaring from the Treetops." *New York Times Book Review*, 27 May, 14.

———, ed. 1970. *The Penguin Book of Irish Verse*. Harmondsworth, England: Penguin.

Kenner, Hugh. 1972. *The Pound Era*. London: Faber and Faber.

———. 1983. *A Colder Eye*. New York: Knopf.

Kiely, Benedict. 1970. "A Raid into Dark Corners." *The Hollins Critic* 7, no. 4: 1–12.

Kierkegaard, Soren. 1941. *Sickness unto Death*. Translated by Walter Lowrie. Princeton: Princeton Univ. Press.

Kinzie, Mary. 1988. "Deeper than Declared." *Salmagundi* (Fall): 22–57.

Lawrence, D. H. 1931. *Apocalypse*. London: Heinemann.

Lomas, Herbert. 1987. "Two Faces of Yeats." *London Magazine* (July), 92–94.

Longley, Edna. 1982. "*North*: 'Inner Emigré' or 'Artful Voyeur?' " In *The Art of Seamus Heaney*, edited by Tony Curtis, 63–95. Bridgend: Poetry Wales Press.

Lowell, Robert. 1944. *Lord Weary's Castle* and *The Mills of the Kavanaughs*. New York: Harcourt, Brace and World.

———. 1973. *The Dolphin*. New York: Farrar, Straus and Giroux.

McClatchy, J. D. 1987. "The Exile's Song." *New Republic*, 21 Dec., 36–39.

Magnusson, Magnus, and Hermann Palsson. 1960. Intro. to *Njal's Saga*. Harmondsworth, England: Penguin.

Mailer, Norman. 1968. *The Armies of the Night*. New York: Signet.

Mallarmé, Stephen. 1956. *Selected Prose Poems, Essays & Letters*. Translated by Bradford Cook. Baltimore: Johns Hopkins Univ. Press.

———. 1977. *Mallarmé, The Poems*. Translated by Keith Bosley. Harmondsworth, England: Penguin.

Martz, Louis. 1954. *The Poetry of Meditation*. New Haven: Yale Univ. Press.

Merton, Thomas. 1972. *Seeds of Contemplation*. Wheathampstead, England: Anthony Clarke.

Milton, John. [1637] 1983. *Milton's "Lycidas": The Tradition and the Poem*. Edited by C. A. Patrides. New rev. ed. Columbia: Univ. of Missouri Press.

Morrison, Blake. 1982. *Seamus Heaney*. London: Methuen.

O'Brien, Conor Cruise. 1972. *States of Ireland*. London: Hutchinson.

O'Brien, Flann. 1951. *At Swim-Two-Birds*. New York: Walker and Co.

O'Keeffe, J. G., ed. and trans. 1913. *Buile Suibhne (The Frenzy of Suibhne) being The Adventures of Suibhne Geilt, A Middle-Irish Romance*. London: Irish Texts Society; David Nutt.

Oldfather, C. H. 1933. Intro. to *Diodorus of Sicily*. London: Heinemann.

O'Riordain, Sean. 1942. *Antiquities of the Irish Countryside*. London: Methuen.

Parini, Jay. 1980. "Seamus Heaney: The Ground Possessed." *Southern Review* 16 (Winter): 100–23.

Paulin, Tom. 1986. "New Look at the Language Question." In *Ireland's Field Day*. Notre Dame: Univ. of Notre Dame Press.

Pei, Mario. 1949. *The Story of Language*. New York: J. B. Lippincott Co.

Pinsky, Robert. 1987. "Responsibilities of the Poet." *Critical Inquiry* 13 (Spring): 421–33.

Plato. 1961. *The Collected Dialogues of Plato*. Edited by Edith Hamilton and Huntington Cairns. Princeton: Princeton Univ. Press.

"Poet Wearing the Mantle of Yeats." 1987. *The Observer*, 21 June.

Puttenham, George. 1589. *Arte of English Poesie*, quoted in *A Book of English Pastoral Verse*. New York: Oxford Univ. Press.

RD. 1987. "Double Time." *The Boston Phoenix*, 18 Sept., sec. 3.

Richardson, William. 1983. "Lacan and the Subject of Psychoanalysis." *Interpreting Lacan*. New Haven: Yale Univ. Press.

Ricks, Christopher. 1979. "The Mouth, the Meal and the Book." *London Review of Books*, 8 Nov., 4–5.

———. 1984. *The Force of Poetry*. Oxford: Clarendon Press.

Riffaterre, Hermine. 1983. In *The Prose Poem in France*. Edited by Caws and Riffaterre. New York: Columbia Univ. Press.

Roethke, Theodore. 1975. *The Collected Poems of Theodore Roethke*. New York: Anchor.

Ross, Anne. 1967. *Pagan Celtic Britain*. London: Routledge and Kegan Paul.

Rowe, A. L. 1975. *Jonathan Swift*. New York: Charles Scribner's Sons.

Sacks, Peter. 1983. *The English Elegy*. Baltimore: Johns Hopkins Univ. Press.

"Semaphores of Hurt." 1972. *Times Literary Supplement*, 15 Dec.

Shelley, Percy Bysshe. 1945. *The Complete Poetical Works of Percy Bysshe Shelley*. Edited by Thomas Hutchinson. London: Oxford Univ. Press.

Snyder, Gary. 1969. *Earth House Hold.* New York: New Directions.

Spender, Stephen. 1973. "Can Poetry Be Reviewed?" *New York Review of Books,* 20 Sept., 8–14.

Spenser, Edmund. [1596] 1970. *A View of the Present State of Ireland.* Oxford: Clarendon Press.

Steiner, George. 1967. *Language and Silence.* London: Faber and Faber.

Stevens, Wallace. 1972. *The Palm at the End of the Mind.* Edited by Holly Stevens. New York: Vintage.

Synge, John. 1935. *The Complete Works.* New York: Random House.

Theresa, Saint. 1958. *The Interior Castle,* edited by Hugh Martin. London: SCM Press.

Vendler, Helen. 1988. "Second Thoughts." *New York Review of Books,* 28 Apr., 41–45.

Vico, Giambattista. 1982. *Selected Writings.* Edited by Leon Pompa. Cambridge: Cambridge Univ. Press.

Warmington, E. H. 1970. Intro. to *Tacitus, Agricola, Germania, Dialogus.* London: Heinemann.

Weiskel, Thomas. 1976. *The Romantic Sublime.* Baltimore: Johns Hopkins Univ. Press.

Whitaker, Thomas. 1964. *Swan and Shadow.* Chapel Hill: Univ. of North Carolina Press.

Yeats, William Butler. 1937. *A Vision.* New York: Macmillan.

———. 1955. *The Letters of William Butler Yeats.* Edited by Allan Wade. New York: Macmillan.

———. 1959. *Mythologies.* New York: Macmillan.

———. 1965. *The Variorum Edition of the Plays.* New York: Macmillan.

———. 1983. *The Poems.* New York: Macmillan.

INDEX

211

SEAMUS HEANEY, POET OF CONTRARY PROGRESSIONS
was composed in 10 on 12 Galliard on a Merganthaler Linotronic 300
by Partners Composition;
with display type in Weiss #1 by Dix Type;
printed by sheet-fed offset on 55-pound, acid-free Antique Cream,
Smyth-sewn and bound over binder's boards in Joanna Arrestox B,
with dust jackets printed in 2 colors
by Maple-Vail Book Manufacturing Group, Inc.;
and published by
SYRACUSE UNIVERSITY PRESS
SYRACUSE, NEW YORK 13244-5160

RICHARD FALLIS, *Series Editor*

IRISH STUDIES presents a wide range of books interpreting important aspects of Irish life and culture to scholarly and general audiences. The richness and complexity of the Irish experience, past and present, deserves broad understanding and careful analysis. For this reason, an important purpose of the series is to offer a forum to scholars interested in Ireland, its history, and culture. Irish literature is a special concern in the series, but works from the perspectives of the fine arts, history, and the social sciences are also welcome, as are studies that take multidisciplinary approaches.

Selected titles in the series are:

Beckett and Myth: An Archetypal Approach. Mary A. Doll

Celtic Contraries. Robin Skelton

Children's Lore in "Finnegans Wake." Grace Eckley

Cinema and Ireland. Kevin Rockett, Luke Gibbons, and John Hill

The Figure in the Cave and Other Essays. John Montague

Finnegans Wake: A Plot Summary. John Gordon

Frank O'Connor at Work. Michael Steinman

In Minor Keys: The Uncollected Short Stories of George Moore. David B. Eakin and Helmut E. Gerber, eds.

Irish Literature: A Reader. Maureen O'Rourke Murphy and James MacKillop, eds.

James Joyce: The Augmented Ninth. Bernard Benstock, ed.

Selected Plays of Padraic Colum. Sanford Sternlicht, ed.

The Irish Renaissance. Richard Fallis

Yeats. Douglas Archibald

Yeats and Postmodernism. Leonard Orr, ed.